D. H. Lawrence

D. H. LAWRENCE
The failure and the triumph of art

ELISEO VIVAS

Northwestern
University
Press
EVANSTON

Copyright ©, *1960, by Northwestern University Press*
Library of Congress Catalog Card Number: 60–10049
Printed in the United States of America

FOR MARTA ELVIA

Preface

THIS STUDY is not concerned with Lawrence the man. His life has been thoroughly examined by a large number of biographers, friendly and unfriendly; he has been psychoanalyzed, criticized, evaluated, loved in public posthumously; he has been worshipped from a distance as the lovable angel that at times he was, and he has been despised as the demon that he also was. His every move has been charted, his reading scrutinized, his formidable battles with his wife recorded, and his novels have been corrected by checking them against the facts he used as matter for them. We know he cooked, trimmed hats for Frieda, built chicken coops, baked bread in old-fashioned ovens and fell into sadistic tantrums; and we also know that he could be tender after his explosions. Sometimes the same event has been recorded by several hands—the "last supper" episode at the Café Royal, for instance.

A distinguished English philosopher of our age, Bertrand Russell, has put on record his intense dislike of, and his utter failure to understand, Lawrence; an English economist, John Maynard Keynes, from the lofty height of his aesthetic and intellectual superiority, condescended to notice Lawrence's reactions to the economist's precious set of aesthetes. Recently his most indefatigable biographer, Harry T. Moore, has added to two very useful books on Lawrence a third; and more recently still, another biographer, Edward H. Nehls, has given us a very valuable composite biography in three volumes. If there is information on his life that has been overlooked, letters that have not yet been printed, surviving relatives and friends not yet interviewed, vital statistics not yet published, it is not likely that they shall alter the picture we have of Lawrence's work and of his character. But if there is such data, it is not the writer of this book who would be interested in finding it.

This work is centrally concerned with Lawrence the "poet"— which is to say, the maker, the artist. It attempts to discriminate between his successful and his unsuccessful art. But it is essential, of course, to realize that the word "poetry" is used in this book as a short and convenient term to refer to the whole of imaginative literature, whether written in prose or verse. Lawrence's verse, or what he took to be verse, is not examined here for several reasons. One of these, although purely subjective, acts with a strong operative force: I find Lawrence's verse embarrassing. I respond to it as one responds to a *gaucherie* committed in public. The embarrassment comes from the sight of a major artistic talent trying his hand at something which I do not believe he could do well. Lawrence seldom had the inspiration and the discipline to write verse of distinction. Some of his verse is unutterably tender and fully controlled, obviously the product of genuine inspiration: "Have you built the ship of death, oh have you?" But Lawrence's best writing is found in his prose. I am not unaware, of course, that he began his career as poet by writing verse, that distinguished editors published it, and that fellow poets acclaimed it as excellent. But I must stick to my opinion. If I am wrong, no harm can come of it, for he has received ample attention as a writer of verse. Another reason for my ignoring his verse is that its substance, when it deserves notice as such, is not essentially different from the substance of his fiction. It is in the great works of fiction that we find what in a different language of criticism would be called "his vision of the world."

But although my fundamental interest is in Lawrence's poetry and particularly in its substance, I am not, nor could I be, altogether indifferent to biographical data when his aesthetic failures can be traced, as in the last analysis they must be, to subjective factors; nor could I disregard his "ideas" although I find many of them of little value and some of them pernicious. Unfortunately Lawrence had ideas—mere opinions, that is—on anything and everything. Modifying for our purposes what Eliot said about Chesterton, Lawrence's head teemed with ideas but it did not always give evidence that it could think. Without discrimination, many students of Lawrence have taken all his ideas—to which they refer as his "philosophy"—seriously, forgetting that Lawrence himself, at his best, had a deep-seated and, in my opinion, justified repugnance towards ideas—although, as any one acquainted with the man would expect, not always towards his own ideas. But occasionally with a cruel, because lucid, self-knowledge he acknowledged his own theoretical incompetence. Earl Brewster tells us that when he "urged Lawrence to write at length on his philosophical and psychological conceptions, he would shake his head and say: 'I would contradict myself in every page.'"

When one looks at his "love ethic" carefully, or at any other identifiable body of ideas put forth by him, it becomes clear that it is a mixture of sense and nonsense, when it is not a mixture of wisdom and corruption. This is true not only of his erotic philosophy but also of his "vitalism" and of his opinions on economic, social, and other problems. On the other hand, it is not altogether possible to go along with the accepted opinion in our day that his notorious "philosophy of the blood" is without qualification pernicious. I shall show that while it has its ugly aspects, it also contains an indispensable modicum of wisdom.

After this has been noted, it should remain undeniable that the highest value of Lawrence's work lies in his poetry. He was a *poet*—what could we say that would be more honorific? Only that he was a saint—and that, not even Mr. Leavis would claim for him. He was a poet and that is more than enough. At his best— which unfortunately was not often—Lawrence himself was not unaware of the central, the indispensable, function of poetry. In the Preface to Harry Crosby's *Chariot of the Sun* he wrote: "The essential quality of poetry is that it makes a new effort of attention, and 'discovers' a new world within a known world." The quotation marks with which he harnessed the key term are of great interest: he was obviously aware of the fact that it was not an ordinary discovery that the poet made since the poet is a genuinely creative man. It is a pity that this was not a consistently guiding insight of his. Expatiating, what Lawrence is telling us is what we know from other sources, that the function of the poet is to sweep away the "ideas" that darken and falsify our vision. He tears the horny cataract of conceptual abstractions from the soul's eyes, the worn-out categories, the stereotyped modes of response to the living world, the brittle formulas. In their place he gives us fresh, quick, tender, unmediated revelations of the world of nature and of man. Having freed us from our "ideas," he substitutes his own freshly organized experience, through which we are able to understand aesthetically, to grasp by immediate apprehension, those aspects of contemporary experience that without his aid would remain for us threatening and oppressive because they would remain chaotic. The poet's organization constitutes a discovery, but one that is creative. And because it is both, his central function is to define an important aspect of the human condition of his age by giving it form, and substancing that form with the matter of his own experience. The lenses he offers us we use as a fresh and adequate categorial scheme, by which we grasp the world anew; with it we now sense what he sensed, and when we respond properly to his work we use it later, much later, to judge as best we may what he sensed and grasped—*later*, for during the time we are in intimate relationship with his work, if we know how to respond to it, all we do is behold. Without these lenses, purblind, we would stumble in the dark, not realizing the true shape of things. For this reason if we dismiss Lawrence—if we dismiss Gide, Céline, or, changing the scale, if we dismiss Paul Bowles (and I put beside Lawrence one poet whom the majority of critics will think of equal stature to him, another who is of lesser and still another who is of much lesser stature than he) we deprive ourselves of the means of grasping the specific process of decomposition of values through which we are living.

Because, as I shall indicate presently, one of my ends in writing this book was to "test" a theory of criticism I espouse, my interest in Lawrence has been limited to that part of his work that I considered relevant to my end. For that reason I have not examined all of his work. His first two novels I have not examined at all. The work of a talented beginner, they can have only biographical interest. Had they not been written by Lawrence they probably would not be kept in print. *Sons and Lovers* is Lawrence's first artistic success of magnitude, but it is not fully mature Lawrence. He did not come to full possession of his poetic power and insight until *The Rainbow* and *Women in Love*. After writing these two novels his work deteriorated as art—with the exception of a few short stories which, however perfect in their kind, are minor. It is therefore on the relatively major novels only that I have put the greatest effort. The rest of the work has been considered, for much of it is of importance, although it lacks the perfection I find in his two great novels. But the emphasis has been on the defects of these lesser novels.

To his committed admirers, no doubt, and to those critics who, like Mr. Hough, have offered us a complete analysis of his whole *oeuvre*, this approach will appear a good illustration of the inevitable and undesirable consequence of the application to a major poet of what my friend Professor Nathan A. Scott, Jr. has aptly called "a rigid adherence to an aesthetic rigorism." I do not conceal, indeed I would fully acknowledge, that I have tried to apply with as much rigor as I could summon, a demanding criterion. My justification is this: we are inevitably the victims of the definitions we use to our advantage. Fully aware of the price I was paying, I have accepted the strictures and limitations of the aesthetic that I have used as guide. The alternative was to abandon all effort to stick to a definition or, put in nicer terms, to use the word "art" in a wider sense. I own that such an approach would have a number of advantages: it would have made my work considerably easier, and it would have protected me from the possibility of being dismissed as narrow; it would also have allowed me to ascribe to Lawrence's work values that within the definition I chose I must deny to it. I would have been able to take him seriously as a sociologist, as a historian, a psychologist, a political theorist, and, indeed, an all-round polymath, a universal guru. But, alas, these advantages I must eschew. Besides being anti-Lawrentian in spirit—and this is not a consideration that would have greatly influenced me—it would have forced me to deny the unique value I believe poetry to have.

I would be, however, less than candid with my reader if I did not make explicit my conviction that an aesthetic—any aesthetic, whether it be that of a philosophical giant like Kant or Schopenhauer or that of a mere professor of philosophy in the twentieth century—is inevitably, and cannot but be, a Procrustean bed in which we force a work of art to lie down in order to cut it to a size we can manage. This holds, in my opinion, for any philosophical theory. I leave it to the scientists to decide whether it also holds for scientific hypotheses. No "philosophy"—whether it be an ethic, a philosophy of religion, or a vision of the world claiming adequacy to the actual world—can be adequate to it.

I do not say this out of cynical misology or tired skepticism. Nor do I think it is an expression of an anti-intellectual or an irrational streak in me. I say it out of a radical conviction I have long espoused that the data to which the thinker turns, whether it is reality or that aspect of the real that is art, is larger and more complex than any theory that can possibly be devised, and in the last analysis it remains, therefore, intractable. In any case, I do not know of a coherent aesthetic that completely "saves the appearances" of art, no matter how many epicycles we add to the orbit, no matter how much we fix up the theory, unless we are willing to accept *ad hoc* repairs that are a camouflage for radical incoherence—something I will not do so long as I am aware of what I am doing. But the emphasis in the preceding sentence is on the term "incoherence," for a syncretistic critic can and does easily save all the appearances—at the price of fundamental coherence.

Stated differently, art gives the lie to a given aesthetic method, just as life gives the lie to a given ethic, and religion to a given theology. But in saying that art gives the lie to theory I am not belittling theory, unless I belittle a human product in marking the consequences of the fact that it is indeed the product of a human being. A complete and perfect adequation between a segment of reality (or all of it) and a system of ideas must be sought at all costs. A serious thinker does not hesitate to espouse a system of ideas because he knows that his aims, coherence, and adequacy are in the last analysis unreachable ideals, any more than a serious lover gives up his worship because he knows that disease and finally death will give the lie to his conviction that he has found perfection.

I hope it is true that although rigorism cuts out much that Lawrence and his admirers have called art, no harm can in the end accrue to Lawrence from my effort. Of late, Lawrence has been the object of much critical and popular recognition. It has become more and more clear every day that Lawrence will survive any amount of criticism, however demanding. It is no longer possible to write, as Middleton Murry wrote in 1936: "Since I became a peripatetic lecturer in America, I have been shocked by the relative lack of interest in D. H. Lawrence." Nor is it necessary to say, with Mr. Leavis, only three years ago, that it is important to "win recognition for the nature of Lawrence's achievement as novelist," or as anything else. Bertrand Russell—whom no one could accuse of being a Lawrence fan—gave him almost two-thirds of a page in *A History of Western Philosophy*—and demonstrated thereby his lack of understanding of his ex-friend. I had already written this preface when I came across an advertisement in *The Times Literary Supplement* (London) announcing the publication of a study of the "development of the religious, secular and humanist traditions of European thought, exemplified by moralists and moral philosophers from Plato to D. H.

Lawrence." When Lawrence's name can be coupled with that of Plato in a study published by the Cambridge University Press, it is obvious that we no longer have to look in order to realize that he has come through—we *know* it.

The writing of this book has had for me another value—a purely personal, subjective one. I undertook it for the sake of my own intellectual well-being. Too long have I lived with Lawrence, feeling always the need to make clear to myself and my students the basic ground for my divided attitude towards him. But I could not be sure of what I thought about him before I wrote it down, put it into some sort of order, and surveyed it from a few feet away. I cannot quite say with Mr. Leavis that Lawrence has been a major factor in my life. But he has been a factor, and not altogether an unimportant one. I began reading him in the early, also my own early, twenties, and began reading him for a reason that I am confident must be unusual: I wanted to learn the English language, and found his lexicon the purest. But gradually my interest expanded to include the poet, the maker. I have read him on and off, the reading broken by periods of indifference and often of something that amounted to revulsion, ever since. I wrote my first essay on Lawrence—fortunately buried in an inaccessible and forgotten "little mag"—in 1925. And since 1935 I have been discussing him in one of my courses. Until I finally came to grips with Lawrence, I was bound to suffer from tensions that called for resolution. And nothing that I have read on him has fully resolved them. I have been forced, therefore, to make the effort on my own.

The writing of this work had still another value for me that I think worth mentioning. It has long been my opinion that a professional aesthetician who does not try his hand at criticism shirks the full responsibility for his theory. Military trainers tell us that the battle is the pay-off. I agree. It is the pay-off not only for the success of the training but for the quality of the theory that controls its conception and development. To write *about* art, but never to come to critical grips with it, is to run to the rear when the shooting begins. For this reason I hope that what vanity there is in the claim will be excused, or at least understood, when I say that by applying to Lawrence certain ideas on art that I entertain, I have been able to arrive at discriminations that otherwise would have escaped me. The analysis, as I see it, does not detract from other values of Lawrence that other approaches may reveal; but it helps us to assess the value I discover in his work the more justly, and to conclude that he is as important as those who admire him take him to be—but on grounds that I take to be somewhat different from theirs.

The organization of this book calls for a word of explanation: I start with those aspects of the poet that seem to me to be failures. I go from there to the novels that appear to me to represent his best work. Had I treated his work chronologically, the greater part of the book would have been anti-climactic.

I would like to extend my grateful acknowledgment to the publishers who have given permission to quote material from their books: to The Viking Press, Inc., New York, for *Aaron's Rod, Kangaroo, Women in Love, Etruscan Places, Apocalypse, The Letters of D. H. Lawrence* (edited by Aldous Huxley), *Sons and Lovers*, and *Rainbow*; to Alfred A. Knopf, Inc., New York, for *Assorted Articles, Morning in Mexico, St. Mawr, The Plumed Serpent*, and F. R. Leavis' *D. H. Lawrence: Novelist*; to Julian Press, Inc., New York, for Ira Progoff's *Jung's Psychology and Its Social Meaning*; and to Sheed & Ward, Inc., New York, for Mircea Eliade's *Patterns in Comparative Religion*. Thanks is given also to *Bucknell Review* for their permission to include in this book "The Two Lawrences" which first appeared in their publication in March, 1958; and to *The Sewanee Review* for their permission to use material from my review of F. R. Leavis' book, *D. H. Lawrence: Novelist* (LXV,1: Winter, 1957), and for "The Substance of *Women in Love*" (LXVI,4: Autumn, 1958).

It is a pleasure to be able to express my gratitude to those people who have helped me in the writing of this book: to Dean Simeon Leland, The College of Liberal Arts, Northwestern University, who gave me a leave of absence in the fall of 1958 to finish a manuscript on which I had labored many summers; to Dean Moody Prior and Assistant Dean Robert H. Baker of the Graduate School, Northwestern University; to the reader whose careful reading of the manuscript saved me from many stylistic errors; to my friend, Professor Murray Krieger, to whose brilliant and powerful mind I owe much stimulation; and to my wife, who not only helped with the editorial and physical work but to whose critical mind I am deeply indebted.

6 January 1960
Evanston, Illinois   Eliseo Vivas

Contents

Contents

D. H. Lawrence

The Two Lawrences[1]

CAN THERE be doubt at this late date that D. H. Lawrence is one of the most important writers in the English language in the first half of the twentieth century? Whether he has a permanent place in the history of English literature only those endowed with the power of prophecy can say with assurance. I believe he has; but I do not take my attitude as anything more than a belief grounded on hunches. We can, however, say with authority—the authority of a judgment that now has general critical support—that with Yeats, Eliot, and one or two others—perhaps Pound or Faulkner, but who else?—Lawrence was one of the constitutive writers of our generation. I use the word "constitutive" in somewhat the same sense that contemporary neo-Kantian philosophers employ it: the world in which we live is not entirely made up out of our own minds, but the character that it appears to have, for those who have read Lawrence seriously, it has in part by virtue of his work.

Mr. Leavis has recently written that *The Rainbow* and *Women in Love*, which he correctly considers Lawrence's best novels, "have had essentially no recognition at all." But a less ardent admirer of Lawrence would acknowledge that if we judge by critical interest Lawrence has at last come to occupy the place in English literature that he unquestionably deserves. Father Tiverton may be right when he points out that Lawrence did not compel his successors to write like him; what he did was to make it impossible for them to write like his predecessors. But a writer's

3

importance cannot be judged exclusively by his influence on other writers. When we consider the changes that have taken place between the year 1911 (when Lawrence's first novel appeared) and the present, it seems that this is as much Lawrence's century as that of any other writer of the period. For he was one of the writers who helped give form to the sensibility we now possess and who helped define the values and concerns that are the substance of our lives. If it is true, as Ezra Pound has put it, that artists are the antennae of the race, we can say of Lawrence that early in our century he thrust his long, tremulous filaments into the future and brought back to us a report of what we were gradually to find there as the years went by.

But we shall miss Lawrence's positive value as well as overlook the threat he represents if we center our critical interest exclusively on the biographical or psychoanalytic aspects of his work: the gossipy game of discovering who were the originals for the characters of his novels, or of finding the neuroses that are expressed in them; the dreary and often trivial game—in certain quarters considered "scholarly research"—of ascertaining whether Lawrence did or did not read Zelia Nuttall or Bernal Diaz del Castillo. If we are to take Lawrence seriously, we must read him as Mr. Leavis, Father Tiverton, Mr. Hough, and only a very few others have read him: as a writer who discovered by means of the creative act the structure of experience and who, by embodying it in his art, achieved a vision of life.[2]

Not that we can afford to do without the biographical labors of his friends and enemies; or that we can ignore the literary psychoanalysis that is so freely practiced on him. There is urgent need for these kinds of investigation. But the essential task is that of examining Lawrence's art and not his sick soul. The latter is of objective importance only when it becomes the source of traits discernible in the work itself. What is of undisputed importance is the work itself. Do we have an adequate knowledge of Lawrence's vision of the world? Do we know how perfect or imperfect it was? The critics I have mentioned have in the last few

years addressed themselves to this question. But I do not believe
that these men have said the last word on Lawrence, simply because on such a subject there is no last word. If a man is a poet of
Lawrence's stature, no age, no critic, no reader definitively
"places" him. It is a job that has to be done again and again—a job
that we must do, not for the sake of the poet, but for our own
sake. In the process of this continued critical definition and re-
definition, we may not arrive at a final estimate of his value, but
we do something at least as important: we redefine our heritage
and, in so far as it is given to us to do so, we enlarge our vision.
No doubt in doing so we run the risk of inflicting a radical in-
justice on the poet, hastening to read into his work our own inchoate aspirations and our fears. But this is inevitable and, in any
case, the dialectic of criticism tends to make the necessary correc-
tions.

[2]

When we try to read Lawrence objectively, in order to discover the nature of his gift to us, we do not find it easy to do.
The best of contemporary criticism rightly frowns on the facile
separation of substance and form. Sophisticated critics today quite
automatically harness the word "message" with quotation marks.
They shun the word "moral" when used as a synonym of "message." It is a basic assumption of contemporary criticism, and a
fully justified one, that poetry with a moral is bad poetry and
that if it is good poetry the moral has been artificially tacked to
it by the writer or the reader. No critic well grounded in contemporary aesthetics would find an "ethic" in genuine poetry.
If he found it, he would suspect the quality of the poetry. Nevertheless, the first and the most difficult problem that the critic of
Lawrence has to face is that of distinguishing in his work poetry
from prophecy, art from message; of distinguishing aesthetic vision authentically revealed from propaganda, of distinguishing
the world he discovered in and through the act of creation from

his criticism and his turgid lucubrations. The created world will
be found at its best to be a powerful aesthetic organization of
values and disvalues, the matter of experience as grasped by a
gifted mind and transmuted and informed by it. What the poet
gives us is what he brings up from the depths of his creative imagination, in the ideal isolation of his perfected form and informed
substance. True, the matter the poet works with is the stuff of
his experience of life and of art; but if he is an artist, the act of
creation *adds* to his experienced matter to make up a literally new
product: the informed substance of his poetry. The addition
makes this product more than an imitation or reflection of what
exists; it is literally an addition, the manifestation of the freedom
of his spirit. The vision the poet offers us has order and splendor,
whereas the objects of our vision are incomplete, opaque, vague.
The first and most important step in arriving at knowledge of ourselves and of the world is to apprehend both immediately in
their own terms as objects of the act of aesthesis. It is at this point
that the work of the poet comes to its full non-residential utility:
we do not see the world reflected in it, we see the world by
means of it. And the difference between the alternatives is radical.
It is in this special sense that the poet's world is normative.

[3]

Father Tiverton asserts that it is not possible to separate art
from message in Lawrence, and in a sense he is right. But he himself has noted adversely certain features of Lawrence's thought
and called attention with sympathy and sensitivity to others.
Again, the refusal to make the separation overlooks two facts.
The first is that Lawrence did not always produce "pure" art;
and the second is that Lawrence himself advised us to make the
separation and gave us essentially valid reasons for doing so. The
reader will probably remember the last two lines of the essay on
"The Novel": "Oh give me the novel. Let me hear what the

novel says. As for the novelist, he is usually a dribbling liar." ³
This statement, expressing in two lines the truth of the so-called
intentional fallacy long before those who baptized it wrote
their controversial essay, represents no mere passing thought of
Lawrence's, but a considered insight, as fundamental to his
aesthetic as it is to any aesthetic worth serious consideration. All
we have to do to verify this assertion is to remember the first chapter of *Studies in Classic American Literature:* "Art speech is the
only truth. An artist is usually a damned liar, but his art, if it be
art, will tell you the truth of his day. . . . The old American
artists were hopeless liars. But they were artists in spite of themselves."

That art tells "the truth" is something that a reader acquainted
with contemporary aesthetics would hesitate to assert in the
facile way in which Lawrence asserts it. Having pointed out the
impropriety of his use of the word "truth" in this connection,
however, we need not scruple to employ it; the word stands for
something real and important, although it would take a close and
prolonged analysis to define it. But that the intention of a work, if
it is art, will often be in conflict with what the artist takes to be
his intention is as well known today as it is easy to prove.

In the same chapter of *Studies* from which this quotation was
taken, Lawrence writes that "the proper function of a critic is to
save the tale from the artist who created it." Agreed. But there is
a catch to the statement. For a critic can save the tale only if he
recognizes art, and he cannot recognize it unless he has an idea
of what art is prior to his recognition that a particular thing is indeed art. All this we have long known, for Plato made it perfectly clear in one of his most popular dialogues, *The Phaedo.*
But it is a truth that entails coming to terms with abstract and difficult problems of aesthetics.

The distinction between the dribbling liar who is the novelist
and the truth of the novel applies to Lawrence as much as it does to
"Old Leo" and the others against whom Lawrence employed it so

brilliantly in his essay on "The Novel." But before we apply it, it is desirable to take a closer look at it, for it expresses the basic distinction with which I shall be working in this work.

In the essay on "The Novel" Lawrence traces the distinction to a conflict between "the passional inspiration" of the artist, as he calls it, and his didactic purpose or philosophy. He writes: "It is such a bore that nearly all great novelists have a didactic purpose, otherwise a philosophy, directly opposite to their passional inspiration. In their passional inspiration, they are all phallic worshippers . . . yet all of them, when it comes to their philosophy . . . are all crucified Jesuses. What a bore! And what a burden for the novel to carry!" [4] There is an important insight here. The terms in which the insight is couched are not theoretically felicitous, and the assertion that what makes a novelist a dribbling liar is the conflict between his philosophy and his phallic worship is one of those irresponsible generalizations that frequently open Lawrence to easy attack. But we often find novels that contain conflicting intentions, and this is the important point. Exactly how these intentions are to be defined is something to be found by an analysis of each novel.

It is, then, in the work itself that we shall find the clash between the liar and the poet. What turned so gifted an artist into a liar is the subject of biographical inquiry. That there are two Lawrences has long been known: indeed, one could without artifice distinguish more than two. Katherine Mansfield found three. But for our purposes two are enough. How, then, shall we explain this conflict? From the objective point of view the conflict can only be a failure of integration between form and substance; or, more precisely, a fault in the transmutation or transubstancing of the matter of experience into the informed substance of art. The matter is whatever the artist uses—passion or ideology or anything else, if there is anything else; in any case, we recognize the fault when the work fails to function in the aesthetic mode, when it arouses emotion or insinuates questions concerning matters of fact or of value that prevent the intransitive contemplation that is the proper reaction to art as art. The objective failure is, of course, finally to be traced to subjective sources: to divided vision, to a clash of allegiance in the artist himself between the creative act of aesthetic apprehension and his own commitments as a moralist or a political or religious man or some other sort of sectarian.

Here we cross from the field of criticism into that of biography. A complete explanation, demanded by the mind, forces us to discover the cause of the aesthetic fault. But if there is a fault in the vase because the hand of the potter trembled, we shall find the cause in him, in his relations to society or in the state of his body, in short in data that is not aesthetic. Ultimately it is in the stresses and strains between the espousals and the commitments of the artist as practical man and as artist that we find the objective conflicts expressed in his work. That the account of such clashes and stresses is bound to be only speculative and is not susceptible of verification is unfortunate; but it is not something we can remedy. In general terms, the subjective clash is to be accounted for in the following manner: the matter of experience attempts to reveal itself in the creative act, but the non-aesthetic demands of the artist predominate or at least are strong enough to prevent a fully adequate aesthetic transmutation of matter into informed substance. The moralist or the practical or the religious man or the political man is offended or bruised by what the poet is on the verge of creatively discovering and attempts to bring it into harmony with his non-aesthetic commitments. In a genuine artist the clash is never radical; it is never a question of unconditional surrender. Nor does it appear to him as a conflict between aesthetic and non-aesthetic demands. It appears as the travail and turmoil of the creative act. This is the reason the artist has a hard time against the dribbling liar. His business is to submit, with humble docility, all that comes up as matter for his work, to the demands of the whole. The liar adds his own matter, and the artist in his humility and his impersonality does not recognize what the liar offers and fails to see the manner in which it is of-

fered. For the artist is capable of an impersonality that the dribbling liar in him resents; this impersonality ignores the liar's pet
notions, his wounds, his vanities, his loves and hates, in favor of
something that, gestated in the depths of the artist's mind, seems
nevertheless alien to him—and, indeed, is, since it possesses a
self-sufficiency all its own. To the degree that the artist fails to
digest his experience aesthetically and that bullying passion and
autocratic ideology take over, the product is a "dribbling lie"
—or, as I shall call it, impure art. In Lawrence we find both forms
of impurity: excess of passion and the autocracy of ideas, both
of which are the result of his failure to bring the prophet to heel.
There are other faults in his work, but the most serious faults are
caused by the dribbling liar.

It follows from what has been said that, properly speaking,
poetry is not a medium for the communication of "ideas," for the
exposition of a "philosophy." We can, of course, speak of a philosophical poet. We can expound the philosophy of Shakespeare's
plays, of Conrad's novels, of Eliot's verse. But we then use the
term in one of two senses: we mean that the poet's revealed vision
is grounded on a number of presuppositions, either moral or
cosmic, which he takes for granted and which function as principles by means of which he selects the matter he chooses to
transmute into informed substance. Or, probably more often, we
mean that more or less automatically we evaluate in terms of our
own standards the revealed vision. In the latter sense, Shakespeare,
say, is a philosophical poet. But he expresses as many philosophies as there are critics who interpret him.

Lawrence drew, from a different point of view, essentially the
same distinction when he wrote, in a well-known passage of the
"Foreword" of *Fantasia and the Unconscious*, that his verse and
novels are pure passionate experience and that his philosophical
ideas "are inferences made afterwards from the experience." Had
this always been the case he would have always been a poet.
Through the writing of *Women in Love* this was, by and large,
the case; Lawrence was a "pure" artist and his novels did not

drag with unnecessary philosophical messages. The impurities we find in the works written prior to *Aaron's Rod*, and we find many, are relatively minor. But after *Women in Love* Lawrence's prophetic urge took over. This is not to say that his later work is entirely unpoetic. Some of his short stories—whatever their relative merit as compared with his major novels—are pure poetry.

These observations require a careful qualification. Lawrence wrote, and the preceding discussion has been carried on, as if the relation between poetic substance and conceptual content were a simple matter of either/or, whereas it can only be one of degree. Actually, the matter of experience that goes to make up the substance of a work of literary art must already be conceptually structured to some extent. Even the best of poets (a poet so pure that what Mr. Eliot said of Henry James would apply fully to him: one with a mind so fine that no idea could violate it) cannot help acquiring in his practical, non-poetical, living more or less rudimentary or finished "philosophical" notions by means of which his experience is given some sort of order prior to its substantiation and information by the creative act. Even when young Lawrence was living in his parents' home, visiting Jessie Chambers at the farm, he was reading a great deal, as we know, and he was "thinking" after his fashion, which is to say that he had ideas of all sorts, that he had already begun to pick up a philosophical attitude towards life. His mind was not, it could not be, so fine that it was ideologically vacuous in an absolute sense. The ideas that serve as matter for the making of his poetry perform two legitimate functions: one, already indicated, is that of serving as principles of selection. But they may perform this function wrongly: when they reject matter on moral rather than on aesthetic grounds, they turn the poet into a dribbling liar. The ideas themselves may also function as matter to be transmuted into informed substance and to be revealed in the poetry in the opinions of the "actors" or in the principles of their actions. In his poetry Lawrence's ideas are not merely dressed up in false dramatic face: Mr. Pessimism, who is bound to commit suicide at the end of the tale, or Miss Chastity who, being naive, is victimized by Sir John Lecher.

If Lawrence wants to call his art "pure experience" there is no law to prevent him from so doing, nor is there any harm in it, so long as we make clear that the expression is being used in the sense gathered from the considerations I have tried to elucidate. But neither Lawrence nor any one could take his art as "pure" in the sense that it was altogether free from conceptual structure. That it could never be. In this sense, "pure" experience is utter mindless chaos: the blooming and buzzing confusion of which we used to hear when William James was still read by American philosophers.

[4]

If Lawrence was not always a successful artist, how can we account for his failure? The causes, of a biographical nature, are obscure and can only be put forth diffidently, for they are speculative interpretations of facts that are complex, vague, and, at this date, beyond adequate authentication. A complete account of them would involve the writing of a critical biography. Here all I can do is to give a succinct outline of several of the factors that I take to be the most important. But I must make it quite clear that in broaching the topic I am undertaking a job of critical spelunking. I am inviting the reader to go down with me into a cave where we shall be lighted by the dim and wavering flame of a quasi-psychoanalytic candle. If the image is objectionable, let me put it more literally by saying that we are about to enter a region of pure speculation in which facts, such as they are, are inherently susceptible to the most conflicting and weird interpretations.

The biographical data required are already at hand. Everywhere we pan in Lawrence material we strike pay dirt. But it would be folly to forget that the word "perhaps" darkens the whole discussion. Speculations of this sort are necessary, they are often illuminating, but they can neither be taken to be uninterpreted fact nor be put forth as scientific hypotheses.

The investigation would begin with an analysis of Lawrence's childhood, interpreting along orthodox lines Lawrence's attachment to his "genteel" mother and his intense hatred of his working-class father. The investigation would next emphasize the alienation that this relationship probably generated. His alienation, his acute sense of social inferiority, and his ambivalent attitude towards the upper classes, which he discloses with candor and pathos in the "Autobiographical Sketch" published in *Assorted Articles,* are probably allotropic manifestations of a complex reaction. To this alienation his superior talent and his mother's ambitions for him no doubt contributed. The investigation would then move on to an examination of later events: his protracted and unsatisfactory love affair with Jessie Chambers, the death of his mother, the final brutal break with his childhood sweetheart, and his relatively easy success as a writer at the beginning. From here the investigation would take up the central event of his life, Frieda. None of these experiences could be expected to lead to a facile "adjustment" to his world. On the contrary, they all tended to intensify his acute sense of difference between himself and others. Then comes the suppression of *The Rainbow,* with both its immediate consequences and the threat it carried to his future as artist. All of these events are taking place at the time when many educated people are reacting from the aestheticism of the nineties—the business of the gem-like flame and the pallid art for art's sake. If I am not utterly wrong, this aestheticism was to evolve by a devious process into the hedonism of the Russell-Keynes group, for which the economist has left us an unconvincing apology. Lawrence, when he came into contact with the followers of G. E. Moore, sized them up immediately and accurately and reacted with deep repugnance towards them. But those who could not accept the aesthetic hedonism of G. E. Moore's disciples did not have at hand an adequate aesthetic that would provide them with something they badly needed—a sharp definition of art and a clear distinction between what is art and what is something else. Nor did the times allow those who reacted against Moore's aestheticism to realize the need for such an aesthetic. The need for it was not perceived and the hammering out of it did not take place until twenty-five years later (counting, of course, in good round numbers) when the problems of paraphrase, of the intention of the work as contrasted with that of the artist, and of intrinsic as against extrinsic criticism, and the like, came up for serious and protracted discussion.

When Lawrence begins his career as a poet, in spite of his shrewd distinction between the dribbling liar and the poet, he has no scruple in using art as means for non-aesthetic ends, and acts as if he believed, with the majority of his contemporaries, that anything is art that can be called art—and, of course, there is no human product that cannot be called art. The end of art, furthermore, is for him and his contemporaries the good life, and anything that is revolutionary, anything that appears to be an innovation, anything that can be claimed to be a release from Victorian norms is good. Lawrence, although he had very little respect for most of his fellow artists, was born to "The Pompadour Café"—the Café in *Women in Love* in which the scene of Gudrun's snatching Birkin's letter from Halliday took place. He was part of the avant-garde; he did not need an introduction to it, he required no initiation; Lawrence took readily to the group of well-born and not so well-born men and women whom he met after the publication of his first novel and whom he used as matter for some of the characters of the books. In *Point Counter Point* Huxley pictures Lawrence as ill at ease and antagonistic to the London bohemians from whom he is distinguished by his vitality. This is no doubt true to the biographical fact. But it does not contradict the contention that Lawrence was a bohemian. What else can we call this rootless, wandering expatriate, living into the twenties on nearly nothing, if not a citizen of that demi-republic of letters that had, and I am told, still has, enclaves in London, Paris, Florence, and Taos? When the war ended he escaped from England and the Pompadour Café—again, so to speak—and started a tour that finally took him completely around the world: to Italy, to Ceylon, to Australia, to Taos, to "old Mexico," and finally to Europe to die. But what good did it do him to escape physically?

But I am going too fast and am in danger of losing my trail. The war brought the great trauma, the slow, pitiless, and final break with his world. During a war everybody feels the urge to do something in some way or other—or nearly everybody. In 1914 the youth of England went to the trenches to die, and died. Or, like Middleton Murry, found useful work to do at home. But Lawrence would not help. He was opposed to the war although he was no pacifist. He refused to serve. Nor would he keep quiet about his refusal—and with a German wife he could not get by unnoticed. Why did he take the position he did? One word seems to account for it—"alienation." Because I judge this subject to be of great importance I intend to consider it at some length in its proper place (Chapter II, section 2).

Whatever was back of Lawrence's attitude towards the war, Lawrence opposed it with intense passion and intense terror in his soul. But he could not stand idly by. Something had to be done. But what can a writer who is married to a German woman do when the world is out to destroy him or, what adds up to the same thing, when he thinks it is: when it pushes him around, snoops into his private life, denies him the means of making a living, and forces him to undergo degrading medical examinations? There is nothing to do but to attempt to flee. But Lawrence was not allowed to leave England while the war was going on. He escaped, nevertheless, in imagination: he planned a Utopia and discussed it, apparently seriously, with friends whom he appointed as disciples. Most of the prospective pioneers knew better than to submit their lives to his management: Katherine Carswell had a good excuse—she had a husband. Murry had another excuse; and so for the rest but one. Dorothy Brett was ready to follow him. One can without impropriety say, since she herself left us the account of her relation to Lawrence, that she was ready to chase him to the end of the world with a yearning heart and a trumpet ready

to the ear to catch his every word. It would all be hilarious had it
not involved so much gratuitous pain. In the meantime, while
waiting to ship to Florida and start his happy little colony—in
the swamps, among the noble Seminoles, one supposes—he undertakes the reform of England in collaboration with Bertrand Russell. The brief friendship and quarrel with Russell appear to the
reader today as pathetic and comic. But not so to Russell, who
nearly forty-five years later has given strong expression of his
hatred of the artist and his ideas.

Once Lawrence, forced by his opposition to the war, became a
reformer, he never gave up the role. Give a man who has the
need to dominate others the chance to lead the world out of its
mess, and the need will never subside. It seeks satisfaction by any
means at hand. Having tasted that kind of intoxicating blood, our
bengal is never satisfied with anything else. Art, pure art, is by
comparison an insipid quarry. He tells us somewhere that he
used his novels as means of shedding his sickness. This is true. But
he also puts his novels to other uses. He will reform mankind,
just as he will tell Bertrand Russell what and how Russell may
think.

Because *Women in Love* had been conceived earlier than the
brutal trauma he underwent during the war (originally, as everybody knows, this work and *The Rainbow* made up one single
novel), the prophet did not meddle with this book. But from
Aaron's Rod on, this statement does not hold. *Kangaroo* is hardly
a novel. It is at best an effort, a futile effort, to solve a problem.
After *Women in Love*, Lawrence is not able to inform the matter
of his experience with the success he had achieved earlier. We
find a continuous development in stylistic gifts. Some of the short
stories are quite successful, and in everything he writes are to
be found, in profusion, vignettes and even expository paragraphs
that are evidence of his mastery over the language. They are
pure poetry. Several chapters of *Morning In Mexico* are magnificent, although it would not be astonishing to me if anthropological
students of the Southwest found his interpretations of the Indian

dances offensive to their scientific consciences and even utterly fantastic. As late as the posthumous *Apocalypse*, we find whole paragraphs that constitute triumphant evidence of what a gifted man can do with the English language. But on the whole the poet has lost control. He is too deeply involved in a bitter struggle against forces that he feels threaten him to handle them as he handled his experience up to and including *Women in Love*.

This passionate desire of Lawrence to do something about the world was not subject matter that could be transformed into substance—or at least that *he* could transform. It was, for him, too definitely addressed to practical ends. What he could and did do was to handle with a messianic fervor subjects he had formerly handled aesthetically. He changed settings. He took Aaron and Lilly to Florence, he took Lovat and his foreign wife to Australia, he went with Kate to "old Mexico." He added to his interest in love a strong sociological and political interest that he had not shown in his earlier work. The dances of the Indians of the Southwest gave him a clearer grasp than he had previously achieved of the insight that one of the profound needs of modern man is a religion that will enable him to re-establish his broken connection with the Cosmos. And thus, Lawrence managed to give himself and those of his readers who do not grasp the distinction between quasi-art and art in the most exacting sense, the impression that he was growing prodigiously in an aesthetic sense. But the rate of growth, *exception fait* of his increasing mastery over language, was negligible.

A detailed examination of the work that Lawrence did after *Women in Love* will show that, whatever its many incidental aesthetic excellences and whatever its ideological value, on the whole it fails to come up to the purity exhibited in his two greatest works, *The Rainbow* and *Women in Love*.

PART ONE

The Failure of Art

CHAPTER ONE

Aaron's Rod

IT IS not easy to bring to mind a writer of the stature of Lawrence, whose work is as uneven as his. In all of his books, even in *The Lost Girl*, which he wrote as a pot-boiler, there are pages that give evidence of his superb mastery over language. But if we expect an object of art to be an organic whole, to be free of padding, to be the product of sustained inspiration, and thus to be the source of an intransitive experience embodying immanent meanings—if this is our notion of art, the difference between his best, as represented by *Women in Love* and *The Rainbow* and some of the short stories on the one hand and the poor work on the other, is abysmal. And the worst of his novels is, in my opinion, *Aaron's Rod*. I make this statement fully aware of the fact that Middleton Murry said of this novel in *Son of Woman*, that it was "the greatest of his novels," and that in his *Reminiscences of D. H. Lawrence*, published two years later, he reiterated his judgment by coupling it with *Fantasia of the Unconscious* as "the two finest of his later books." [1] And I also say it fully aware of the fact that Mr. Leavis praises it highly. Middleton Murry's attitude is probably accounted for in terms of his complex and messy friendship with Lawrence and the feeling that he was himself as closely implicated in the problem the book discusses dramatically as was Lawrence. For this assumption there is circumstantial evidence in the discussion of *Aaron's Rod* in *Son of Woman*, since Middleton Murry takes the writer Lilly to be Lawrence, and it is not difficult to surmise that Aaron was a portrait, in part at least, of

Lawrence's best friend at one time. But subjective interpretations of the book need not obscure for others its fundamental weakness, a radical incoherence in substance.

The novel is a thoroughly prosaic account of the events that led Aaron, after leaving his wife and children, to go to London and, after an illness in London, to Italy. One of Lawrence's critics has correctly observed that its machinery creaks disgracefully: "Our story will not yet see the light of day." ". . . Our story continues by night." "Don't grumble at me, gentle reader, and swear at me that this damn fellow wasn't half clever enough to think all these smart things . . ." The writing is utterly flat: " 'I don't say so. But—' exclaimed the flush, full blooded Robert, who was nothing if not courteous to women."

But it is not merely a question of technical clumsiness and of flat writing. The book shows no trace of creative imagination whatever. It is a mere transcription, mere reportage. We do not have to identify the original of Lilly, "the dark, irascible little man," a rootless and drifting writer, and his Norwegian wife. We need not perceive that we are presented here with another version of the couple we are to meet in Lawrence's next novel, whose slight physical changes and new aliases are the merest pretense at concealment. We do not need the key with which his letters and his biographers so generously provide us, in order to realize that the other characters of this flat book are taken directly from life and stuck into the novel. This is not true of his successful novels, but it is of *Aaron's Rod*. In this book the stuff of the drama, whether a faithful record of actual events or sheer invention, lacks that which lifts the matter of experience into the substance of poetry. The stacking of the sheaves in *The Rainbow* was probably lived by Lawrence, and the scene in which Birkin shatters the image of the moon in the pond in *Women in Love* may also have been lived by him. But this is wholly irrelevant for the reader of *The Rainbow* and *Women in Love*. For whether lived or invented, the scenes reverberate with dense meanings, each fully realized, utterly self-sufficient; confronted with them, even if we are reading with minimal attention, we recognize them at once as our only and exclusive object of interest. And the result is that in retrospect the whole book remains a luminous realization, a coherent whole that retains its power of attracting us. Nothing like that is to be encountered in *Aaron's Rod*.

But the worst defect of the book is its radical incoherence. This defect shows itself in two closely connected senses: in its utter lack of form and in its failure to elucidate an important point in which the reader is legitimately interested, the grounds on which Aaron leaves his wife and children.

The form of the book, if one can apply this term to it, is the formlessness of the picaresque, a narrative made up of a series of incidents whose only unity is the thin thread imparted to it by Aaron's presence in the chapters of the book. Some of these incidents, such as the brilliant sketch of the two young Englishmen, have no relation to the development of Aaron's story. They are, for all their individual worth, pure padding. The book contains one pseudo-symbol or quasi-symbol, the flute, through which Aaron expresses his spiritual needs, through which he earns his living after leaving his wife, and through which, as might be expected, the obvious Freudian meaning is conveyed.[2] But the symbol is concocted and fails to organize the story. In its Freudian meaning it is utterly incongruous when we consider that one of Aaron's traits seems to be frigidity or fear of women, connected with a repressed, latent homosexuality. As the golden bowl is central to James's novel, so are water and the moon central to *Women in Love*, bringing together into a concentrated focus the substance of Lawrence's great novel. The flute merely baffles.

To the incoherence from which the novel suffers because of its lack of form we have to add the incoherence of its substance. Lawrence sides with Aaron and Lilly, nor is such partiality necessarily to be considered a defect. His business is to exhibit the values and qualities which he takes to give human existence its significance, such as they may be. But Lawrence's partiality for

Aaron does not help us grasp the nature of Aaron's quarrel with his world, particularly with his wife. It is a deep quarrel, and appears all the deeper when it is contrasted with the irresponsible prattle of his friends about bloody revolution and the need to tear the house down. But what is the object of Aaron's grudge? What does he hate and what does he love? And why? The hatred will remain blind until we are permitted to grasp the values precluded from realization by the objects of his hatred. And what justifies the grudge? There is no answer to these questions. Was Lawrence trying to shed his illness in this book? The hurried dumping of his illness not only had no therapeutic value for him, but is the cause of a botched job. Without explanation or warning, Aaron decides not to return to his wife and children. What justifies the action? I am not calling for a *moral* justification for an unmitigatedly caddish act, a justification that will satisfy my notions of the decent treatment a man owes his family and himself. As a critic, what I must ask for is the aesthetic justification; a rendering, in whatever way the author chooses to give it, of that which gives Aaron's action its intelligibility in the story. This justification is lacking because in *Aaron's Rod* Lawrence has not digested the subject he has to transmute to substance.[3] The novel does not give us the means to see what revulsions and what inspirations led Aaron to abandon his family. We are told that he wants to keep the mastery over his soul. "Be damned and blasted to women and all their importances," cries Aaron. "They want to get you under and children is their chief weapon" (Chapter IX).[4] But one is not given even an inkling, in terms of specific acts, of the soul's outrage or humiliation or enslavement, which would enable the reader to understand his revolt. We are told Aaron was outraged. But no *dramatic* evidence is provided. How does a woman get a man under herself? And when a woman gets a man under, exactly what does he lose, what does she gain? In a novel, which is not a philosophical essay, we expect more than abstractions and generalizations.

In Chapter XIII, Lawrence tries to make clear the grounds for

Aaron's flight. The reader will remember that indispensable chapter in Henry James's *The Portrait of a Lady*, in which Isabel stays in the drawing room after her husband asks her to use her influence with Lord Warburton in Pansy's behalf. Osmond leaves and Isabel leans back in her chair and closes her eyes, and for a long time meditates. What she is doing is reviewing her situation and she finally comes to the lucid and shattering conclusion that "she had thrown her life away." The chapter's indispensability rests on the fact that Isabel must at this juncture accept with devastating clarity the realization of the true nature of the man she has married, for everything that follows depends on that realization. Isabel achieves her clarification and the reader shares in it, and he is thus prepared for the discoveries Isabel must make before her education is complete and she is ready for the final decision she must make, that of returning to her husband from London after Ralph's death.

In Chapter XIII of *Aaron's Rod*, Lawrence is up against a problem similar to that which confronted James in *The Portrait of a Lady*. He did not avail himself of several opportunities that presented themselves to him to make clear to his readers the ground of Aaron's flight. And now we have Aaron sitting in a hall at some distance from a burning fire, thinking of his wife and children at home. In eight pages he reviews his life and his relations to Lottie, his wife. But the information we are given does not in the least make Aaron's action more intelligible than it was before, and not long afterwards one comes to the conclusion that Aaron had no grasp of his action. In the chapter in which Isabel reviews her life, it is Isabel who does the reviewing, it is Isabel with whom we are in direct communication, seeing the truth of her plight unfold as she sees it and when she sees it. In *Aaron's Rod* this is the way in which the review begins. But the novelist cannot accomplish the feat of transmitting to us Aaron's grasp of his situation in Aaron's terms and from his point of view. We begin to look at the situation through the eyes of his wife Lottie, and the novelist shifts us back to Aaron. But soon the novelist himself takes over and offers us an explanation that explains nothing.

He realized that he had never intended to yield himself fully to her or to anything: that he did not intend ever to yield himself up entirely to her or to anything: that his very being pivoted on the fact of his isolate self-responsibility, aloneness. His intrinsic and central aloneness was the very center of his being . . .

He coldly and terribly hated her, for a moment. Then no more. There was no solution. It was a situation without a solution. But at any rate, it was now a defined situation. He could rest in peace.

Thoughts something in this manner ran through Aaron's subconscious mind as he sat still in the strange house. He could not have fired it all off at any listener, as these pages are fired off at any chance reader. Nevertheless, there it was, risen to half consciousness in him.
—CHAPTER XIII

When one places these considerations beside Aaron's peculiar relationship to Lilly, one sees that the novel is really an invitation to a Freudian picnic. The situation is defined and clarified in one sense. Aaron has decided he cannot go back to Lottie and has surveyed the reason he cannot. But the definition we are given is not what we require and what the novelist should have given us in order to dispel the irritating obscurity. What we are given is *an abstract discourse*, too vague to be illuminating as philosophy or psychology and too abstract to have the immediacy and resultant conviction of concrete drama. The account floats above the character; it has no anchorage in action nor is it gathered in a system of poetic symbols to give it presentational immediacy. When, in *Women in Love*, Birkin is going through a spiritual crisis, after leaving Hermione, and before Ursula accepts the love beyond love he proffers her, the novelist by a system of powerful symbols gives us a sense, *au fond*, of the nature of Birkin's trouble; we see him shattering the image of the moon, we see him proposing love to Ursula and pointing to the cat, Mino, to make his point, we see him discussing the West African figure with Gerald in

Halliday's flat, we hear him engage in conversations with the other characters—conversations that are sometimes good-natured, sometimes fierce—and all along, by concrete means, we get nearer to Birkin and grasp the nature of his values and of his desiderata. In *Aaron's Rod* we never find out satisfactorily what Aaron means by his "isolate self-responsibility," his "aloneness." We do not find out what the values are whose attraction accounts for his caddishness to his wife.

I am not suggesting that Aaron is not a convincing person. It is not at all a question of Aristotelian probabilities. It is something quite different and much more fundamental: it is a question of intelligibility. Aaron is a puzzle. Cads and villains are convincing enough in art or in life. There is nothing unconvincing about Iago. In life we are satisfied with labeling them and noting under some general rubric the actions we may expect from them. He is selfish, we say of a man. We do not explain him in one sense, yet we do in another, since we subsume him under a general category. If our act of subsumption is challenged, we present evidence: "He is selfish because"—and we cite specific actions that we take to be acceptable to our interlocutor as evidence of selfishness. If we want to account for his selfishness, we ask, How did he get that way? And the possible answers range from Calvin to Thomas Aquinas to Cora Dubois, from predestination to freedom to toilet-training. The novelist need not give us an account in this sense. But if he is not to puzzle us, he has to give us that larger context, the situation within which his characters move, the context which Lawrence gave us in his earlier books and which made Paul, Tom, Lydia, Will, Anna, the Brangwen sisters, Birkin, and Gerald intelligible. Aaron is possible enough. As Lawrence himself puts it in the essay on "The Novel," from which I have already quoted: "So if a character in a novel wants two wives—or three—or thirty: well, that is true of that man, at that time, in that circumstance." Aaron does not want a wife and children. That is true of him. But a few lines earlier in the same essay Lawrence writes: "And this is the beauty of the novel;

everything is true in its own relationship, and no further." [5]

But this is the lack of beauty of *Aaron's Rod*, that the relationships are lacking, that circumstances and convictions have been withheld that would have given Aaron's decision to leave his wife and children its "truth." But what Lawrence means by the "truth" is not clearly enough indicated, although it is suggested: what he means is that the novel is a self-contained universe. When the "truth" of a novel fails to come about we have no barrier between our world and the world of the novel, the distinction between art and life is erased or has not been drawn. Either the actual world enters into the world of art, bringing with it all its heterogeneous problems, its essentially baffling concatenations, its incompletion and its mere unsupported factuality, or art spills into life and acquires its own irreducible opacity. The upshot is that we have no novel, properly speaking. What we have is a number of pressing questions, generated by our contemplation of the no-novel before us.

When the novelist fails to contain the substance of his work in its informing bounds, we are free, or rather we feel pressed, to ask any question that the no-novel suggests to us. The most pressing question *Aaron's Rod* suggests involves the values and attitudes of the man who attempted, but failed, to write the novel. It is the most pressing question, because in *Aaron's Rod* these values have spilled over into the art without having been subjected to the process of informing and transubstancing and the result is that the work is turbid; they are there making themselves felt by their conspicuous presence or by their absence, but in any case obtruding themselves on us, demanding that we look at them. The unexplained caddishness of Aaron forces on us a suspicion that some values are being presented in, and some are being withheld from, the novel, in which we have a serious moral interest.

But before we look into Lawrence's values and attitudes, let me push one possible irrelevance aside. If we remember the circumstances in which Lawrence wrote *Aaron's Rod*, we may feel inclined to account for it in terms of these facts. With these facts on hand, the parlor psychoanalyst can turn the problem into a genetic question and derail us from our objective by offering us an alleged explanation of the meaning of Aaron's decision. This explanation is so obvious that we need not sketch it here. But even assuming that the literary critic, with his second-hand psychoanalysis, can get at these reasons, their discovery does not in the least illumine or nullify the question that confronts us. For that question is addressed to the grounds of our puzzled dissatisfaction with the work of art.

In order to answer our question we have to keep in mind the conclusions already reached in respect to *Aaron's Rod*. No ground is offered, we saw, for Aaron's desertion of his family. For if we accept as adequate ground his expressed desire, reiterated in various occasions, "to keep the mastery of his soul and conscience and actions," we have to ask exactly what is the meaning of this conviction of his and what is its validity for him. If we say the intense desire to be free is enough to justify his leaving his wife and children, we are saying that *a man who does not feel any obligations does not have any*. This is a theory that subjectivist moral philosophers maintain, or is a consequence of their theory. Its error is to be traced to the utter contempt of experiential data that *soi-disant* empirical philosophers show when engaged in their intellectual games. We do not know in what sense Aaron's wife, Lottie, was an impossible person. But even if she was, and Aaron was justified in leaving her, the manner in which he chose to do it heaped on her humiliation and injury, and the conclusion must be that Aaron is no less contemptible than the Bricknells and their set. To the serious reader, endowed with moral responsibility, what *Aaron's Rod* signifies is the widening area of infection which is poisoning our society.

The defense of Lawrence—not of Aaron—that readily comes to mind at this point is that he faithfully reports on a state of affairs and does not hold it up for admiration; this is the way things are, and it is not his business to conceal them; nor would we want him to lie to us about what he sees. "If a character in a novel wants two wives—or three—or thirty; well, that is true of that man, at that time, in that circumstance." But the criticism to which *Aaron's Rod* is open is that Lawrence defends Aaron's action. He not merely presents an aspect of experience, he presents it in such a manner that one is fully aware that he is trying to make a case for Aaron, and he does so in spite of the fact that he is not able to tell us what grievances Aaron had against his wife. When Aaron returned to his home he performed an act of cruelty whose nature is not sensed by Lawrence any more than it is by Aaron. Lottie asks him what she has done to deserve such treatment from him. Aaron thinks to himself, "Telling isn't so easy—specially when the trouble goes too deep for conscious comprehension. He couldn't *tell* what he had against her" (Chapter XI). The italics are the novelist's, not mine. That Aaron might not have been able to express what he had against his wife is an unexceptionable point. What the reader must object to is that Lawrence is not able to tell him what Aaron had against Lottie—except in the most general and abstract terms. But when, in *The Rainbow*, Will and Anna quarrel, when in bitterness and anger "she jeers at his soul," we are fully given the grounds for their estrangement; and we are fully given them, not in general terms but in the dramatic terms appropriate to the novelist. The same is true of Ursula and Birkin in *Women in Love*. There is a scene in Chapter XXIII of *Women in Love* in which Ursula and Birkin engage in an extremely bitter quarrel, the prima facie grounds of which, at least, are fully exhibited. The ultimate root of the conflict is not disclosed, and one is left wondering why Ursula throws at Birkin that he is foul and obscene and perverse. But at least we know why the quarrel began: it began because Birkin had promised to be at Shortlands for dinner and would not stay with Ursula as she wanted him to.

Not only, then, is Lawrence taking sides in the abandonment of his family by Aaron, but he does not see that leaving the act without explanation makes it appear purely arbitrary. But this is

not the way Lawrence proceeds throughout the novel. When he
has Jim Bricknell complain that life is slipping by and he needs
love, Lawrence does not merely present a scene, as a radiologist
might show an X-ray plate. He evaluates that scene, by rendering
Jim's weakness in such a way that it comes to us as weakness. The
writer's contempt for Jim cannot be missed. Again, when the
Bohemian set, after the opera, play at being "bolshy," the treatment of the scene does not conceal that these people are not serious,
that they are irresponsible. And in exactly the same manner
Lawrence approves of Aaron's leaving his wife. But there is an
important difference. His evaluation of Jim is not puzzling: Jim is
a weak man who cannot walk without a woman by his side to
hold his hand. And it does not matter whether the reader agrees
or disagrees with Lawrence that this is a legitimate ground for
condemnation of Jim. The reader may disagree with Lawrence's
evaluation, but he is not puzzled. This is not true in respect to
Aaron. The trouble between him and Lottie goes too deep for
Aaron's comprehension—and seemingly, it also goes too deep for
Lawrence's comprehension.

Because Lawrence is not content to present the reader with a
scene but confronts him with a puzzling ethical problem, the question must be asked whether men are justified in acting as Aaron
did. Mr. Leavis defends Lawrence's attitude towards Aaron and
Aaron's action in the following manner:

It is a familiar situation, a familiar kind of life—frustrating deadlock.
The presenting of it transcends ordinary moral judgments; to judge
Aaron selfish and irresponsible for leaving his wife in the lurch with
the children on her hands (though he provides for her financially),
or to say that, whatever the total account of rights and wrongs might
be, plainly the domineering, demanding, complaining woman was at
fault and had made his life intolerable, wouldn't, we know, be to the
point. The presenting sensibility and the inquiring intelligence engaged
are, of course, profoundly and essentially moral; the moral concern
goes far deeper than the level of those judgments. What is wrong
here? What laws of life have been ignored that there should be *this*

situation, this dreadful deadlock between a man and a woman? These questions give the informing preoccupation.[6]

An adequate discussion of Mr. Leavis's effort to defend Lawrence's treatment of the deadlock between Aaron and his wife is impossible here, for the paragraph raises enough questions for an extended treatise on moral philosophy. I shall confine my comments to one question and two remarks. How does Mr. Leavis know that Lottie was a domineering, demanding, complaining woman? We are given only a brief account of the relation between them before Aaron leaves Lottie and the account does not present a complaining, domineering, demanding woman. They have been married twelve years and had two daughters, and Lottie is afraid, when Aaron returns to the house, that the men want to get rid of him. The evidence for the domineering, complaining, demanding woman was not obtained by Mr. Leavis from the text. Then where did he obtain it?

My first remark is this: Mr. Leavis reminds us several times throughout his book of the advisability of never trusting the artist but trusting the tale. But Mr. Leavis seldom stops to hear what the novel says and is quite ready to listen to what the novelist says. Had he listened to the novel and not to the novelist, he would have noticed a significant fact: namely that Aaron's reaction to Lottie, his sense of frustration with her and the children, was illumined by the strange relationship between Lilly and Aaron. He would have noticed particularly Aaron's statement to Lilly, when the latter took him into his apartment, to the effect that his illness was the result of giving in to Julia when she forced him to make love to her. One does not have to read the novel as if it were autobiography, as Middleton Murry does, to come to the suspicion that Aaron's attitude towards his wife Lottie had deeper roots than the fact that Lottie was a domineering, demanding, complaining woman.

My second remark refers to the grounds on which Mr. Leavis defends Aaron's action and by implication Lawrence's approval of it. If we must ask what "laws of life" which transcend "ordinary moral judgments" have been violated by Lottie in her treatment of Aaron, the answer cannot give us "the informing preoccupation." In any case the appeal from morality, whether ordinary or extraordinary, to life, is inadmissible. What does the contrast consist in, suggested by the qualification of morality by the adjective "ordinary"? But let that pass. What we cannot let pass is that the appeal from morality to life is not what it pretends to be, for life itself, outside the moral law, or laws, cannot have primacy over morality. Outside morality, which is to say, considered in abstraction from the values it makes possible, life itself is, if I may be forgiven the tautology, value-free. I must point to the obvious tautology because it is the failure to see it that makes Mr. Leavis' defense of Lawrence inadmissible. And it is in turn the failure to see the tautology that opens Lawrence's values to criticism.

When a writer, whether novelist or critic, defends "life" against the attacks of a moral code, he cannot be construed as appealing to mere life against the constraining or killing demands of morality. He must be construed as defending one conception of the good life against another conception, one deemed less defensible. Life qua life is value-free, is a mere biological process, and whatever differences there may be between the biological processes of a human organism and those of a non-human organism, in terms of complexity, qua organic processes there is no difference. Quantitatively a unicellular organism may be considerably different from a human organism, since the former is relatively simple as compared to the latter. But what makes the difference of interest to the moralist is that the human organism is more than a mere organism, for it is capable of espousing values, while the monocellular organism, presumably, is not. The quarrel, then, between the moral vitalist and those who disagree with him concerns the values espoused. Vitalism is a plausible moral stance—but not because it appeals to *life* but because it appeals to *a kind* of life, one considered by the vitalist to be good. Its plausibility derives from the implicit assumption that abundance of life is abundance of realized values. But whether or not this is the case is not something we can decide by an appeal to life. In respect to morality the vitalist is, in one sense, on the same plane with the ascetic and life-denying values of, say, the Plato of the *Phaedo*. For it is not life but the good life that both are interested in. The difference lies in the values that the vitalist would prefer to see realized, as against those that his opponent would.[7]

But another defense of Lawrence is possible. It is made by Father Tiverton in answer to a somewhat similar criticism, and I have already touched on this question from a different point of view. But we must return to it and consider it again, not only because it is important for our understanding of D. H. Lawrence, but because it has general applicability. Considering as we did (the defense runs) the substantive values involved, and disregarding the form, we are shattering the unity of substance and form, and committing a fallacy. But is the matter that simple? Form and substance are indissoluble when art is perfect, but even then only at the ideal moment of successful aesthetic apprehension. But it is precisely the criticism here leveled at D. H. Lawrence that aesthetic apprehension is not possible because the art is not perfect. In *Aaron's Rod* the values fall apart from their form, from their poetic embodiment; they are added, and one is not able to find a connection between the ideas and the novel. A series of incidents are contrived in order to thrash out a number of ideas defended or attacked by characters who are in no way connected with the ideas put forth. When in *King Lear* Gloucester advances the opinion that the late eclipses of the sun and moon portend no good, this is not something that is just put in his mouth to fill time, to pad the scene. It is revelatory of Gloucester's character and important in respect to events that will soon come to pass. And the same is true of the bastard's soliloquy that follows. Man is for the villainous bastard a master of his fate; he makes his future, the stars do not make it for him, and this again is an opinion that is related to subsequent events. Nothing like that can be said of

Lawrence's characters in *Aaron's Rod*. There is no organic relation between ideas and characters. As I shall have occasion to point out more fully later, in his successful books there are, in a sense, no *characters* either. But, then, the ideas that the "agonists" put forth in these books are related to the kind of experience they undergo. The ideas help present the fluid aspects of personality of which they are the expression.

Equally unintelligible is the nature of the relationship between Aaron and Lilly. Let us recollect the facts: Lilly, the "dark, ugly man," who is a writer, and married to a Norwegian woman, Tanny, meets Aaron through the Bricknells and their set. When Lilly's wife, Tanny, goes to Norway to visit her people, Lilly comes to London and takes a room over Covent Garden market. One cold grey afternoon in early April, he sees from his window a crowd hovering around a man who seems to be drunk and whose identity Lilly discovers by his voice to be Aaron. With the help of a policeman, Lilly takes Aaron to his room, where he finds out that Aaron has the flu. Aaron explains he is sick because he allowed Josephine Ford, who is engaged to Jim Bricknell, to seduce him. He reiterates that he would have been all right if he hadn't given in to her. Lilly persuades Aaron to stay in his apartment, and undertakes to nurse him back to health. One early afternoon, with the sun shining into the room, Lilly decides to rub Aaron with oil.

Quickly he uncovered the blond lower body of his patient, and began to rub the abdomen with oil, using a slow, rhythmic, circulating motion, a sort of massage. For a long time he rubbed finely and steadily, then went over the whole of the lower body, mindless, as if in a sort of incantation. He rubbed every speck of the man's lower body —the abdomen, the buttocks, the thighs and knees, down to the feet, rubbed it all warm and glowing with camphorated oil, every bit of it, chafing the toes swiftly, till he was almost exhausted. Then Aaron was covered up again, and Lilly sat down in fatigue to look at his patient.

. . . I wonder why I do it. I wonder why I bother with him. . . .

Jim ought to have taught me my lesson. As soon as this man's really better he'll punch me in the wind, metaphorically if not actually, for having interfered with him. And Tanny would say, he was quite right to do it. She says I want power over them. What if I do? They don't care how much power the mob has over them, the nation, Lloyd George and Northcliffe and the police and money. They'll yield themselves up to that sort of power quickly enough, and immolate themselves *pro bono publico* by the million. And what's the bonum publicum but a mob power? Why can't they submit to a bit of healthy individual authority? The fool would die, without me: just as that fool Jim will die in hysterics one day. Why does he last so long!—CHAPTER IX

As if to emphasize the meaning the scene embodies, Lilly washes and darns Aaron's socks. As Aaron gets better, the two discuss women and they agree that women want to get men under and use children as means to their ends. And the question we must ask here is, How we are to read this chapter? In the juxtaposition of the relationship between the two men and their reflection on women, are we to find more than Lawrence actually says? Or should we take it literally? But such scenes as this cannot be taken by us, men of our age, as having surface meaning only. We quite naturally and effortlessly see certain scenes as sometimes attempting to cover meanings which at the same time they suggestively reveal. And the difficulty here refers to our inability to decide, while staying within the context of the story, how much we shall read out of the scene or, what perhaps adds up to the same thing, how much of what we tend to read into it, is illegitimate and how much is legitimate. Beyond this question lies another: To what extent and in what manner is Aaron's rejection of his wife connected with his relationship to Lilly?

 Kangaroo

THE MOST damaging indictment that must be brought against the autobiographical novels of Lawrence is that the fable never achieves organic wholeness, and what he succeeds in offering us is a series of episodes strung along in the picaresque manner; nor can one find any aesthetic reason why one episode takes place now and another later. This is probably the reason Richard Aldington says that *"au fond, Kangaroo is a travel book like Sea and Sardinia."* [1] The truth of this statement lies in the fact that most of the episodes that make up the book have no genuine dramatic significance in themselves; their significance lies in the fact that they are means of letting the "characters" express their opinions. I emphasize the lack of organization of *Kangaroo* reluctantly because Graham Hough, after pointing out that to a superficial glance *Kangaroo* "is even more desultory in plan and mixed in content than *Aaron's Rod*," goes on to say that "further reading shows an underlying unity of a kind not immediately obvious." That unity, or form, he tells us, was for Lawrence "the following out of an authentic process of living growth." [2]

I do not doubt that had Lawrence undergone "an authentic process of living growth," "the following out" of it might have successfully informed the account of his Australian experience. But the remark can be accepted only if we overlook two important considerations. The first is that it is not easy to see how the growth could account for the padding which the novel exhibits. The most obvious example of this padding occurs in the last few pages of Chapter VIII entitled "Volcanic Evidence." What sort of "growth" does this material represent? I find it difficult to be-

lieve that the inclusion of a newspaper article in the body of the
novel—quite apart from the question of the article's being admissible as serious science—is evidence of Somers-Lawrence growth,
for neither Somers nor Lawrence was dedicated to growth
through the acquisition of knowledge. Lawrence sticks to the
solar plexus. But Mr. Hough's remark also overlooks a fact borne
out by both the intrinsic evidence of *Kangaroo* and the abundant
extrinsic evidence available to us in terms of letters and the accounts of his biographers—the fact, namely, that Lawrence at
the time of his visit to Australia, and even earlier, had not been
exactly "growing" but had been undergoing a disrupting ailment
of the soul that he was desperately trying to understand and to
remedy, and that, if he mastered it at all, he only mastered it towards the very end of his life, after his return to Europe from
Mexico.

Up to the time when he began to compose himself for
death, the most we can say is that Lawrence had periods of health
and of superb but not of sustained creativity. The story, "The
Woman Who Rode Away," for instance, which Mr. Hough ad-
mires highly, is an imaginative enactment of a need to give up, a
deep expression of death wishes. It is as if Lawrence could carry
on no longer and sought in the sacrifice of his heroine the peace
he craved. What we know of his ailment in Taos and in "old
Mexico" confirms the surmise. Particularly after Frieda left
him in Mexico, Lawrence had a very hard time. For this reason I
do not believe we can speak of "growth" without extensive and
careful qualifications. Both *Aaron's Rod* and *Kangaroo* constitute
an artistic debacle. What Lawrence pointed out about Tolstoy and
others in the essay on "The Novel" applies to himself. Lorenzo
has gone the way of "old Leo." The passional inspiration no
longer flows along aesthetic channels. Lawrence has turned practical.

Kangaroo is, in a sense, an accurate account of the life of Lawrence and Frieda in Sydney, a record of their capacity to respond
lyrically to land and sea and sky, and occasionally even to respond

with warm friendship to their Australian acquaintances. It is also an account of the fun the couple were capable of enjoying at times, as well as of moments of erotic satisfaction. But it is also a record of the relentless struggle that went on between Lawrence and Frieda and that frequently broke out into bitter quarrel. It is also a statement of their fundamental incapacity to show any genuine charity towards their fellow beings, of their inverted snobbishness, their violent reaction to what they took to be the unbuttoned, back-slapping, plebeian nature of the Australians, and the Australian cockney accent and "colonial humor."

However, when I say that it is an accurate record of the Lawrences' life in Sydney, I do not mean that I have checked, or that I would be interested in checking, the events recounted in the no-novel against available documents in order to ascertain that the work is historically "accurate." What I mean is that the book has an extremely autobiographical "feel" about it. It is this "feel" that is of interest to the critic. It is also strongly conveyed to the reader by *Aaron's Rod* and *The Plumed Serpent*. But it is not conveyed by *The Rainbow*. And while, on extrinsic grounds, we know that the matter transmuted into the substance of *Women in Love* is drawn from actual experience, I do not find the autobiographical "feel" in this novel.

If we consider the novel to be an accurate account of the life of the Lawrences, a chapter in *Kangaroo* depicting the struggle between Harriet-Frieda and Somers-Lawrence repays examination. It is entitled "Harriet and Lovat at Sea in Marriage," and it opens with an essay, two or three pages in length, on the three possible types of marriage (Chapter IX). The only way I can refer to it accurately is to use a slang expression: it is pure *corn*, and as such it stands at the head, as far as one reader is concerned, of all the many expressions of bad taste that Lawrence has left us. There are three courses open "to a sincere man when he marries a wife," we are told: To become: "(a) the lord and master who is honored and obeyed, (b) the perfect lover, (c) the true friend and companion." The introductory essay ends: "I would recommend perfect-companionship to all those married couples who truly and sincerely want *to get on*"—the italics are furnished by the marriage counselor. Lawrence then goes on to recount the adventures of "the good bark *Harriet and Lovat*, and how it arose from the waves like Aphrodite's shell as well as Aphrodite, in the extremest waters of perfect love." If until now the reader has kept a hard grip on his tendency to squirm with embarrassment for Lawrence when he reads him, he will not be able to do so from here on. For Lawrence tells us that he has "not made up [his] mind whether she was a ship, or a bark, or a schooner, technically speaking. . . . Or perhaps she was a clipper, or a frigate, or a brig." All that he insists on is "that she was not a steamboat with a funnel." The bark is "pushed into the bays and creeks of the Pacific ocean of marriage, lord-and-masterdom." But then it finds itself in "a wildly stormy strait, like the Straits of Magellan, where two fierce and opposing currents meet and there is the devil of a business trying to keep the bark of marriage, with the flag of perfect-love at the mast, from dashing on a rock or floundering on heavy seas." The vessel runs into fair weather and foul, her sails are slit, some of them are carried away in a blizzard. From the Pacific she sails into the Atlantic, E N E, and the dialogue between Harriet and Somers pushes the embarrassment close to the limit of one's endurance. The figure of the ships is juiced to its last drop. All of this from a man who is infuriated by the names of Australian bungalows and vacancy signs.

But mixed with this embarrassing corn there is another trait of Lawrence which in fairness ought to be pointed out. Lawrence is sometimes capable of devastating self-knowledge. At the end of the nautical chapter we run into the following comment:

Him, a lord and master! Why, he was not really lord of his own bread and butter; next year they might both be starving. And he was not even master of himself, with his ungovernable furies and his uncritical intimacies with people: even people like Jack Callcott, whom Harriet quite liked, but whom she would never have taken seriously.

Yet there was Lovat pouring himself out to him. Pah—believe! How could one believe in such a man! If he had been naturally a master of men, general of an army, or manager of some great steel works, with thousands of men under him—then, yes, she could have acknowledged the *master* part of the bargain, if not the lord. Whereas, as it was, he was the most forlorn and isolated creature in the world, without even a dog to his command. He was so isolated he was hardly a man at all, among men. He had absolutely nothing but her. Among men he was like some unbelievable creature—an emu, for example. Like an emu in the streets or in a railway carriage. He might well say phoenix.— CHAPTER IX

But *Kangaroo* is autobiography in another sense: it is the fulfillment of the complex and strong yearnings Lawrence had for power, the yearnings he had to be master and make others his slaves. He did not hesitate to put it down in plain words that he wanted to subordinate the life issue of inferior beings to the responsibility of a superior being. "Why can't they submit to a bit of healthy individual authority?" we have seen Lilly asking himself after rubbing Aaron with oil in *Aaron's Rod*. And in *Kangaroo* in one of the skirmishes between Harriet and Somers, the latter asks:

"Am I disinterested?"
"No"—she hesitated—"not when you want just *power*."

Somers retorts:

"But I don't want just power. I only see that somebody must have power, so those should have it who don't want it selfishly, and who have some natural gift for it, and some reverence for the sacredness of it."—CHAPTER V

But it is of course he, Somers-Lawrence, who had the gift and the reverence, and it is Lawrence who decides that Somers-Lawrence has the gift.

But matters are never simple with Lawrence. While he craved power over individuals, he was also revolted by the intimacy that the relationship towards the disciple forced on the master; and while wanting power, he hated passionately the shenanigans of politicians and the hypocrisies of labor leaders, the do-gooders and the social activists. He dreamed of founding a colony in Florida composed of a few autonomous individuals, all equal and independent, but headed of course by Lorenzo, who naturally would be more equal than his followers.

[2]

Lawrence also craves love, and he craves it with the same mixture of a capacity for self-deception and an almost cruel, because utterly lucid, insight into himself, the same ambivalence and the same entanglement of urge and counter-urge that we find in his craving for power. But the love he craves is eros and never agape. Of the latter he knew nothing, and what he thought he knew about it made him loathe it. He could not conceive how a person would want to give himself or herself to another for the other's sake—unless the person gave herself or himself to him, Lawrence. He could not understand how one could feel the outward thrust in which the self recedes because the needs of the other come forward and the loving self, by an act of projection, becomes identified with that other. However that act is explained, whether naturally or otherwise, it is not in the gratification of sensation, in pleasure, in the release of tension, that it has its center of gravity. The center of gravity is out there, in the other, in the fulfillment of his or her needs, in the increase of his or her well-being, the relief of his or her pain. All this we have long known and had it confirmed in our generation by men like Bergson, Nygren, de Rougemont, D'Arcy and the many others who have written on this topic. The monistic error of Freud, the simplistic reductions of the naturalist, will of course remain to plague us and to distort our conception of experience and thus often to mislead our behavior. But it will not change the fact that agape is something different both in nature and in origin from eros.

It must be said in Lawrence's favor that while he loathed agape he was quite clear as to the nature of eros. He knew that eros remains reflexive. About this Lawrence is utterly lucid. In *The Rainbow*, after a love episode between Ursula and Anton, we are told:

So, shaken, afraid, they went back to her parents in the kitchen, and dissimulated. But something was roused in both of them that they could not now allay. It intensified and heightened their senses, they were more vivid, and powerful in their being. But under it all was a poignant sense of transience. It was a magnificent self-assertion on the part of both of them, he asserted himself before her . . . she asserted herself before him. . . . And after all, what could either of them get from such a passion but a sense of his or of her own maximum self, in contradistinction to all the rest of life?—CHAPTER XI

A human being in the grip of lust—and on such an occasion he is hardly human, he is close to a mere animal—wants another as the means of release of tension that the possession of the other brings. This is the rapture, the ecstasy of erotic love. It is a loss of self, but not because another self has been found and the self has gone towards her or him and has achieved fulfillment in the service of the other. It is the loss of self because the pleasure which is the release of tension thrusts from consciousness all other objects and pleasure alone remains. After all, what can any one get from such a passion but satisfaction and the accompanying sense of one's own maximum self? When the intense pleasure begins to fade, tender friendship comes in, the friendliness of two people who love each other without urgent erotic need. Lawrence wanted eros in its naked manifestation when passion wells up, powerful and peremptory. In the last chapter of *Aaron's Rod*, Lilly admonishes Aaron with all the schoolmasterish finger-wagging with which the ventriloquist Lawrence makes his dummies speak. The passage is too long and too repetitive to cite in full, but three selections from it should give a fair sample of its flavor and its substance:

"No, you're not. But you've a love-urge. And perhaps on the recoil just now. But listen to me. It's no good thinking the love-urge is the one and only. *Niente!* You can whoosh if you like, and get excited and carried away loving a woman, or humanity, or God. Swoop away in the love direction till you lose yourself. But that's where you're had. You can't lose yourself. You can try. But you might just as well try to swallow yourself. You'll only bite your fingers off in the attempt. You can't lose yourself, neither in woman nor humanity nor in God. You've always got yourself on your hands in the end: and a very raw and jaded and humiliated and nervous-neurasthenic self it is, too, in the end. A very nasty thing to wake up to is one's own raw self after an excessive love-whoosh. Look even at President Wilson: he love-whooshed for humanity and found in the end he'd only got a very sorry self on his hands.

"So leave off. Leave off, my boy. Leave off love-whooshing. You can't lose yourself, so stop trying.

". . . Remember this, my boy: you've never got to deny the Holy Ghost which is inside you, your own soul's self. Never. Or you'll catch it. And you've never got to think you'll dodge the responsibility of your own soul's self, by loving or sacrificing or Nirvaning—or even anarchising and throwing bombs. You never will. . . ."

Aaron was silenced for a moment by this flood of words. Then he said smiling:

"So I'd better sit tight on my soul, till it hatches, had I?"

"Oh yes. If your soul's urge urges you to love, then love. But always know that what you are doing is the fulfilling of your own soul's impulse."—CHAPTER XXI

Here, in one short sentence, we find the heart of the Lawrentian wisdom on the subject of love. "Always know that what you are doing is the fulfilling of your own soul's impulses." If *Aaron's Rod* were pure art in the sense already specified, I could not say that this admonition is an expression of Lawrence's "wisdom." But the novel is a didactic tract, and as such it calls for the comment that it is an expression of Lawrence's unmitigated, immature, foot-stamping, table-pounding, fretting, pouting, cry-baby, petu-

lant selfishness—a sheer, uncomplicated, unrestrained, colossally
arrogant, self-centered selfishness.

The rationalized counterpart of this attitude towards love involves the error that Bishop Butler once and for all laid to rest,
namely, the belief that because all our actions and affections have
their source in the self, they are all equally selfish. Even those
who hold to the view in spite of, or in ignorance of, Butler's ex-
posure of it, are more or less ashamed of the fact. We have generally a feeling that if we cannot help being selfish, this is something to regret, or to conceal, not to plume ourselves with. It was
Lawrence's great discovery that we ought to nurse our selfishness,
to exult in it, and to preach it to others. But Lawrence's position
is not the outcome of philosophizing, of recognizing on intellectual grounds first the necessity and advisability of fierce individu-
alism, and of espousing it as a consequence of the philosophical inquiry afterwards. There may be philosophers who take vital moral
positions, whatever they are, as a result of inquiries they carry on,
even if in my reading I have never come across such men. But if
there are, Lawrence certainly was not one of them. Why then
does Lawrence loathe agape as profoundly and bitterly as he
does?

There is in *Kangaroo* a detailed account, extending through two
chapters, of the alleged grounds of his revulsion against the old
ideals. But before turning to these chapters, it is helpful to recall the events preceding the account. Through Jack Callcott,
Somers has met Kangaroo, who has offered Somers his love and
has tried to attract him to the rightist Diggers. And through
Trewellan, alias Jaz, Jack's brother-in-law, Somers has been introduced to Willie Struthers, head of the socialists and of the labor
people. During the interview, Struthers pleads with Somers that
he accept the editorship of a paper that would bring his message
to the people. On the night of that same day, Somers visits Kangaroo and tells him of the visit to Struthers. A quarrel follows, and
Somers who, like Paul Morel, Lilly, and some other of his cen-

tral heroes, gives one the impression of being a physical coward, leaves Kangaroo's rooms in terror. ". . . By bad luck it was Saturday night when Sydney is all shut up and the big streets seem dark and dreary, though thronging with people"; he is moved with an intense fear. "One could feel such fear in Australia" (Chapter XI). (Kate was to experience a similar kind of fear in Mexico.) This leads Somers in the beginning of the next chapter, entitled "The Nightmare," to remember the "different deep fears" he had felt elsewhere, particularly in England, during the years of 1916–1919.

The only value I can find in the minute account of Somer's experience during these years lies in the fact that it is a thinly disguised autobiography, and therefore throws light on the factors that finally led one of the superb artists England produced in our age to transmogrify himself into a preacher. We know of course that it bears an almost one-to-one correspondence to the experience of Lawrence himself and his German wife in Cornwall, London, and in the Midlands after they were proscribed from Cornwall. But here again the knowledge is not essential to our conviction that this chapter is autobiographical. That conviction emerges from the chapter itself, from its failure to achieve self-sufficiency as art.

In 1916 Somers was summoned to join the army. Let us remember that Richard Lovat Somers is no more of a pacifist than Lawrence was. "He was no Quaker, to believe in perpetual peace." What is more, Somers hated the German militarists and thought them to be "mechanical bullies. They had once threatened to arrest him as a spy, and had insulted him more than once." The actual experience to which Lawrence here refers had taken place before the war, during his first trip to Germany with Frieda, and the details are well known. What is of interest is his reaction to the German militarists and to the English. Of the former he tells us, in the sentence immediately following the last quotation, "Oh, he would never forgive *them* in his inward soul." But notice what follows:

. . . The industrialism and commercialism of England, with which patriotism and democracy became identified: did not these insult a man and hit him pleasantly across the mouth? How much humiliation had Richard suffered, trying to earn his living! How had they tried, with their beastly industrial self-righteousness, to humiliate him as a separate, single man? They wanted to bring him to heel even more than the German militarist did. And if a man is to be brought to any heel, better a spurred heel than the heel of a Jewish financier. So Richard decided later, when the years let him think things over, and see where he was.—CHAPTER XII

Therefore when the war came, Somers' instinct was against it. When the Asquith government so softly foundered, he began to suffer agonies. But when the Asquith government went right under, and in its place came that *John Bull* government of '16, '17, '18, then distress gave way to agony. The humiliation Richard had suffered trying to earn a living corresponds of course to the difficulties Lawrence ran into after the publication of *The Rainbow*. To this was added the humiliations inflicted on the occasions he was summoned for military service. The first summons he did not resent. The two doctors who examined him were gentlemen "who knew the sacredness of another naked man." Nevertheless on returning home he made up his mind that if he was called again he would go, but he would never serve. The second summons and examination seems to have gone off relatively easily, but the last was for Somers-Lawrence a shattering experience. Two full pages describing the physical examination precede this summing up of the experience:

He dressed and waited for his card. It was Saturday morning, and he was almost the last man to be examined. He wondered what instructions they had had about him. Oh, foul dogs. But they were very close on him now, very close. They were grinning very close behind him, like hyænas just going to bite. Yes, they were running him to earth. They had exposed all his nakedness to gibes. They were pining, almost whimpering to give the last grab at him, and haul him to earth, a victim. Finished!

But not yet! Oh, no, not yet. Not yet, not now, nor ever. Not while life was life, should they lay hold of him. Never again. Never would he be touched again. And because they had handled his private parts, and looked into them, their eyes should burst and their hands should wither and their hearts should rot. So he cursed them in his blood, with an unremitting curse, as he waited.—CHAPTER XII

To the suffering and humiliation of these examinations we must add the treatment Richard Lovat Somers and Harriet received in Cornwall. They were the victims of snooping by neighbors, the police searched their home, and the general attitude of the in- habitants was unfriendly. The result, it will be remembered, is that the Somers, like the Lawrences, were proscribed from Corn- wall, and went first to live in the Midlands and then in London. Even in his own Midlands he could not stay.

He went out into accursed Derby, to Harriet. She was reassured again. But he was not. He hated the Midlands now, he hated the North. They were viler than the South, even than Cornwall. They had a uni- versal desire to take life and down it: these horrible machine people, these iron and coal people. They wanted to set their foot absolutely on life, grind it down, and be master. Masters, as they were of their foul machines. Masters of life, as they were masters of steam-power and electric-power and above all, of money-power. Masters of money-power, with an obscene hatred of life, true spontaneous life.
. . . This was his home district—but from the deepest soul he now hated it, mistrusted it even more than he hated it. As far as *life* went, he mistrusted it utterly, with a black soul. Mistrusted it and hated it, with its smoke and its money-power and its squirming millions who aren't human any more.—CHAPTER XII

Somers and Harriet finally returned to London, where they were not yet free from persecution. Earlier, before he moved to Corn- wall, I believe, he had decided that:

In the winter 1915–1916 the spirit of the old London collapsed; the city, in some way, perished, perished from being a heart of the world,

and became a vortex of broken passions, lusts, hopes, fears, and hor-
rors. The integrity of London collapsed, and the genuine debasement
began, the unspeakable baseness of the press and the public voice, the
reign of that bloated ignominy, *John Bull*.

No man who has really consciously lived through this can believe
again absolutely in democracy. No man who has heard reiterated in
thousands of tones from all the common people, during the crucial
years of the war: "I believe in *John Bull*. Give me *John Bull*," can
ever believe that in any crisis a people can govern itself, or is ever fit
to govern itself. During the crucial years of the war, the people chose,
and chose Bottomleyism, Bottom enough.—CHAPTER XII

It is necessary, although not very pleasant, to examine in detail
the dreary and distorted picture Lawrence gives us of those dark,
miserable years. "The well-bred, really cultured classes were on
the whole passive resisters," he writes in the paragraph immediately following the last quotation. And a few pages later, when
the Somers arrive in London, after their proscription from Cornwall, Lawrence tells us he found ". . . an atmosphere of terror all
through London, as under the Czar when no man dare open his
mouth. Only this time it was the lowest orders of mankind spying
on the upper orders, to drag them down" (Chapter XII).

That Somers-Lawrence perceived terror in London I do not of
course question. And if Lawrence were writing pure fiction that
would be the end of the matter. But Lawrence, as we have seen, is
not writing fiction—even if he thought he was, which I doubt.
And yet, read as history, as we are forced to read it, it sounds
distorted. I have no desire to deny that the warring nations went
mad during the war. It happened here in the United States a little
later than in England—the vast majority here, too, went on a
binge, an orgy, of hatred. And those who lived here through
those years cannot have forgotten the mass hysteria, the frantic appeals to patriotism, the ravings during the five-minute speeches
in the movies, the hysteria of the school assemblies, the banning of
Mozart, Beethoven, Brahms, and Wagner. They cannot have forgotten the contributions of scholars to prove with devastating eru-

dition and irrefragable logic that if you scratched a German you
found a Nietzsche or a Treitschke and if you scratched deeper
still you found a primitive Hun. One remembers the atrocity
stories, the collective insanity that moved the peoples engaged
in the conflict and even the neutrals during the war. I am prepared to believe that something like what I saw here in the
United States was to be seen in England, in spite of the cultural differences between the two nations. But precisely this fact, the collective insanity, gives Lawrence's picture the lie. The "well-
bred, really cultured" English classes were not on the whole, I
dare say, passive resisters any more than the American upper
classes were. It was not the workers alone who died in Flanders or
wherever the war was fought, not they alone who went into a
Walpurgis night of hatred. The "well-bred, really cultured" English classes were caught up in the frenzied madness as much as
any one else—with the understanding, of course, that the madness increased in direct proportion to the distance from the front
lines; for it has been said, and there is no ground for doubting it,
that those who were busy killing and keeping themselves from
being killed could not afford the luxury of hatred.

Lawrence, however, might answer that those who went on the
grand binge of hatred were not well bred, were not really cultured. But who, then, were the members of this class and how
many of them made it up? Lawrence and the other members of the
small group to which the Lawrences belonged: a girl from New
Zealand who, as a short story writer, fully deserves the minor
reputation she still enjoys, the man with whom she was living
who achieved rank as a critic, a Russian writer, and an English
pacifist who was already a philosopher of stature, and was by then
beginning to show that he was thoroughly alienated from his
own class—these and a few others were the members of the "well-
bred, really cultured classes." So be it. But let us be clear about
the people to whom Lawrence is referring. This is the small group
—or "class" if we must call it that—that had a "gay evening,"
when the Somers-Lawrences returned to London, "in a gorgeous

commotion in Somers' rooms: four poets and three non-poets, all fighting out poetry: a splendid time" (Chapter XII).

As for the atmosphere of terror, I have no doubt Lawrence-Somers and Harriet-Frieda felt it, and no doubt their friends, the few poets and non-poets, also felt it. But the majority, the Hun-haters, probably felt no more terror than the members of a Southern mob, in years I hope now altogether past, who are about to lynch a victim. The terror is felt, alas, for such is the nature of the world, neither by the mob that mills in front of the jail, nor by the conniving sheriff who pretends hypocritically to resist while egging the mob on. It is felt by the victim waiting in the cell and by those who scurry to their shacks, blow out the lamps, shut tight the doors and windows, and sit with vacuity in their hearts and perhaps with shame because they are glad that it is not they but someone else who is to be snatched by the beastly mob. It was Lawrence-Somers who felt the terror, not those who terror-ized him. Indeed he seems to have realized this, for in the same chapter he tells us that "Everybody in London was frightened at this time, everybody who was not a rabid and disgusting so-called patriot." If you allow for the bias Lawrence shares ex-plicitly with his hero, Somers, the statement is probably true; but, of course, the great majority were patriots.

But even before the experience of the last medical examination and even before the troubles with the neighbors and the authori-ties had come to the surface in Cornwall, Somers had decided (as, earlier, we have seen Lawrence himself decide) that he would report when summoned but would not serve. His earlier "in-stinct" against the war developed into a powerful hatred of it and of those that backed it, which is to say, a hatred of all England:

"Once," he said to Harriet, "that they have really conscripted me, I will never obey another order, if they kill me . . ."

"If ever," he said, looking up from his own knees in their old grey flannel trousers, as he sat by the fire, "if ever I see my legs in khaki, I shall die. But they shall never put my legs into khaki."—CHAPTER XII

We ought not to be surprised to find that Somers-Lawrence's feelings during this period are chaotic, and that his reaction to the hatred he felt surrounding him and to which he responded in kind, roils the bottom of his soul and stirs to the surface attitudes and drab, chaotic passions that a well-bred and truly cultured man, if he has them, keeps a tight grip on. The following passage in which Somers-Lawrence tears his soul and exhibits it to us without restraint or dissembling is all the more revealing since it is put into the middle of the narrative and yet has no prima facie connection with the narrative or with the development of its hero. It is interesting to us, however, on two counts: it gives us a powerful sense of the trauma of the war years for Lawrence, and it reinforces the feeling that becomes stronger the more carefully one reads Lawrence, that there were at the bottom of his soul, as there may be at the bottom of all souls, powerful, demonic forces. Lawrence, unlike the majority of men, was not unaware of them, but felt a fascination for them and on occasion responded to them, at least in his imagination.

The old Celtic countries have never had our Latin-Teutonic consciousness, never will have. They have never been Christian, in the blue-eyed, or even in the truly Roman, Latin sense of the word. But they have been overlaid by our consciousness and our civilisation, smouldering underneath in a slow, eternal fire, that you can never put out till it burns itself out.

And this autumn Richard Lovat seemed to drift back. He had a passion, a profound nostalgia for the place. He could feel himself metamorphosing. He no longer wanted to struggle consciously along, a thought adventurer. He preferred to drift into a sort of blood-darkness, to take up in his veins again the savage vibrations that still lingered round the secret rocks, the place of the pre-Christian human sacrifice. Human sacrifice! He could feel his dark, blood-consciousness tingle to it again, the desire of it, the mystery of it. Old presences, old awful presences round the black moor-edge, in the thick dusk, as the sky of light was pushed pulsing upwards, away. Then an owl would fly and hoot, and Richard lay with his soul departed back, back into the blood-sacrificial pre-world, and the sun-mystery, and the moon-power, and the mistletoe on the tree, away from his own white world, his own white, conscious day. Away from the burden of intensive mental consciousness. Back, back into semi-dark, the half-conscious, the *clair-obscur*, where consciousness pulsed as a passional vibration, not as mind-knowledge.—CHAPTER XII

The memory of his experiences makes Somers realize that he "felt broken off from his fellow-men." His ties to England, he felt, were broken and he felt without his people and his land. And in Chapter XIII, entitled " 'Revenge!' Timotheus Cries," he tells us that Somers realized further that after leaving England, in 1919, wherever he was, "in Sicily, or Switzerland or Venice or Germany or in the Austrian Tyrol, deep in his unconsciousness had lain this accumulation of black fury and fear, like a frenzied lava quiescent in his soul." The quarrel with Kangaroo brings Somers' pent-up fear to the bursting point. He tries to reckon it up, and the conclusion is that he realizes that the old ideals are dead, "the ideal of Love, Self-sacrifice, Humanity united in love, in brotherhood, in peace—all this is dead." And Somers goes on, "How do we know? By putting off our conscious conceit and listening to our own soul." But how do we know we have put off *our* conscious conceit and are listening to *our* own souls? Obviously, it is not quite as simple as it sounds. Lawrence has to acknowledge that men and women persist in the dead ideal. But in the service of the defunct ideal they find themselves, we are told, utterly humiliated, *sold*. And the result—and here, as I have done elsewhere, I am following Lawrence almost *au pied de la lettre*—is that when men find out they have been sold, something breaks in their tissue, and the black passion fires their blood. The result, in turn, is that they desire revenge on all that the old ideal stands for. This is what in fact Kangaroo and Willie Struthers, the leaders of the rightists and the leftists in Sydney, stand for: they are the vengeful mob. Somers asks whether he himself is Timotheus, crying *Revenge!* And he answers, "Oh, revenge, yes, he wanted to be avenged" (Chapter XIII). This is Lawrence's explanation of the

Somers-Lawrence loathing of agape. But is it the whole story? The reader of Chapters XII and XIII of *Kangaroo* is left with two questions. Does Lawrence's account of his war experience furnish us with an adequate explanation of his attitude? And, assuming the old ideals are dead, what ideal does he propose to put in their place?

The answer to the first question is of course, no. Lawrence's explanation of Somers' attitude is an elaborate hitching of the cart before the horse. It was not his experiences during the war that led to his loathing of agape, of the old ideals of Love, Self-sacrifice, and a Humanity united in Brotherhood. It was his loathing of Love, Humanity, and Brotherhood, a loathing which was an important part of his alienation syndrome, that led to his war experience, his discovery that London was in the grip of terror, and his strong reactions to the medical examinations. And it was these reactions that led his neighbors and the authorities in Cornwall—in the midst of the war hysteria, the early air raids, and the submarine scare—to distrust him and to search him and finally to proscribe him from the coast, where, so long as he stayed, he was a burden and an irritation to them. The hysteria, the fear, the apprehension cannot be denied. But did not the foreign looking man with the beard and the German woman represent a threat to a people in danger? One night in London, Somers-Lawrence and Harriet-Frieda see in the sky, like some god-vision, a Zeppelin, and the searchlights catching it so that it gleamed like a manifestation in the heavens. As Harriet looks up at the far-off Zeppelin, she says to Somers, "Think, some of the boys I played with when I was a child are probably in it" (Chapter XII).

Is it altogether a wonder, then, that the English, menaced as they had not felt menaced in a century, should fear the bearded man who, as Lawrence himself tells us, looked a stranger to them, and the foreign wife? But this point is of no great importance. It is not a question of placing blame upon the Somers-Lawrences or upon the English who, through the draft board and the police and military authorities, as Somers-Lawrence thought, were persecuting the couple unjustly. What is important to notice is that Lawrence's alienation did not start with the war, or with the suppression of *The Rainbow* and the years of poverty before the war. It had roots that stretched farther back into his past.

This opinion is confirmed by considering his ambivalent attitude towards the working class: he loathes it, but he feels himself to be a member of it when he is forced to choose between it and the middle classes. Consider his yearning for distinction, for aristocratic appearance: his narcissistic pictures of himself in the novels expressed this yearning with pathos. Consider his reactions to the suave, young aristocrats that he occasionally encountered in his peregrinations over the face of the earth: in the picture of the two young lords in *Aaron's Rod*, done with a devastating candor of which he is so frequently capable, we see how much he envied the wealthy young men. Consider his hatred of his father. Consider his difficulties with Jessie. Consider his inability, until his mother's death and his finding of his wife-mother Frieda, to cut the umbilical cord. Surely we know enough about the man, his background, his childhood, his years at school and his early struggles in London, to know that his alienation was not caused by the war. It had its roots way back in his past. What the war did was merely to bring on an added trauma, a more severe one, one that brought up all the dregs of hatred and frustration and rejection, and left him—but for the moments of preternatural lucidity, the halcyon hours of which we find record here and there in his novels and in some of his short stories—in a turbid and angry mood until his very last days.

It is this alienation, given the sensibility and the superb artistic talent and the deep religious instinct of the man, that leads Lawrence to define reality as sensation, as the inward surge of emotion at its most intense, and that with inescapable logic leads him to find the moment of intense sensation in the moment of erotic ecstasy and in the explosion of hatred. And it is this effort, bound to fail as it was, that leads to the exacerbation of his feeling of isolation. And it is this vicious circle that he attempts to escape by exercising dominion over others. Of all the false and pernicious theories that Lawrence propounded, none is more deplorable than his belief that the great secret of life, the way to self-fulfillment and sincerity and integrity, is for a man to stand alone as his own judge of himself, absolutely. None of his pernicious theories was as devastatingly disproved by his own experience, by his craving for friendship and love, by his need of Frieda. And the reason for the magnitude of the error is that this belief is deceptively similar to an important truth with which it can be easily confused: certainly, for all their similarities, there is a difference, and a radical one, between integrity, sincerity, respect for ourselves, on the one hand, and on the other the autocracy of the dominant impulse of the moment, which was all that Lawrence meant by standing alone and being the judge of himself, absolutely.

Here, then, we have the key to Lawrence's hatred of agape. There is a deep and persistent need in man to surrender his selfhood, and Lawrence felt it often and gave it candid and lucid expression. But he sought for it in eros where it is not to be found. The unappeased need made itself felt in him with relentless ache, and turned to hatred and to self-hatred. Oppressed by a sense of social inferiority, he fastened his hatred without difficulty upon an external object—the democratic mob. But endowed with acuity and a candor that never quite forsakes Lawrence the artist, he hated himself without difficulty. He hated himself because of his lust for power, for which he had at the same time contempt; because of his cowardice, of which he was ashamed; because of his poisonous capacity to make himself offensive, of which he was perfectly aware, and with which he endowed his narcissistic and counter-narcissistic image of himself, Richard Lovat Somers.

[3]

I have not yet discussed an important aspect of the views expressed in *Kangaroo*. When Somers first meets Willie Struthers, the leader of the socialists, they agree that what is needed is a new bond to unite men. The principle on which socialism shall be built is the mate principle. Richard wanted this mate trust called into consciousness and highest honor, as we are told, and by offering him the editorship of a paper, Struthers offered him the means of bringing his message before the workers. But what is this mate principle in which Struthers and Somers believe? It is to be distinguished, we are told, apparently without awareness of what the words entail, from the theoretical socialism started by Jews like Marx, which appeals only to the will to power in the masses. Socialism, by making money the whole crux, has cruelly injured the working people of Europe. As against it, what Somers and Struthers want to arouse in man is the latent power that is in him today, to love his near mate with a passionate, absolutely thrusting love. The mate principle is what Whitman called "love of comrades," and this is to be the new tie between men, the new democracy. In so far as I am able to gather anything clear and concrete from the vague and abstract discussion, what the two men want seems to be something that I have already alluded to: the more or less explicit yearning for a homosexual relationship in Lawrence, whose exact degree of sublimation it is not possible for us to determine from what he says about it.

There is another factor to be considered. Somers rejects the political programs of both the rightist and leftist leaders because he knows that human trust and love break down, because love smashes those whom it brings together, because it cannot be absolute although it seeks to be. Apparently giving us Somer's reflections, Lawrence tells us that the individuality which each man has, and which makes him a wayward, willful, dangerous, untrustworthy quantity to every other individual, is bound to react at some time against every other individuality without exception— or lose its own integrity. Hence, to set up love as an absolute is wrong. But man must have an absolute, Somers continues. Where shall he find it? In God Almighty, Somers believes. Does not this, again, seem to give the lie to my contention that Lawrence hates agape? The answer is again that it does not, for the God he is

thinking of is "the Dark God" of which he often speaks. I shall
consider Lawrence's religious ideas at some length later on. Here
it is simply necessary to make clear that the God Somers wishes
to serve is the God from whom the dark, sensual passion of love
emanates and not only the spiritual love of Christ. He wants men
once more to approach the fulfillment of their sensual passion in
an attitude of reverence for the sacred Dark God, the ithyphallic,
membrum virile erectus, of the first religions. Once more one is
led to ask, How foolish, how wrong, can a brilliant man get?
Contemporary liberal philosophers would knock God down from
the altars and would put in His place a generic, universal, indeterminate "man," neither black nor white, neither tall nor short,
who is everyman. It is this fiction they would have us worship.
The Communists are somewhat more restrictive: not generic
"man" but the worker. And the Nazis are more restrictive still,
for they would have had us worship Nietzsche's blond beast. All
of which is stupid and catastrophic enough. But the lingam!
Would it not be wise to ask us to take our sensuous Dark God,
the lingam, back to the cave, or better, if we can carry it, while
we swing from branch to branch, back to the trees?

[4]

If the chunks of ideology we find in the *olla podrida* that is
Kangaroo were merely the views of its characters, the adverse
critic of Lawrence could be disposed of by pointing out to him
that the novel is not a treatise. The critic could in turn ask why
Lawrence picked on such muddleheads whose thoughts are so
turgid and so silly. If *Kangaroo* were a novel and not a pseudo-
novel, the fact that Lawrence picked the characters he did would
not threaten the aesthetic quality of the work. But the book is not
a novel. Lawrence obviously took the ideas that he put into the
mouths of his characters seriously. True, afterwards, in a well
known, often quoted, letter to Bynner, speaking of *The Plumed
Serpent*, he repudiated some of the ideas that he put forth in *Kan-*

garoo as well as in the Mexican novel. But when he was writing *Kangaroo* and the Mexican novel he was utterly serious about the ideas he put in the mouths of his characters. He was not ridiculing Somers, Kangaroo, and Jack when, during the luncheon at which Somers first meets Kangaroo, he launches them forth into an abysmally profound lucubration on Kangaroo's "attempt," to which he had been helped by Somers' articles on Democracy, published in an "absurd international paper" printed at the Hague. It is Lawrence himself who is talking through the mask of his characters when he pontificates upon the secret of all life as obedience to the urge that arises in the soul. These pseudo-characters are not figures who speak and act out of their own aesthetic self-sufficiency. They are not fictional characters, they are megaphones to carry to the world the living truth that Lorenzo, gone the way of old Leo, preaches.

We do not have to base this conviction on the fact, easily verified, that in his essays and letters Lawrence discusses problems similar to those aired in the novel; nor need we base it on the fact that Somers and his wife seem like slightly altered photographs of the couple who, in 1922, spent some time in Australia, and the events of whose life correspond fairly closely to those of R. L. Somers and Harriet. Neither do we need to base it on the fact that Knud Merrild transcribed whole pages of *Kangaroo* as bona fide accounts of the discussions he heard Lawrence carry on with Frieda. The conviction is based on the novel alone. It emerges from our reading of it. We look in it for what we found in *The Rainbow* and to a lesser extent perhaps in *Women in Love*, for the quality by which we recognize poetry. But we do not find it. We look for the self-sufficiency of the story and its characters, we look for the splendor and the ease of the still wings of the poet wheeling in the upper air. But we do not find it. Instead of the immobile wings in the blue we see the harrassed flapping of an ambitious chicken that can only rise a few feet above the ground: the long dreary lectures, the reiteration of opinion, the sophomoric philosophizing.

Take for instance, these few lines out of a longer disquisition introduced, a few paragraphs earlier, with the ominous device: "Richard knew this. But he had learnt something else as well." Among other things, he had learned that "the human heart must have an absolute. It is one of the conditions of being human. The only thing is the God of all passion . . ." (Chapter XI). And so on for eighteen more lines. This may be true, and it may be very important for us to know it, but if we take it in its context we get a very definite sense that not only did Richard Lovat Somers know it but that Lawrence wanted us to know it; and he wanted us to know it, not in order to know Richard but for its own sake, because he wants us to accept it. And here is the difference between art and message. The book is as chock-full of sermons as a vicar's library. And some of them are as interminable and as dull as the unashamed article, at its worst, can be.

Take Chapter XVI, as another instance. It is introduced as follows: "The thing that Kangaroo had to reckon with, and would not reckon with, was the mass spirit." This is the excuse for a long dissertation on the mob, which moves on to a disquisition on the study of collective psychology, quotes D'Annunzio's version of that dear old chestnut about *l'anatomia presuppone il cadavero*, takes up the problem of humane sciences, goes on to man, returns to the mob, expounds a glandular theory of neurasthenia, enters the vast sea of religion, moves on through problem after problem, page after page for ten and a half pages, and in the same discursive mode, gives us in one page the quiddity of Richard's philosophy stated as a development of the theme: "What Richard wanted was some sort of a new show: a new recognition of the life mystery, a departure from the dreariness of money-making, money-saving, money-spending." One reader at least is left unimpressed by such sciolistic erudition. But whether this is a correct judgment or not, it is clear that Lawrence, while giving us what Richard wanted, also gave us what he, Lawrence, very much wanted us to accept and to believe.

[5]

But is this all we can say about *Kangaroo?* No. Something must also be said of the spoor it leaves behind. What sort of universe does it reveal? What is Lawrence's world like, as it comes through in this book? An artist—whether poet or painter or composer—leaves us with a coherent sense of what his created world is like. This sense does not come from any one scene or figure or movement. It comes from the whole. One remembers the brilliant, gay, sensual, sometimes sentimental world of Renoir, or the intense living solidity of Cezanne. In retrospect one remembers the ordered, lucid, compact world of Jane Austen, a world in which the evil of nature or man does not cast its shadow, and in which the fundamental problems of morals are blended with those of manners, a world in which the central problem men and women face is that of undergoing the moral education required to discover the genuine values society would have them actualize. In contrast one remembers the intense, dense, surcharged world of Dostoevski, for whom the soul has infinite depth where the tremendous conflict between God and nothingness is enacted. I may be wrong about any one or all of the characterizations I have set down. If so I can easily be corrected. But the point remains: a work of art, in any medium, reveals a complex, irridescent, and ineffable quality which must be gathered from the work itself. The values are presented positively or negatively by the artist. If art is, as I hold, a revelation of reality—something quite different from an imitation of it—it is this quality that gives us the specific revelation the artist wishes to make. No single artist, no single school or age, of course, reveals reality completely. Art, like philosophy or any human effort to get at the real, is limited by the perspective of the artist. But from his perspective the artist grasps through the act of creation the quality of the world he discovers and offers to our apprehension. We have therefore to ask of an artist whom we take seriously: What sort of world does this artist create, how does experience taste when we crack the shell of his work and chew the kernel? Is the world he reveals and organizes into a constitutive picture of life good or evil? Is it the product of the demonic vision or the saintly, of the heroic or the merely caddish?

What is the dominant atmosphere of *Kangaroo?* Somers reads a newspaper article on the possibility of a volcanic catastrophe swallowing Sydney, Melbourne, Adelaide, or Brisbane, Lawrence tells us. "But he had read this almost thrilling bit of journalism with satisfaction. If the mother earth herself is so unstable, and upsets the applecart without caring a straw, why, what can a man say to himself if he *does* happen to have a devil in his belly!" (Chapter IX). What a man says to himself in the isolation of his own conscience he may not be able to help, and it is, in any case, none of our affair. But what he preaches is very much our affair, and he can help it. The world of *Kangaroo* is a torn world, cracked by hatred, embittered by the absence of charity, a world torn by illicit passions, by blind rejections, a world without pity, an inhuman, demonic world, made what it is by unwarranted claims and by a false sense of superiority. It is no wonder that it is a world that does not come off as viably human. It is a world created by a man with a devil in his belly.

But in a sort of sense it is a world. And it is this power Lawrence had of never altogether failing in his failures that makes him such a formidable challenge to the critic. This no-novel that is a sermon on several of the themes that Lawrence brooded over, this unlovable and disorganized cosmos instinct with hatred, revulsion, and rejection is, nevertheless, some sort of cosmos. In the end one has to admit that for all its faults Lawrence comes close to bringing it off. From the standpoint of workmanship the no-novel creaks almost as badly as *Aaron's Rod;* from the standpoint of unity there is little to be said in its favor and much to be said against it. And yet, there is Aldington's "but." Aldington himself tells us of *Kangaroo* that "It is a strange, fascinating, beautiful, exasperating book thrown together with a carelessness of 'form' which almost goes beyond *Aaron's Rod*." [3] I would not put it in the same terms but essentially I agree with the judgment. And yet, there is always the "but." The hatred one can do without, the sophomoric philosophizing, and the corn are embarrassing; the blatant autobiography shows that Lawrence's creative powers had considerably receded from the high-water mark of *The Rainbow* and *Women in Love*. And yet, in a sense, *Kangaroo* almost achieves the appearance of a world. Autobiographically considered, it is, of course, an important document. And I am also ready to acknowledge that from an aesthetic point of view it cannot be condemned without qualification.

I am not saying, however, that Lawrence gives us *a false picture* of the world. Nor am I saying that in *Kangaroo* he left us the means of constituting our own picture of reality. Ultimately, the judgment that we must pass on the book is neither purely intellectual, as it would be if it were a question of its truth, in the narrow, positivistic sense, nor aesthetic, but moral. The man with the devil in his belly has conceived life in a pernicious manner, and the evil he reveals in the guise of good is dangerous. Lawrence's world, as it comes to us in *Kangaroo*, is not a world in which man's powers and virtues can flower at their best. It has a serious flaw in it. The aspirations it envisages as man's proper end are chaotic, incoherent, evil. Lawrence's world is a world in which man's perennial dream of the good life has turned into a nightmare, a world in which terror and hatred reign in the place of God. But it is, let us not overlook the fact, the world that, partly with Lawrence's help, we have been rearing. And after us the bomb.

CHAPTER THREE

The Plumed Serpent,

THE PLUMED SERPENT is open to many of the criticisms of *Kangaroo*. We can call it a *novel* only in the widest and most permissive use of the term, for it is clearly a book written with the intention of conveying a message. Lawrence wrote this novel with the explicit intention of proposing a program for the regeneration of Mexico and of the world. And his intention is equally the intention of the novel. The program it proposes consists of two parts, a politico-religious one and a sexual one. A leader, who proclaims himself a living God, revives the pre-Columbian religion of the Mexicans, encourages handicrafts, introduces dancers from New Mexico, or precisely, "from the North," to teach the people to dance, and this activity brings about a tremendous revival to a people torn by discord. At the same time, the heroine of the book discovers, through a new love affair, that her sexual relations with her former husband had not been adequate and she learns what a woman may rightly expect from the sexual act.

This novel, unpleasant and defective as it is, develops, then, the two most important themes that preoccupied Lawrence. I shall confine myself, however, in this chapter and the next, to the religious theme. First I shall discuss the defects of *The Plumed Serpent;* next I shall examine Lawrence's religious ideas, relating them to what I call his "American experience"; and then I shall discuss his notorious "philosophy," or "religion of the blood"—a body of ideas that many of Lawrence's critics find the least digestible of his so-called philosophy. The sexual theme, while important, is sub-ordinate in *The Plumed Serpent* to the politico-religious theme. I shall discuss it in the chapter on *Lady Chatterley's Lover.*

The "plot" of the "novel"—if these terms can be applied to the work—consists of a straightforward, chronological account of the experiences of Kate Leslie in Mexico. The widow by her second marriage of an Irish political idealist, Kate first appears in Mexico City with two American friends. They go to a bull fight that revolts Kate, and she leaves before the spectacle is over. Outside the bull ring, while she waits in the rain, she meets a Mexican general of pure Indian blood, Cipriano Viedma, who gives her a ride to her hotel in his car. Subsequently, at the home of Mrs. Norris, an Englishwoman who is an old-time resident of Mexico, she runs again into General Viedma and a friend of his, an *hacendado* named Ramon Carrasco. Sometime later Kate goes to the village of Sayula, on the lake of Sayula, where she takes a house. The village of Sayula is not far from Don Ramon's *hacienda*, and Kate visits Don Ramon and his wife, Doña Carlota, frequently. Before leaving Mexico City Kate had read a newspaper article entitled "The Gods of Antiquity Return to Mexico." It gives an account of a "ferment" in Sayula occasioned by the alleged arising of a man of great stature from the lake, who tells a peasant that he is Quetzalcoatl. The ferment is a well organized movement, initiated and directed by Don Ramon, who is seriously attempting to revive the pre-Columbian gods of Mexico. Don Ramon, supported by the soldiers of General Viedma, has apotheosized himself as the living Quetzacoatl, and apotheosizes his friend Cipriano as the living Huitzilopochtl. The climax of the story takes place when Kate, after much hesitation, accepts apotheosis as the living Malintzi, the wife of Cipriano, the living Huitzilopochtl, and learns to accept the kind of love he offers her, a love beyond love, in which she finds pure fulfillment.

[2]

The most apparent defect of the book is that the ideology, the exposition of which was Lawrence's primary purpose for writing the book, does not emerge from the story. This is to say that the book was not conceived dramatically but conceptually. The characters who put Lawrence's ideas forth speak with the never-deceiving timbre of a ventriloquist's voices. The fable or plot is a mere external instrument by means of which the ideas are conveyed to the reader and the message could have been stated at least as persuasively, clearly, and economically had Lawrence chosen to argue his ideas in conceptual terms.

Because the primary interest centers in the exposition of an ideology, the characters are mere dummies. Some of them were taken directly from life. And if we need to go to the *Letters* and the biographers to learn their real names—Bynner, Johnson, Mrs. Nuttall, Vasconcelos—we find from the book itself that they were people Lawrence knew. But Lawrence and Frieda are not to be found in *The Plumed Serpent* in the identifiable way in which we find them in *Kangaroo.* Kate is Frieda as Lawrence wanted her to be, accepting his conception of the sexual act, but she also reports many of Lawrence's own reactions to Mexico and its people. Ramon is the exponent of Lawrence's ideas, but so also are Kate, Cipriano, and Teresa. Although Ramon has a major role in the book, Lawrence never shows us Ramon from the inside, in the way in which he shows Kate or the Brangwens of *The Rainbow.* So that while in a sense the novel pulses with life, in another it does not have any. The characters drip the life from which they were taken: indeed they stand in an unseemly puddle of life; but they lack the "life" that is given to a character by art. The only person whom we see from the inside is Kate. The others are mere phonographs expounding Lawrence's ideas.

Like *Kangaroo, The Plumed Serpent* is enveloped in a heavy atmosphere of frustration, anger, despair, misanthropy. Early in the novel Kate reflects: "There is so much in the world that one wants to avoid, as one wants to avoid the lice that creep on the unwashed crowd" (Chapter II). And a little later: "Off she drove back to her hotel, once more in a towering rage . . . she felt she would die. Burning, furious rage" (Chapter III). These are statements about Kate's feelings when she is still in Mexico City, be-

fore her departure for Sayula. But matters do not improve when
Kate arrives at the lake. She is frequently beset by fear, anger, irritation, or a dragging sense of frustration. Mexico moves her
deeply and so do its people, but the response is seldom one of joy
or sympathy or glad acceptance. The people terrify her or irritate
her; she objects to all of their ways, even the way they worship.
True, Lawrence's extremely sensitive response to the spirit of
place is fully aroused by the land itself; but although there are moments in which Lawrence expresses a natural piety and a deeply
lyrical response, which dispel the darkness, the dominant mood is
given the novel by Kate's fear, anger, irritation, and her dragging
sense of frustration. The misanthropy is, indeed, radical. Thinking about the fight that Don Ramon is putting up to save Mexico
and the nearly mortal wound he received during the attack on the
hacienda, Kate thinks: "Let the beastly world of man come to an
end if that was its destiny, as soon as possible" (Chapter XXV).
Even Don Ramon, the leader of the movement that is going to save
Mexico, shares Kate's misanthropy: "Oh, if only the world would
blow up like a bomb," he exclaims at one point (Chapter XVIII).
And in a conversation between Ramon and Kate in Chapter XVII,
in which echoing her remarks, Ramon says: "So you must hate
people and humanity. . . ."

These many misanthropic expressions pose a problem. Contrary to some aestheticians who have maintained that art flows
out of love only, I see no reason why a novel cannot be written in
which the characters feel a strong misanthropic repugnance to
their world. A philosopher asserting that art flows from love has
not looked at Goya, has not read Dante with care, has ignored
Kafka, has looked carelessly into Swift, has not heard of Céline.
The doctrine, making an empirical claim, is a deduction from a
system and it oversimplifies man and the creative process. Art has
many sources and love is only one of them. It is not, therefore, the
novel's total rejection of the world that constitutes the problem.
The problem is that the reader becomes more and more convinced,
as he gets into the book, that here he is confronted with another

effort on the author's part to shed his illness, and that unfortunately the author succeeds all too well in dumping his illness before the reader's eyes and nose. A man has a right to seek health by any means within his reach, so long as he keeps within the law. But to call attention in public places to infected sores and soiled surgical bandages can hardly be said to be one of the basic rights of man. Lawrence left the matter of his sick experience untouched by the creative process, he failed to achieve the proper aesthetic distance, he did not recollect his experience in tranquillity: put it any way you choose, it is all the same. The central matter of the Mexican novel is an incongruous mixture, unmistakable for anything but what it is—the expression of Lawrence's yearnings and frustrations. Here is the desire for power he had already exhibited in *Kangaroo,* the yearning for a satisfactory solution of his sexual problem, with which we made acquaintance in *Aaron's Rod;* here is the misanthropy, unqualified and unexplained, the rejection of the world and the longing to belong in it; here is the assumption of superiority to all men, a silly claim that would be laughable were it not pathetic; and here is Lawrence's strong and polyvalent reaction to Mexico and its people. These traits and symptoms are conspicuously Lawrence's.

Another artistic defect of the book is the egregious bad taste Lawrence permits himself to display. Readers of *The Lost Girl* remember the Indian act of the vaudeville team with embarrassment. The Natcha-Kee-Tawara Troupe, whose act, we are told, "had its beauty," is pure corn—let me insist again on the *mot juste.* But the Natcha-Kee-Tawara Troupe does not elicit the embarrassment elicited by the lack of taste displayed in *The Plumed Serpent.* Here is a writer seriously proposing a program for the regeneration of a nation and of the world the heart of which consists of men painted as savages, with befeathered foreheads and loin-cloths. But aesthetically and intellectually this is nonsense because we cannot conceive of painted, naked savages as noble primitives. What power and virtue his life may have had in isolation from the white world, the American Indian loses that power and that virtue when we contrast him with the white. His nobility is veined with ferocity, his innocence turns out to be ignorance, and the alleged simplicity of his life conceals complications that arise from his inability to deal successfully with the power and the blandishments of white civilization. To believe that a contemporary society can be saved by instituting a synthetic savagery is to display a failure of intelligence, and to see in white men and their troops, who have streaked their faces with garish colors and shed their clothes, power, or beauty is a failure of taste. Consider the following scene—but consider it as it is intended, as a program to regenerate a nation. If in that light it is not worse than silly, I simply do not know what the word "silly" means:

A flute sounded the summons to close the doors. The drums of Quetzalcoatl ceased, and from the towers was heard again the wild bugle of Huitzilopochtl.

Then down the centre of the church, in silence, bare-foot, came the procession of Huitzilopochtli, naked, save for the black loin-cloths and the paint, and the scarlet feathers of the headdresses. Cipriano had his face painted with a white jaw, a thin band of green stretched from his mouth, a band of black across his nose, yellow from his eyes, and scarlet on his brow. One green feather rose from his forehead, and behind his head a beautiful head-dress of scarlet feathers. A band of red was painted around his breast, yellow around his middle. The rest was ash-grey.—CHAPTER XXIII

This is not the only instance of men painted like savages in the Mexican novel. In the church he has taken from the Catholics for his new religion, Don Ramon officiates adorned "with three green parrot feathers erect on the brow," and he makes a serious attempt to go native in his own *hacienda*, by dressing in the costume of the Indian peon. Cipriano, in loin-cloth, befeathered and streaked with paint, dances grotesque dances, to the reader's embarrassment, and Lawrence asks us to believe these dances have the power of revitalizing the General and his soldiers and of instilling discipline in them. All of this is in bad taste, because it elicits on the part of the reader embarrassment for the writer.

But there is a question here of more than mere bad taste in the superficial meaning of the words. It is a question of the failure of fundamental intelligence, of lack of common sense. For what we are confronted with is Lawrence's failure to distinguish between a genuine and a phony activity. The primitivism is ridiculous because it is ersatz, and Lawrence does not see that it is ersatz and fails to grasp the fact that ersatz primitivism is sterile and ridiculous. He takes the factitious atavism, the fabricated rites, the barely disguised homosexuality of the ceremony by means of which Ramon turns Cipriano into a living God, and the sexual act in which Cipriano indulges with Kate before the image the night of his apotheosis—he takes all these monkeyshines seriously. The more one considers the matter the more puzzling it becomes. How can a man endowed with such luminous intelligence and with such sensibility as Lawrence's, a man who made the claim to superior taste that he made, write this stuff down and publish it?

On the other hand it must be acknowledged freely that the book contains many virtues. In spite of the misanthropic atmosphere, the bad taste, the ersatz nature of its primitivism (which I shall discuss extensively later), the book is a powerfully authentic record of Lawrence's complex Mexican experience, and some of that experience was eminently worth recording. But since *The Plumed Serpent* is not a self-contained work of art and since the reader is seldom free from the sense that he is reading about Lawrence and his experiences, the question arises as to whether Lawrence's Mexico was not the product of Lawrence's projection, of his "empathy" in the original and not the degenerate sense of this word. The problem is given weight by the fact that the reader of Lawrence has encountered the moods of this people and the qualities of this land in other fictionalized accounts of Lawrence's experience in other places, and that he remembers Lawrence's superb ability to objectify his purely subjective reactions, to see idiosyncratic responses as if they were indeed the qualities of

things and people. On the other hand, we are also well acquainted
with the poet's power of creative observation, his superior sensibility, his unerring grasp of the spirit of place to which most of us
are simply blind. But however we finally take the Mexican record, its authenticity cannot be doubted. In this respect there is
nothing phony about the book.

Even more than is usually the case with Lawrence's books, the
vignettes strewn throughout *The Plumed Serpent* are extraordinarily beautiful. The sketches of the land and people are the product of a creative mind working at its best on the lyrical plane. As
a poetical documentary, *The Plumed Serpent* is almost as good as
anything he ever wrote. In this respect it comes close to rivaling
Mornings in Mexico—although in another respect, as I shall note
below, it cannot stand comparison with it. The beauty and the
freshness of the country after the rains, the tenderness of the
tropical dawn, the hot emptiness of morning as it turns to burning
mid-day, the sketch of the mother ass and foal, and the picture of
the urchin dragging the water-fowl to the lake—all this and much
more comes to us enveloped in the translucence of pure lyrical
poetry. But in Lawrence we must always expect conflict, and the
vignettes done out of love clash violently with those that convey
the terror, the anger, the bitterness, and the frustration that he
often experienced and that in Mexico he seems to have felt more
frequently and more deeply than in Australia or elsewhere. In any
case, vignettes are not enough to give us a novel. There is great
beauty in the book, but the book is not an organic work of art.
What Lawrence says of Sayula applies to *The Plumed Serpent*:
"Since the rains, the trees in the broken gardens of the lake front
had flamed into scarlet, and poured themselves out into lavender
flowers. . . . Wonderful splashes of color. But that was all:
splashes!" (Chapter XIV). Splashes of beauty, no matter how
vivid and abundant, do not make a novel. Mr. Harry T. Moore—
to whose biographical research we are deeply indebted—informs
us that when the book was first published, Knopf listed it as a
novel but later it was put under the category of belles-lettres.

[3]

It may be hard to believe, but Lawrence was entirely serious when he proposed as a remedy for the regeneration of Mexico the revival of the pre-Columbian gods. And he intended the program of reform not only for Mexico but for the whole world: each country was to revive its old, pre-Christian gods. This is Lawrence's intention and the intention of the book. In a letter to Curtis Brown, his agent, he speaks of *The Plumed Serpent* as his "most important novel so far." [1] And in a letter to Secker, calling for a missing galley of the novel, he writes: "I still say, this is the most important of all of my novels." And just before closing this letter, he writes: "Tell the man, the very nice man, in your office, I *do* mean what Ramon means—for all of us." [2] It is true that these letters are written in July and October of 1925 and that by July 1927 he writes to Trigant Burrow about "the hero illusion," [3] and that in March 1928, in a frequently quoted letter to Bynner, he makes the statement, that "the hero is obsolete, and the leader of men is a back number." [4] But when Lawrence wrote the novel he did not take the hero to be obsolete and he seriously believed that the principle of the primal blood (as regards which he was not steadily of one mind even while writing the novel) was to be fulfilled through the revival of the old gods: by the same means all social and personal problems would be automatically resolved and men and women would be able to find something supremely valuable to live for.

However naïve or irresponsible it may sound to us, Lawrence's thinking, when he proposed the revival of the old gods of the pre-Columbian world, was based on two ideas that in his mind were related. The first was his conception of the religion of early man, which, although it manifested itself differently in different cultures, was at bottom one. He took that early religion to be a powerful, life-giving religion. The second was that Christianity was dead. It was not able to touch the heart of the Mexicans. We are told in so many words that Jesus was never the Saviour of the

Mexicans. They needed the old gods. In a conversation with Kate, Don Ramon puts the essence of his and Lawrence's thought on the subject of religion in a few words. "We must change back to the vision of the living cosmos." This is also what Doña Carlota, Ramon's first wife, tells Kate that Ramon wants:

He says he wants to make a new connection between the people and God. He says himself, God is always God. But man loses his connection with God. And then he can never recover it again, unless some new Saviour comes to give him his new connection. And every new connection is different from the last, though God is always God. And now, Ramon says, the people have lost God. And the Saviour cannot lead them to Him anymore. There must be a new Saviour with a new vision.—CHAPTER X

Elsewhere we read:

For Jesus is no Saviour to the Mexicans. He is a dead god in their tomb. As a miner who is entombed underground by the collapsing of the earth in the gang-ways, so do whole nations become entombed under the slow subsidence of their past. Unless there comes some Saviour, some Redeemer, to drive the new way out, to the sun. But the white men brought no salvation to Mexico. On the contrary, they find themselves at last shut in the tomb with their god and the conquered race.—CHAPTER VIII

It is not clear to me whether it is Kate who is thinking these thoughts or whether they are an editorial comment by Lawrence. The passage is probably intended as a record of Kate's thinking. In any case, it is what Ramon himself thinks. Elsewhere, in a conversation between Ramon and his first wife, he amplifies his views and tells her that

Quetzalcoatl is just a living word, for these people, no more. All I want them to do is to find the beginnings of the way to their own manhood, their own womanhood. Men are not yet men in full, and women are not yet women. They are all half and half, incoherent,

part horrible, part pathetic, part good creatures. Half arrived . . .
I mean all the world.—But these people don't assert any righteousness
of their own, these Mexican people of ours. That makes me think that
grace is still with them. And so, having got hold of some kind of clue
to my own whole manhood, it is part of me now to try with them.
—CHAPTER XIV

There are other passages to the same effect, for the book is
somewhat redundant, as if Lawrence could not trust the reader to
get the point and felt that he had to hammer it in by repeated
blows. This last passage is as good as any to show how Ramon
and Lawrence believe that the manhood and womanhood that
Lawrence thought we have lost are to be regained through relationship with a living God. The dances, the liturgy, the elaborate
ceremonies, the hymns, and the rhythmic, untiring drums put us,
Lawrence would have it, in touch with the heart of the cosmos.
As already noted, Don Ramon imports Indians from the north to
teach the Mexicans how to dance, in order to restore them.

He had the wild Indians from the north beat their drums in the
barracks-yard, and start the old dances again. The dance, the dance
which has meaning, is a deep discipline in itself. The old Indians of
the north still have the secret of animistic dancing. They dance to
gain power; power over the *living* forces or potencies of the earth.
And these dances need intense dark concentration, and immense endurance.—CHAPTER XXII

These, then, are Lawrence's ideas regarding religion, as we
find them in *The Plumed Serpent*. But as one might have expected,
Don Ramon's effort to revive the old religion of pre-Columbian
America has to contend with two powerful and well entrenched
forces: the politicians and the Church. To the socialists Ramon
writes an open letter:

What do you want? Would you make all men as you are? And when
every peon in Mexico wears an American suit of clothes and shiny
black shoes, and looks for life in the newspaper and for his manhood

to the government, will you be satisfied? Did the government, then, give you your manhood, that you expect it to give it to these others?

It is time to forget. It is time to put away the grudge and the pity. No man was ever the better for being pitied, and every man is the worse for a grudge.

We can do nothing with life, except live it.

Let us seek life where it is to be found. And, having found it, life will solve the problems. But every time we deny the living life, in order to solve a problem, we cause ten problems to spring up where was one before. Solving the problems of the people, we lose the people in a poisonous forest of problems.

Life makes, and moulds, and changes the problem. The problem will always be there, and will always be different. So nothing can be solved, even by life and living, for life dissolves and resolves . . .

Therefore we turn to life; and from the clock to the sun and the stars, and from metal to membrane.—CHAPTER XXII

In an effort to bring the Church into his movement, Don Ramon has an interview with the "Bishop of the West." He tells the Bishop (whom he, an *hacendado* who should know the appropriate forms, addresses as "Father") that

We are in Mexico for the most part Indians. They cannot understand the high Christianity, Father, and the Church knows it. Christianity is a religion of the Spirit, and must needs be understood if it is to have any effect. The Indians cannot understand it, any more than the rabbits of the hills. . . . We must speak to the Mexicans in their own language, and give them the clue-word to their own souls. I shall say Quetzalcoatl.

Don Ramon argues that the Church ought to be really catholic, universal, and hence it ought to be the Church of Mohammed as well as of Jesus, and of Buddha, and Quetzalcoatl and all the others—"*that* would be the Catholic Church, Father," Don Ramon urges.

To this argument the best Lawrence's Bishop can answer is: "Alas, my son, I know the Apostolic Church of Christ in Rome, of which I am a humble servant. I do not understand these clever things you are saying to me" (Chapter XVII).

Not even Lawrence could imagine that the "Bishop of the West" would be convinced by such arguments. What enables the movement to succeed is Cipriano's army—for we are to suppose, as the book closes, that not only has Kate conquered her individualistic demand for frictional sexual satisfaction and found fulfillment in submission to Cipriano, but that Don Ramon's movement is a success.

Lawrence does not realize how much he spoils the presentation of Ramon's and his own side by putting into the Bishop's mouth a weak reply. But I have a hunch that the difficulty was not primarily an aesthetic one. In his treatment of the Catholic Church, Lawrence was plainly beyond his depth.

[4]

What can be said of Lawrence's program?

Let us note, first, that one probable reason for Lawrence's seriousness was that he was not burdened by too much erudition and felt quite free to pick and choose. The pre-Columbian religion of the valley of Mexico, which Ramon and Cipriano revive, is not that of which Bernal Diaz, Father Sahagun, and others left us a record. Lawrence does not propose to bring back the stinking pyramids of skulls, the cages of the victims waiting for the obsidian knife, the wild priests with hair clotted with human blood smelling death, the blood-madness of the Aztec world, the collective psychosis that led this people to keep the river of blood flowing with ever-increasing volume from their sacrificial altars, the insane cruelty which we find recorded in what we know of their culture and powerfully expressed in their art—these features, which were as much a part of their culture as the admirable ones, Lawrence overlooked. That this was not all there was to Aztec culture we know. When the Spaniards brought down the empire of the Aztecs they found in the valley of Mexico highly developed artistic refinement, luxury and polish in their lives, a developed polity, and the admirable wonders of the city on the lake. But Lawrence noticed only a very small number of the gods from a pantheon that, in Father Sahagun's account, was as richly peopled with divinities as any ever imagined by man. If *The Plumed Serpent* were art, the reference to the reality of the Aztec culture would be utterly irrelevant. But Lawrence intended the book seriously as a program of reform. For that reason we are forced to ask whether the organic character of a culture can be as blandly disregarded as Lawrence evidently assumed it could be. Could the old gods be revived without bringing back the old rivers of blood, the death madness Cortez encountered in the wonderful city on the lake?

The next observation is best divided into a negative and a positive part. Negatively it must be noted that *The Plumed Serpent* constitutes a representative instance of one aspect of Lawrence that makes him difficult to read. He wants to give back *life* to the Mexicans. Let us assume that we know what he meant by "life," and that the Mexicans lacked it—although in the book itself there is evidence that in several senses of the term, the Mexicans did not lack life. Let us also grant, what seems to be true, that the modern world tends to kill the life of men, in the sense that it interposes between man and the universe an impermeable barrier, the product of science and technology. Nevertheless, does it not seem inadmissible to believe that once life has been found, all other problems that confront modern man—even the problems of the twenties, for those of our mid-century are more serious and more difficult—will solve themselves as a consequence? Isn't it obvious that this is irresponsible nonsense? But this was no mere trivial idea of Lawrence, thrown off in a thoughtless moment and therefore not to be taken seriously by us. We shall encounter the same nonsense in *Lady Chatterley*.

On the positive side we must recognize here in passing that what Lawrence had to say about religion in *The Plumed Serpent* and elsewhere cannot be dismissed as utter nonsense. But I shall examine fully his views on this subject in the next chapter and to a lesser extent in Chapter VIII.

The third observation calls attention to Lawrence's conception of Ramon Carrasco as saviour or redeemer of his people. One expects a saviour or a redeemer to love the people whom he seeks to save or redeem, to be outraged by the iniquities of which they are the victims or moved by the usual motives ascribed to men who seek to save or redeem a people. Don Ramon does not love the people at all and he is not fundamentally concerned with their fate, their happiness, their improvement, nor does he make a pretense of acting from the motives that we are wont to assume move reformers or revolutionists. In a conversation with Kate he says: "About the great mass I don't care. But I don't want everybody poisoned" (Chapter XIV). Ramon, however, does care about the mass; he cares a great deal and he cares deeply. But his is a negative care. Ramon's attitude is almost identical with that of Kate, who frequently feels towards the mass a deep revulsion. There is, of course, an identification of sorts between the *hacendado* of Spanish ancestry and the Indian peons whom he has known since childhood and presumably understands; and Cipriano assures Kate that Don Ramon knows his Mexico. But the typical Lawrentian misanthropy cannot be dissimulated or spirited away. And whether we take the book as art or as propaganda, it forces on us a problem. As art a misanthropic saviour constitutes an incongruity within the context of the novel that requires fuller treatment than it is given for us to accept in the proper aesthetic mode of response. Here, again, it is not a question of Aristotelian probabilities. But even if it were, in these post-Freudian days of ours there can be no a priori ground on which to reject a misanthropic saviour. The problem arises from the fact that the source of the misanthropy is not explored. As a practical program, the fact that it is proposed by a misanthropic saviour forces us to question the motive behind Lawrence's desire to save Mexico and the world. And when we ask this question, other questions force themselves on our attention that are as unpleasant as they are difficult.

Why should a man want to save mankind if he is not concerned with its welfare, if all he wants is to avoid being poisoned? A man in fear of being poisoned gets away, if he can, from those who may poison him. A rich *hacendado* can get away. And a wandering, rootless writer also can. The *hacendado* can liquidate his wealth and go off to the wilderness where men and their poison are not to be feared. And the rootless writer can go back to his ranch in Taos, leaving Mabel and her friends below to their fates.

But of course we know that the matter is not that simple. For a man can say that he wants to avoid being poisoned and he may believe that he means it, and yet his statement may be a means of covering from himself and others what he really wants. What Lawrence had been wanting for quite some time was what Lilly in *Aaron's Rod* wanted, and what Lovat Somers in *Kangaroo* wanted: that others submit themselves to him, for he possessed "a bit of healthy individual authority." Lawrence, with his double vision—a vision that gives him and his reader, frequently, a pitiless objective disclosure of himself—is not ignorant of the fact that his concern for the betterment of humanity is motivated by the lust for power. In the novel, in answer to Kate's question as to what Ramon really wants, Lawrence has Doña Carlota exclaim: "Power! Just power! Just foolish wicked power. As if there had not been enough horrible, wicked power let loose in this country. But he—he—he wants to be beyond them all. He—he—he wants to be worshipped. To be worshipped!" (Chapter X).

The short outburst, ending with Doña Carlota's going off into shrill, wild laughter, punctuated by hollow, ghastly sobs, gives us the feeling of *déjà vu*. We have been through the identical scene or a very similar scene before, although the situation is superficially different and the characters have different names. In *Kangaroo* we have heard Harriet-Frieda throw it up directly at her husband that what he wants is power. And this is what he, Lawrence, whether under the name of Lovat Somers or of Ramon Carrasco, wants.

Lawrence's craving for power goes along with the insistence on his own superiority which I have already mentioned. In *The Plumed Serpent*, Don Ramon does not make the claim of being superior, as Lilly does in *Aaron's Rod*. It is Kate who perceives his superiority and informs the reader of it. This is a decided improvement upon *Aaron's Rod*, where Lilly-Lawrence pouts because he is not accepted as the greater soul in preference to Lloyd George and the other politicians. Kate is aware of a unison between Ramon and Cipriano on the one hand and their followers on the other—a "soft, quaking deep communion of blood-oneness" (Chapter XXVI), which sometimes revolts Kate. But in spite of the unison, Kate comes at last to perceive that "not in the blood nor in the spirit lay [Ramon's] individuality and his supremacy, his godhead. But in a star within him. . . ." And she then realizes that some men are born divine, while others are slaves or should be slaves. We, the readers, might have an easier time of it, and might go so far as to crave submitting to a bit of healthy individual authority, if we could recognize Ramon's divinity and felt within ourselves that we were born slaves. But we are an irreverent, contumacious lot, and remembering Ramon's painted face, his breechclout, and his feathers, we have all we can do to suppress our jeers.

The last observation about Lawrence's program refers to his account of the relation between the Roman Catholic Church and the people of Mexico. Confronted with his assertion that Jesus cannot be a Saviour to the Mexicans, one is led to ask whether he ever visited a church in Mexico and saw the people worshipping —I mean the Indians in *huaraches* and white cotton trousers and shirts? He must have witnessed them worshipping for he was a thorough tourist and a very keen observer. And Kate is irritated by their worship. We must therefore conclude that his preconceptions blinded him. His notion that Jesus is not a Saviour to the Mexicans is a theory made up entirely out of his own head, and one that has very little to do with Mexican reality. The less privileged classes of Mexico—the Indian peasant and perhaps, though to a lesser extent, the city worker—are a deeply pious people; nor does the persecution of religion initiated by the revolution seem to have made much headway. I am not speaking of a minority of militant and more or less literate Marxists or of intellectuals. I refer to the majority of the population. The Mexicans are a deeply religious people. They pray to God, to Jesus Christ, to the Virgin of Guadalupe, and to the saints.

What they actually are doing when they pray is, in the absence of sociological data carefully gathered, a matter for guess. I would hazard the guess that the Indians of Mexico have remained very much the old polytheists that they were when Cortez brought down the empire of Montezuma. It could not have been difficult for the Mexicans to transfer their allegiances from their native gods to the gods of the conquerors. For the elaborate and subtle theology preached by the conquerors could not have meant much to them. What touches them and has meaning for them—what I believe touches the illiterate not only of Mexico but of the rest of Spanish-America—are the visible symbols: the pictures or statues of the Father, the young Jesus, the bleeding Christ on the cross, who for most North Americans is horrible, the Dove, the Lamb, the Virgin, and the saints. Which is to say that the Mexican Indian remained after his conversion as much of a polytheist as he was before Cortez. I once broached this notion in the form of a question to the late Robert Redfield—an anthropologist who knew his Middle America if anyone knew it—and he agreed. The Puritans would have had a much harder time converting the Mexicans than the Roman Catholics, particularly the Spanish Catholics. (Not that I would accuse the Puritans, already under the heavy indictment of puritanism, of the intention of converting the Indians. We know they behaved in a much more Christian way than the cruel Spaniards did. That is the reason, of course, why so large a number of Mexican Indians survive, while the North

American Indians came within a hair's breadth of going the way
of the grizzly and the buffalo.)

I say, "particularly the Spanish Catholics," because I suspect
there was and there is an affinity of a subtle kind between the
conquistadores and their descendants and the conquered Mexicans and theirs—a subtle bond through their attitude towards
blood and death. The Spanish Christ—and Unamuno made it
clear that the bleeding Spanish Christ was the Christ of the Spaniards and not a catholic Christ—was made to order for a people
who were as obsessed with death and blood as the aboriginal Mexicans.

Be that as it may, the conversion of the Mexicans was the ex-
change of one polytheism for another. It is, of course, true that
the Roman Catholic church teaches trinitarian monotheism, insists
that the saints are not to be adored, and holds that one does not
pray to the visible symbols. But this doctrine involves the grasp
of subtle concepts and fine philosophical distinctions, and it is
not likely that an illiterate Indian is concerned with the nature of
his act and its intention when he prays. When a Mexican Indian
prays, when a member of the unprivileged orders of Spanish-
America prays, I do not believe we can meaningfully ask whether
he is giving to the saints what belongs to God or not. I doubt
whether it is a question he could understand. I am not saying that
the underprivileged Indian is less intelligent and that his failure to
grasp the distinctions taught by Catholic theologians is the result
of his lack of intelligence. All I am saying is that these are subtle
questions to which the Indian does not turn his intelligence.

On these grounds, it would seem, the Carrasco-Lawrence notion that Jesus is no Saviour to the Mexicans, that the Roman
Catholic Church does not possess the key word to the Mexican
soul, is an opinion concocted by Don Ramon (another of whose
aliases is Don Lorenzo) out of his own lucubrations and not an
opinion that either Don Ramon or Don Lorenzo drew from the
reality before his eyes. It is simply false.

But let me be clear on one point. I am not arguing for or against the Roman Catholic Church when I speak of the contemporary polytheism of the Mexican population. I am not a Roman Catholic, although being of Venezuelan birth and ancestry I was brought up one. What I am doing is merely asserting what I take to be the truth. Again, it would be irrelevant to assert the point if *The Plumed Serpent* were a genuine novel. In a novel a man may have as large a harem as he happens to have and that is the end of the matter and a church may be as dead as it happens to be, and that too is the end of the matter. But in *The Plumed Serpent* that cannot be the case, since the very nice man in the office was assured that Lawrence does mean what Ramon means—for all of us. Nor is it a question as to whether the doctrines of the real church are true or its teachings pragmatically useful for mankind, irrespective of the heterogeneity of cultural reality and the variety of character types. These questions are all irrelevant. What is relevant is whether the Roman Catholic religion has been accepted by the Mexicans and meets their needs. And the answer is that it has been accepted and so far as one can see it seems to meet their needs. That it meets their needs because in the process of accepting it the Mexicans have interpreted it in their own terms—that is another question. And whether it ought or ought not to meet their needs, as humanists and Marxists argue, on the ground that needs ought not to be satisfied by spiritual "opium," that is still another question.

Fortunately, there is reliable evidence on some aspects of this question. Thus, it has long been known that in rural areas of Middle America the old pagan and the Christian religions live in comfortable symbiotic relationship. Oliver La Farge has studied this relationship for Santa Eulalia, Guatemala, an Indian settlement immediately south of the Mexican border. [5] Nor is it likely that this phenomenon stops at the political frontier between Guatemala and Mexico, for I doubt whether the frontier exists as an operative cultural reality for the people of the region. For this reason I take it that we can generalize from La Farge's evidence.

In view of his evidence, the old gods cannot be revived because they have never been altogether dead. And the Roman Catholic religion is the religion of the Mexicans and it was not difficult for them to accept it, once they had to, because it could easily be interpreted by them in terms they could handle.

CHAPTER FOUR

The Plumed
Serpent, II

Do THESE criticisms mean that the diagnosis and the remedy presented in *The Plumed Serpent* are to be rejected in their
totality, to be scorned as nonsense? Taken literally, the answer is,
of course, yes. But we need not take the novel literally. We can
take from the program the central valid insight and ignore the
clownish trimmings, the bad taste, and the silly political and social
ideology. When the abstracting and selecting has been duly performed, we are left with Lawrence's assertion that the modern
world needs a new religion and that central to that religion must
be the recognition of the place of sex in human life. This is not a
silly thesis.

To discover the source of his insight and to understand it, we
have to turn back to a religious experience that Lawrence had,
not in Mexico, but in New Mexico. This experience, which arose
out of a permanent and a deeply rooted need in Lawrence, was
authentic when it took place, and thoroughly satisfactory; it continued to satisfy him for a long time. Furthermore it was an
experience whose value transcends its autobiographical import. It
has a claim to our attention because it has value for us. If the Mexican novel has value (outside the vignettes and the splashes of
beauty already recognized), its value lies in the fact that it points
to this experience, demanding of us that we analyze it seriously.
For the novel is an attempt to dramatize that experience.

The religious need was a basic need of Lawrence, a permanent

one, although at times recessive. But as I shall show in this chapter, New Mexico revived it. It led to the three brilliant sketches
of the Indian dances that he collected in *Mornings in Mexico* [1] as
well as to the unfortunate breechclouts and painted faces of
Ramon and Cipriano. The effort to turn the matter of his experience into art did not come off in the novel, as I hope I have
shown. But the sketches are one of the high points of his writing and give us the best statement we have of what he understood
by religion.

Because we need a name for this experience, I shall refer to it
as "the American experience," but the term designates, in this
context, not only his experience in New Mexico but also in "Old
Mexico." It should be noted that the United States is for Lawrence
almost entirely New Mexico, more specifically Taos and the
dancing Indians. What he saw of the rest of the country must
have contributed to his American experience, but if it did, its influence is not discernible as such.

It is impossible to read the three sketches of the dances in
Mornings in Mexico and not realize the importance of the American experience for Lawrence. But his mind was not a roll-top
desk with pigeonholes where different kinds of experiences were
tucked away in isolation from one another. The dances and the
New Mexican landscape were integrated with his profound response to Mexico. And we cannot read Kate's reaction to the land
and the people of Mexico and doubt that Lawrence's Mexican experience was as profound as his New Mexican experience had
been. Lawrence saw something in Mexico that I believe it is easy
to overlook and that the superficial tourist fails to perceive.
His keen sensitivity to the spirit of place revealed to him the
terror, the cruelty, the untameable savagery of the land and its people. Under the thin film of impeccable courtesy and specious
friendliness, he saw the unapproachable monadic inwardness, the
radical indifference of each man for the rest.

The importance I attach to Lawrence's American experience is
not merely an inference based on my reading of Lawrence's writ-

ings on "America," although I would not in principle distrust such an inference. The importance is clearly and explicitly recognized by Lawrence himself in the essay on New Mexico, probably written sometime in 1928.[2] He writes: "I think New Mexico was the greatest experience from the outside world that I have ever had. It certainly changed me forever. Curious as it may sound, it was New Mexico that liberated me from the present era of civilization, the great era of material and mechanical development." Lawrence goes on to say that Sicily or Ceylon did not change him. Neither did Australia. And he continues: "But the moment I saw the brilliant, proud morning shine high up over the deserts of Santa Fe, something stood still in my soul and I started to attend."[3] Lawrence adds that "for *greatness* of beauty" (emphasis on "greatness" is his) he never experienced anything like New Mexico. And commenting on a statement made by Leo Stein to the effect that it is the most aesthetically satisfying landscape Stein knows, Lawrence says that for him "it was much more than that. It had a splendid silent terror, and a vast far-and-wide magnificence which made it way beyond mere aesthetic appreciation." Finally Lawrence comes to the kernel of the meaning of his New Mexican experience. At the end of the paragraph from which this last sentence was taken he writes: "Ah, yes, in New Mexico the heart is sacrificed to the sun and the human being is left stark, heartless, but undoubtedly religious."[4]

At this point I am not able to resist a digression. "The heart is sacrificed to the sun," and "the human being is left heartless." The phrases set the mind off in several directions at once, for they remind one of many of Lawrence's experiences and responses which one recognizes to have had a deep import for him. He is writing these lines in France, but he is writing at the time when the American experience had already been digested, which is to say, had been transmuted and thoroughly synthesized, made into a single, coherent experience.[5] But the phrase reminds one also of "Old Mexico," of the obsidian knife in the bloody hand of the priest, and of the heart, still beating, torn from the victim on the altar. It reminds one of the cruel Aztec world to which Lawrence reacted so profoundly. It also brings to mind by a natural enough association "the old Pyramid of the Sun, at Teotihuacan," to which Lawrence refers twice in the *Letters*, the second time as one of the things that he has known that cannot be unified with others in the world.[6] "Sacrifice" is a word to which Lawrence was responsive; the act somehow quickens him and elicits a strong fascination. We have already seen that Somers wanted to perform a human sacrifice. The story, "The Woman Who Rode Away," to which I have referred as the expression of death wishes and of a diffuse psychic illness, is also the expression of Lawrence's fascination with the subject of human sacrifice. To say that his attitude towards it is ambivalent and that while some of his characters crave it others are horrified by it, is not to alter the facts but merely to state them more accurately. His attitude is a component of his demonic nature; but it is also a symptom of an illness I do not wish to analyze. The phrase, "the heart is sacrificed to the sun," reminds one also that under the influence of Harry Crosby, Lawrence's inclination to sun worship had become a more explicit preoccupation than it had been earlier.

The next paragraph in the essay on New Mexico begins: "And that was the second revelation out there. I had looked all over the world for something that would strike *me* as religious," and he goes on to say that he found it in New Mexico and in the Red Indian (the italics, again, are his).

That Lawrence had searched all over the world for something that would strike him as religious is true; his need did not disappear when he gave up the religious beliefs of his parents. There were periods when he thought sex or love could be substituted for God. At such times he writes, as he wrote to Mrs. S. A. Hopkins on Christmas day of 1912: "I shall always be a priest of love." [7] But he also had periods when he thought he could combine love and religion. In *Kangaroo*, Somers-Lawrence, after flirting with politics, finally chooses the "dark God . . . the God from whom the dark, sensual passion of love emanates . . . the great dark God, the ithyphallic of the first dark religions" (Chapter XI). The effort is again made in *The Plumed Serpent*. There were times when love or sex took a relatively secondary position, although he never quite gave up his concern with sex. At the age of twenty-six he did not know what he meant by God, and wrote his sister: "There still remains a God, but not a personal God: a vast shimmering impulse which waves onwards towards some end, I don't know what— taking no regard of the little individual, but taking regard for humanity." [8] The religious preoccupation finds expression in the letters in statements like the following: "Primarily I am a passionately religious man." "It is an Absolute we are all after." "You must learn to believe in God." "I believe in something supernatural, which is not of human life, neither of religion." Later he writes "And I do think that man is related to the universe in some 'religious' way." And, "there is a *principle* in the universe towards which man turns religiously." [9] But the positive and definitive identification of what he had searched for throughout his life did not come to him in its fullness until he went to New Mexico and to Mexico.

[2]

To achieve a complete examination of what Lawrence meant by "religion," an examination that meets legitimate demands of clarity and coherence is, I fear, not altogether possible. I do not mean that it is not possible for me, with my obvious limitations, to make it clear—that goes without saying. I mean that it is not possible for anyone, even for the best equipped of critics and the most learned Lawrentian scholar. And the reason is that the matter remains somewhat obscure in Lawrence's mind in spite of his efforts to elucidate it. One considers it, one broods about it, and the obscurity refuses to dissipate.

It is not difficult to see that Lawrence's conception of God is intimately related to his lyric receptivity to the beauty and the power of nature. Sensitive to nature's moods, he never forgets our human dependence on it. As his grasp of that dependence matures and deepens, he becomes more profoundly aware of the fact that in the human situation there are forces operative that do not have their origin in it and that, although they may appear to be completely domesticated or socialized, they retain potency by virtue of their transcendent origin.

But the terms I have just used are seriously misleading and I must make the effort to come closer to what I mean. In their abstractness and matter-of-factness the terms caricature an experience which was for Lawrence profoundly stirring, charged with tremendous emotion, engaging his whole organism, and having a revitalizing effect on him that a "pure" aesthetic or a sentimental response to nature could not have. Nor is the word "nature" the right word. Lovejoy aside, the word in its comon-sense acceptance refers today to that which lies behind the billboards as one speeds on the superhighway, or to those areas which are still difficult of access except on horseback or by foot. It refers in short to the world not yet fully a part of our social, urbanized world. But this is a world that is being brought within the frontier of domestication by machinery. Lawrence responded sensitively to this nature —the world untouched by industry, the world of woods and clean waters, of untamed animals: the wider, wild world that frightened as much as it attracted him, the Australia of the bush, the fascinating world of New Mexico, and the wild and frightening world of Mexico. But "nature" meant considerably more than all of this to Lawrence. Back of it was the cosmos, the mystery, the fiery teeming universe at the center of which, for him, glowed a fascinating and impenetrable mystery. The sterilizing and debilitating effects that science has on our attitude towards the universe he managed to a great extent to avoid and he frequently felt the cosmos potent and awesome. He seems to have been able to look on the universe as primitive man probably did. This was "the second revelation," a revelation he had had before but that in New Mexico seems to have come to him more powerfully and more clearly. Part, only a part, of his quarrel with the modern world, with its cerebral approach to man and nature, sprang from his outraged knowledge of what science does to us; because we "understand" the world it loses its mystery and awe for us, and he took this loss to be a great loss.

Lawrence would have it that his response to the cosmos is the response of the "vast old religion which once swayed the earth," and that it "lingers in unbroken practice here in New Mexico," and that it is "older perhaps than anything in the world." [10] His scholarship is irrelevant, although Eliade to some extent confirms Lawrence's notions.[11] What is of interest is what he himself experienced. And this he tells us in magnificent prose in the sketches of the dances in *Mornings in Mexico*. These sketches contain not only an account of what Lawrence saw but also an interpretation of what he took the dances to mean. What he saw—and how much more he could see than the rest of us, these sketches are a witness to—makes hash of any aestheticians's doctrine in which the autonomy and the insularity of the various arts is asserted. Lawrence transcribes into prose the dancing and the ambient scene:

. . . Take the song to make the corn grow. The dark faces stoop forward, in a strange race darkness. The eyelashes droop a little in the dark, ageless, vulnerable faces. The drum is a heart beating with insistent thuds. And the spirits of the men go out on the ether, vibrating in waves from the hot, dark, intentional blood, seeking the creative presence that hovers forever in the ether, seeking the identification, following on down the mysterious rhythms of the creative pulse, on and on into the germinating quick of the maize that lies under the ground, there, with the throbbing, pulsing, clapping rhythm that comes from the dark, creative blood in man, to stimulate the tremulous, pulsating protoplasm in the seed-germ, till it throws forth its rhythms of creative energy into rising blades of leaf and stem.

Or take the round dances, round the drum. These may or may not have a name. The dance, anyhow, is primarily a song. All the men sing in unison, as they move with the soft, yet heavy bird-tread which is the whole of the dance. There is no drama. With bodies bent a little forward, shoulders and breasts loose and heavy, feet powerful but soft, the men tread the rhythm into the centre of the earth. The drums keep up the pulsating heart-beat. The men sing in unison, though some will be silent for moments, or even minutes. And for hours, hours it goes on; the round dance.

It has no name. It has no words. It means nothing at all. There is no spectacle, no spectator.

Yet perhaps it is the most stirring sight in the world, in the dark, near the fire, with the drums going, the pine-trees standing still, the everlasting darkness, and the strange lifting and dropping, surging, crowing, gurgling, aah-h-h-ing! of the male voices.

. . . Mindless, without effort, under the hot sun, unceasing, yet never perspiring nor even breathing heavily, they dance on and on. Mindless, yet still listening, observing. They hear the deep, surging singing of the bunch of old men, like a great wind soughing. They hear the cries and yells of the man waving his bough by the drum. They catch the word of the song, and at a moment, shudder the black rattles, wheel, and the line breaks, women from men, they thread across to a new formation. And as the men wheel round, their black hair gleams and shakes, and the long fox-skin sways, like a tail.

And always, when they form into line again, it is a beautiful long straight line, flexible as life, but straight as rain.[12]

These are the dances as Lawrence saw them performed—or, more precisely, this is what Lawrence reports he saw at the dances. The account seems charged with power and authenticity, and for this reason it is gratifying, but not indispensable, to have the authority of Ruth Benedict support our judgment. "No one," she tells us in *Patterns of Culture*, "has conveyed the quality of Pueblo dancing more precisely than D. H. Lawrence." [13]

What did the spectacle mean to Lawrence? In other words, what was Lawrence's concept of religion? Father Tiverton calls Lawrence a pantheist, but Lawrence himself thought of his religious beliefs as animistic. The question of nomenclature is not very important. What is essential is to bear in mind that his religion was not theistic; he found God in man, in sex, in nature, and in the vast and teeming energies of the cosmos. And since it would rep-

resent nothing but a loss to translate his own magnificent interpretation of it, I reproduce some passages:

But strictly, in the religion of aboriginal America, there is no Father,
and no Maker. There is the great living source of life: say the Sun of
existence: to which you can no more pray than you can pray to Elec-
tricity. And emerging from this Sun are the great potencies, the in-
vincible influences which make shine and warmth and rain. From these
great interrelated potencies of rain and heat and thunder emerge the
seeds of life itself, corn, and creatures like snakes. And beyond these,
men, persons. But all emerge separately. There is no oneness, no sympathetic identifying oneself with the rest. The law of isolation is heavy
on every creature.

How is man to get himself into relation with the vast living convul-
sions of rain and thunder and sun, which are conscious and alive and
potent, but like vastest of beasts, inscrutable and incomprehensible.
How is man to get himself into relation with these, the vastest of cosmic beasts?

It is the problem of the ages of man. Our religion says the cosmos is
Matter, to be conquered by the Spirit of Man. The yogi, the fakir, the
saint, try conquest by abnegation and by psychic powers. The real conquest of the cosmos is made by science.

How to conquer the dragon-mouthed thunder! How to capture the
feathered rain!

We make reservoirs, and irrigation ditches and artesian wells. We
make lightning conductors, and build vast electric plants. We say it is
a matter of science, energy, force.

But the Indian says No! It all lives. We must approach it fairly, with
profound respect, but also with desperate courage. Because man must
conquer the cosmic monsters of living thunder and live rain. The rain
that slides down from its source, and ebbs back subtly, with a strange
energy generated between its coming and going, an energy which,
even to our science, is of life: this, man has to conquer. The serpent-
striped, feathery Rain.

This brings us back to the Hopi. He has the hardest task, the stubbornest destiny. Some inward fate drove him to the top of these parched mesas, all rocks and eagles, sand and snakes, and wind and sun and alkali. These he had to conquer. Not merely, as we should put it, the natural conditions of the place. But the mysterious life-spirit that reigned there. The eagle and the snake.

The Hopi sought the conquest by means of the mystic, living will that is in man, pitted against the living will of the dragon-cosmos. The Egyptians long ago made a partial conquest by the same means. We have made a partial conquest by other means. Our corn doesn't fail us: we have no seven years' famine, and apparently need never have. But the other thing fails us, the strange inward sun of life; the pellucid monster of the rain never shows us his stripes. To us, heaven switches on daylight, or turns on the shower-bath. We little gods are gods of the machine only. It is our highest. Our cosmos is a great engine. And we die of ennui. A subtle dragon stings us in the midst of plenty. *Quos vult perdere Deus, dementat prius.*[14]

Once Lawrence hit upon the nature of "primitive" religion and the function it performed in human experience, he "discovered" it in the Etruscan tombs.

To the Etruscan all was alive; the whole universe lived; and the business of man was himself to live amid it all. He had to draw life into himself, out of the wandering huge vitalities of the world. The cosmos was alive, like a vast creature. The whole thing breathed and stirred. Evaporation went up like breath from the nostrils of a whale, steaming up.

And in another passage he writes:

The strange potency and beauty of these Etruscan things arise, it seems to me, from the profundity of the symbolic meaning the artist was more or less aware of. The Etruscan religion, surely, was never anthropomorphic: that is, whatever gods it contained were not *beings*, but symbols of elemental powers, just symbols: as was the case earlier in Egypt. The undivided Godhead, if we can call it such, was symbolized by the *mundum*, the plasm-cell with its nucleus: that which is the very beginning; instead of, as with us, by a personal god, a person being the very end of all creation or evolution. So it is all the way through: the Etruscan religion is concerned with all those physical and creative powers and forces which go to the building up and the destroying of the soul: the soul, the personality, being that which gradually is produced out of chaos, like a flower, only to disappear again into chaos, or the underworld. We, on the contrary, say: In the beginning was the Word!—and deny the physical universe true existence. We exist only in the Word, which is beaten out thin to cover, gild, and hide all things.[15]

But Lawrence was not only an archeologist, capable of interpreting the nature of a whole culture and the quality of its life by reading the art of its tombs. He was also a higher critic and in *Apocalypse* he finds again what he found in the Indian dances and in the Etruscan tombs:

Perhaps the greatest difference between us and the pagans lies in our different relation to the cosmos. With us, all is personal. Landscape and the sky, these are to us the delicious background of our personal life, and no more. Even the universe of the scientist is little more than an extension of our personality, to us. To the pagan, landscape and personal background were on the whole indifferent. But the cosmos was a very real thing. A man *lived* with the cosmos, and knew it greater than himself.

Don't let us imagine we see the sun as the old civilizations saw it. All we see is a scientific little luminary, dwindled to a ball of blazing gas. In the centuries before Ezekiel and John, the sun was still a magnificent reality, men drew forth from him strength and splendour, and gave him back homage and lustre and thanks. But in us, the connection is broken, the responsive centres are dead. Our sun is a quite different thing from the cosmic sun of the ancients, so much more trivial. We may see what we call the sun, but we have lost Helios forever, and the great orb of the Chaldeans still more. We have lost the cosmos by coming out of responsive connection with it, and this is our chief tragedy. What is our petty little love of nature—Nature!!—compared to the ancient magnificent living with the cosmos, and being honoured by the cosmos! [16]

[3]

Had Lawrence remained content to use his religious experience
as matter for art, one could not quarrel with him: one could only
say that some of his characters respond to the universe in this manner and the question as to whether this is the true nature of a mature religious experience would be irrelevant. But Lawrence's
strong religious interest, transmuted sometimes into art—as it is in
The Rainbow—is put forth in other of his books, as we have seen,
as a true message that we ought to accept. And this forces us to
consider whether or not his conception of religion is indeed true
and valuable.

We must first note with some emphasis that it is not a question as
to whether Lawrence's interpretation of the Indian religion is true
or not. Whatever the anthropologists think of his interpretation of
the religion of the Indians, the valid query for us is whether men
have drawn or thought they drew—for if they think they draw,
they do—strength and splendor from Helios or from the Dragon
Cosmos. And the answer is, of course, that they have. And if we
no longer can draw strength from the Dragon Cosmos, if science
has turned the sun of the Chaldeans into a ball of blazing gas, that
is *our* loss, whatever gain we may reckon it to be in other respects.
There is no question that the Incas drew from their sun-god the
strength they needed to carry on, and that without that source of
strength they could not have been able to conquer and pacify
and extend their empire. And there is no question that the Aztecs
drew from their cruel, blood-thirsty gods the strength they needed
to carry on their wars and capture more victims and spill more
blood to have the strength to build their wonderful city by the
lake, in order to carry on more and more wars until the arrival of
Cortez. And there is no question that science has changed the
Dragon Cosmos into little balls of blazing gas receding into empty
space or whatever is the latest version of the nature and structure
universe—I have not seen anything in the Sunday papers of

late on the subject. But can we return to the Dragon Cosmos by an act of will? And would such a return represent a gain?

The first question I do not believe need detain us at all. Lawrence, who dismissed evolution because he did not feel its truth in his solar plexus, might have been able to return to the primitive religion of early man—assuming that his conception of the early religion is the correct one. But *we* cannot. We *know* the sun is a ball of blazing gas. To assume we can go back to the Dragon Cosmos is on a level with the assumption that we can solve our sociopolitical or economic problems by going back to handicrafts and eschewing commerce and technology. But the second question requires careful examination. For Lawrence is telling us seriously, not that we have lost our religion, but that we have lost the true religion by losing connection with the Dragon Cosmos. And the answer to his criticism is that it is true that we have lost connection with the mystery of the universe, but his animism is no more admissible than his or Ramon's painted face and breechclouts. This is the twentieth century, alas, and we are the children of Darwin and Freud, we live after Hiroshima and Sputnik and some of us create the scientific advances of which we boast and some of us read about them in the Sunday papers. But even at the time Lawrence was writing, it was already too late. This is of course obvious.

But there is more to be said on this question, and that more is best broached, it seems to me, in the light of T. S. Eliot's severe animadversions on Lawrence's views. These are Eliot's words:

I have already touched upon the deplorable religious upbringing which gave Lawrence his lust for intellectual independence: Like most people who do not know what orthodoxy is, he hated it. . . . The point is that Lawrence started life wholly free from any restriction of tradition or institution, that he had no guidance except the Inner Light, the most untrustworthy and deceitful guide that ever offered itself to wondering humanity.[17]

Lawrence, of course, never concealed that he relied on his Inner Light. But reliance on the Inner Light is not necessarily wrong.

What other source of truth does a prophet have when he rises against a moribund orthodoxy or against one that he takes to be dying? Where do new truths come from? Lawrence's error lies, not in its source, but in its partiality and inadequacy to the human situation as it presents itself to Western man in our century. But the question is not so easily disposed of, for we cannot overlook the possibility that, at this late hour in the history of our Western civilization, there may not be available any living forms in respect to which doctrines may be judged adequate or not. Put in different terms, we may say that it is indeed true that Lawrence was a heretic, but the orthodoxy to which he was heretical is not as simply defined as Eliot takes it to be. When Eliot speaks of "tradition" or "institution" one knows very well what he means by it—the triad of Anglo-Catholicism, royalism, and classicism. But the traditions or institutions that these terms refer to do not represent the only traditions or institutions of our Western world, and even if they did, it is too late in our history to assume blandly that they have the undisputed and self-evident authority they once had.

This is hard on men like the writer, who call themselves conservatives, but we shall do a better job of conserving what can be conserved at this late date if we don't try to imitate the ostrich. To speak today of heretics as if there were still a reigning orthodoxy is to misrepresent the facts. Classicism after Picasso? *Gott im Himmel*, we conservatives should have held up all change after Giotto. No, that was already too late. We should have held the line at Altamira! And classicism after *il migglior fabbro?* And royalism, I suppose, of the English variety, *cum* socialism whether Tory or Labor? As for Anglo-Catholicism—what are we going to do, Mr. Eliot, with the non-conformists, Catholics, and Greek Orthodox?

All of this is to say that the problems that Eliot dismisses in his inimitable and magisterial "I-know-and-you-don't" manner, are too complex for that kind of treatment. It is possible that Authority is preferable to the Inner Light, although it seems somewhat naïve to appeal to one Authority in order to discover which of the Authorities ready at hand is *the true* Authority, and although it is quite possible—possible, I do not mean it *is* the case—that the Authority to which we appeal may find that it has the right Authority by appealing to its own Inner Light. However that may be, Lawrence's heresy cannot be disposed of by appeal to Authority, not even Mr. Eliot's Authority.

With these qualifications I can still assert that Eliot is not altogether wrong, and that Lawrence was indeed a heretic. There are a number of views that have been accepted by the West, that define or have defined the civilization of which we are, or our parents were, members. The word "views" is not vague enough for what I have in mind, "attitudes" or "tendencies" may be better. We need a loose and elastic term to speak of the essence of Western orthodoxy, for we cannot have in mind a set of values that can be put into a convenient capsule, into an elegant triad like that of Eliot.

There is, then, or there was, a Western orthodoxy. And one of the basic notions in this body of beliefs is the idea that God is a person and that he is triune. What the theist means by saying God is a person may or may not be sufficiently clear to him; but it is certainly clear enough to enable him to reject Lawrence's conception of God as a vast, shimmering impulse waving on towards an indeterminate end. And God is Providence, and the end He provides for, as the Judeo-Christian tradition asserts, is that of the individual, not that of the species. He is Providence not in the sense that He provides for our whims but, as I understand it, that He provides the end we ought to realize and that He gives us the means and the freedom to achieve that end. Eliot is right. Lawrence was a heretic because he thought he could define his end, and the individual has that end given to him to realize.

Again, Western orthodoxy, after several centuries of intense and searching debate, settled on the notion of the Trinity, a notion frankly declared to be a truth and yet to be beyond rational comprehension. A rationalistic unbeliever will no doubt say that a truth beyond reason is a contradiction in terms. But this is what

the powerful minds that participated in the long controversy finally came to. And only men who pick their theology from Gib-
bon will see in the argument which led to the idea of the Trinity a
gratuitous invention of minds darkened by superstition and af-
flicted with metaphysical logorrhea. The sociologist of religion, in
any case, intent on understanding before he condemns or rejects,
sees in the notion of the Trinity the embodiment of complex experience, which the tradition sought to synthesize without dam-
age to its components. For the tradition, God is Father—the vast
shimmering impulse, the principle of creativity in history and in the
universe. But He is more than a vast shimmering impulse waving
towards some indeterminate end. Western orthodoxy, breaking
with the uncompromising monotheism of the Judaic tradition, asserted that God is Father but also Son and Holy Ghost.

Having said this we have at last arrived at what I take to be the
very heart of the heresy Lawrence espoused. Not only does he
interpret in his own idiosyncratic manner the Father and the Holy
Ghost; he denies the Son. After a fashion he acknowledged the first
and third Persons. His interpretation would have been shocking
not only to Eliot and Bishop Temple but even to his own non-
conformist ancestors. Sometimes, but not often, Lawrence referred to the Son. But Lawrence did not in his heart acknowledge
Him. Lawrence denied Him, and he denied Him because he hated
Him. To acknowledge Him would have meant acknowledging the
role of love—not eros but agape—in our Western world. And to
make this acknowledgement would have involved a repudiation of
his deepest feelings, his radical alienation and his radical misanthropy. Lawrence, a bundle of inconsistencies, was consistent on
one point: he never would give up the assumption of the radical difference between his own superiority and the inferiority of the mob.
He was willing to call himself the priest of love, but the love he
served was eros. Agape he would not and could not serve.

Fortunately we do not have to depend on inferences here, he
himself expressed his attitude clearly. Thus, in a letter to Middleton Murry of October, 1925 he writes: ". . . Must you write

about Jesus? Jesus becomes more *unsympathisch* to me, the longer I live: cross and nails and tears and all that stuff! I think he showed us into a nice *cul-de-sac*."[18] In the essay on "Aristocracy" he flatly asserts the essential difference, a difference in being, in kind, and an infinite one, between some men and the majority.[19] And in *Apocalypse* he writes: "The Christian doctrine of love even at its best was an evasion. Even Jesus was going to reign 'hereafter' when his 'love' would be turned into confirmed power. This business of reigning in glory hereafter went to the root of Christianity, and is, of course, only an expression of frustrated desire to reign here and now."[20]

[4]

Lawrence's attitude towards agape involves more than theological heresy. It is moral defect that has its unlovely side. His defenders have tried to clear him from a charge sometimes brought against him that, for all his contempt of Mussolini, Lawrence had a well developed streak of proto-fascism. He was not, as one might expect, a consistent proto-fascist. But the tendency is there and it is deep-rooted in a psychology incapable of love. It is useless to try to deny it.

This is not all. When we put his scorn for agape together with his attitude towards the infallibility of his feelings, we get an attitude and a body of beliefs that constitutes the least acceptable aspect of his ideology, since they lead him to the conclusion— logical enough given its premises—that any act of his, if authentic, is beyond reproach. This is found stated in his essays and is sometimes turned into genuine art in his novels. In the foreword to *Women in Love* he writes: "Nothing that comes from the deep passional soul is bad, or can be bad. So there is no apology to tender, unless to the soul itself, if it should have been belied." This is a conviction that he frequently put forth and in the novel itself it is turned successfully into art in the scene in which Hermione hits Birkin with the paperweight. Afterwards Birkin reflects: "It was quite right of Hermione to want to kill him" (Chapter VIII). This is Lawrence reflecting for Birkin; and this is exactly what Lawrence himself believed and what he preached outside the novel.

But just how far is Lawrence willing to go? Apparently there was no limit. If Lawrence's deep passional soul prompts him to kill, it is perfectly right for him to do so, and if Lawrence's soul leads him to hate or to love, that, too, is right. And it may have been right for Frieda also, for we remember the time recorded by one of his biographers, when Frieda broke a plate on Lawrence's head while he was washing dishes. But is it right for the rest of us to follow our passional souls? The statement just quoted from the Foreword to *Women in Love* and others that could be cited to support it make no reference to class or race. But we cannot overlook Lawrence's ideas on the natural superiority of some men over others. Lawrence belonged to the natural aristocracy of the world, he and Don Ramon and Don Cipriano and Rupert Birkin and a number of grooms and gypsies and a few others. And it is simply presumptuous of us, and indicative of the fact that whatever our class or condition we are not natural aristocrats but natural plebeians, that we do not realize that what is sauce for the natural wellborn goose is not sauce for the inferior gander. By their failure to recognize the privileges of the natural aristocrats ye shall know the natural hoi polloi.

There are times when the reader of Lawrence is tempted to give up. He asks himself in exasperation, Why bother, why? All this misanthropy, this insufferable, childish arrogance, this kicking of our world's hard-won moral principles—can the beauty he often brings into his pages make up for these ugly qualities? In *Kangaroo* Jack boasts to Richard that during the riot in which the diggers broke up the labor meeting, he had killed three men:

He reached his face towards Somers with weird gruesome exultation, and continued in a hoarse, secret voice: "Cripes, there's *nothing* bucks you up sometimes like killing a man—*nothing*. You feel a perfect *angel* after it."

The text continues:

Richard felt the same torn feeling in the abdomen, and his eyes watched the other man.

Jack continues to exult:

"When it comes over you, you know there is nothing else like it. *I never* knew till the war . . . Having a woman's something, isn't it? But it's a flea-bite, nothing, compared to killing your man when your blood comes up."
And his eyes glowed with exultant satisfaction.
"And the best of it is," he said, "you feel a perfect *angel* after it. You don't feel you have done any harm. Feel as gentle as a lamb all around. I can go to Victoria [his wife], now, and be as gentle—" He jerked his head in the direction of Victoria's room. "And you bet she'll like me."
His eyes glowed with a sort of exaltation.
"Killing's natural to a man, you know," he said. "It is just as natural as lying with a woman, don't you think?"
And still Richard did not answer.—CHAPTER XVI

Richard, it will be remembered, is a pale-faced writer with a dark beard, married to "a Russian-looking" wife, who cannot help reminding us of the author of the novel. And it is Richard who feels the torn feeling in his abdomen. But we cannot have it both ways. We cannot say that Lovat Somers "represents" Lawrence, or is Lawrence's "voice carrier" (as one critic says of Birkin) and say at the same time that *Kangaroo* is art.

In *The Plumed Serpent* we find the same conflict, in the execution scene. Kate's reaction to the killing of the men who assaulted the *hacienda* is one of disapproval. But the author glorifies the scene in the same manner in which he glorifies Jack's killings. Both attitudes were authentically Lawrence's, and we cannot appeal here, in order to clear him of his unlovely traits, to the law of contradiction; for these are matters of psychology in which conflicting attitudes may and do exist at the same time in the same person. Lawrence himself did not hesitate to acknowledge to his friends at times that he had raging murder in his soul. In an undated letter to Lady Ottoline Morel, placed by Huxley immediately after one dated in June 1916, Lawrence makes a pathetic statement, moving in its sincerity and impressive because it is one of those frequent instances in which he saw himself with cruel objectivity. He writes:

I have had a great struggle with the Powers of Darkness lately. I think I have just got the better of them again. Don't tell me there is no Devil; there is a Prince of Darkness. Sometimes I wish I could let go and be really wicked—kill and murder—but kill chiefly. I do want to kill. But I want to select whom I shall kill. Then I shall enjoy it. The war is no good. It is this black desire I have become conscious of. We cant so much about goodness—it is canting. Tell Russell he does the same—let him recognize the powerful malignant will in him.[21]

The authenticity of Jack's feeling arose from his acceptance of the nature of his drive, irrespective of its moral quality, just as the reaction of Somers to Jack and of Kate to the execution arose from their acceptance of their moral natures. But if we look for the source of these accounts we have to admit that both the devil in Lawrence's belly and his need to overcome the Powers of Darkness were undeniable realities of his psychology.

[5]

Thus it is not possible flatly to contradict Bertrand Russell when he tells us that Lawrence's "metaphysical philosophy of 'the blood' " leads straight to Auschwitz. Russell's harsh judgment is misleading if left unqualified, and in this section I shall show that Lawrence's philosophy of the blood is not to be dismissed, as

Russell dismisses it, and others before him have done, as if it were
a malignant throwback to something we have fortunately left behind. But neither can Russell's statement be dismissed as if it were
utterly without foundation.

Here I shall not undertake an exhaustive examination of Lawrence's philosophy of the blood. I shall confine myself to a few
remarks.

The first is that the term "blood" is a metaphorical term which
refers, as "the heart" does, to a psychology that drives a sharp
wedge between reason—or the intellect or the mind—and the
passions, the will and other aspects of the personality, and gives reason the primacy over the rest. But the problem cannot be satisfactorily handled by means of these categories. The important
truth that Lawrence sought to convey in these inadequate terms
can only be exhibited if we find a way of talking about human
living and the human personality that avoids the traditional op-
positions and valuations so deeply rooted in traditional faculty psychology. If Lawrence's philosophy of the blood is a false philosophy, no less false are those philosophies that oppose it in the
manner Russell opposes it, or those that claim for reason a
sovereignty it can only have in respect to knowledge when
"knowledge" is given a rigorously narrow acceptation.

At his best, what Lawrence objected to when he pitted the blood
against reason, was very much what Kierkegaard had objected to
when he attacked The System. The fundamental objection, for
the Dane, is that "thought" is not co-extensive with life, although
the professor who had built The System made one congruous
with the other. This is objectionable because it *substitutes* theology
for the direct encounter with God that Kierkegaard's Knight of
Faith lives for. The precious dialectic of the builder of The System is substituted for the religious experience, and for faith is substituted an explanation of Faith that assigns it to its proper place in
The System. The dialectic is irresistible; it converts actuality into
theory and the living God of Abraham and Paul it turns into The
Absolute, capitalized, of course. Outside It, there is nothing real.

The result is that the rest of the body shrivels while the brain bloats like the belly of a dead fish floating on stagnant water.

In the same manner, Lawrence saw clearly that his friends had substituted conceptual knowledge for experience itself. They somehow sublimated sex and did not love with their bodies but with their minds. The physical union of man and woman took place among them, true enough; but it did not lead to "the death," the *ecstasy*, which the Elizabethans found in it, and it did not because the spontaneity has been drained from the union by the cerebral process to which it has been subjected. The upshot, as Lawrence saw it, was fatal. The awful mystery that men have dreaded, have been fascinated by, and have been compelled to worship, modern intellectuals are no longer capable of discovering. For the mystery they have substituted something which they can have *fun* from. And not only sex, but everything else in life has been subjected to the same treatment; and thus all life, all experience, becomes dry and brittle, because it is transposed to the cold and rarefied heights of the intellect. The process of intellectual levitation is something which modern educated man manages to accomplish in an utterly successful manner. And clever talk—the facile, witty, and irresponsible talk that Lawrence satirized so cleverly, because he could easily outplay the others at their game —is valued, while passion is eschewed.

This interpretation is easily tested by turning to the sketch of Hermione and her friends in *Women in Love*. There is something essentially phony about her purely cerebral avidity for knowledge for knowledge's sake, for ideas. She and her friends, including the sociologist whose prototype in real life was an already famous logician, when looked at carefully, appear to be shrivelled monstrosities, and Lawrence found their precious ideas offensive to his deep sense of the depth and the mystery of life.

Had Lawrence known what we know today, he would have grasped the lack of authenticity of the idea-mongers he despised in terms not open to derision, and thus would have avoided the charge of sheer irrationalism to which he laid himself open. In the medium of which he was master, his presentation of the idea-mongers was irreproachable. The sketch of Hermione and her friends leaves nothing to be desired—as drama. But the conceptual expression which Lawrence gave to what he saw could not have been more unfortunate. To put forth "a philosophy of the blood" was bound to seem archaic and to be profoundly repugnant to his prospective readers, people whose faces are turned the other way, towards reason and science. The modern educated man is for the most part, and still remains in our own day, essentially positivistic. The positivist tries desperately to cover with a thin disguise of confidence in reason his fear of the depths. This is the reason Jung is so harshly dismissed. Men who find in us today traces of our dark past make us radically uncomfortable. We have left all that behind, all that was changed long ago. There may have been monsters in the earth in those days, but the only monsters today live in the delusions of a few irrationalists who are definitely vestigial remainders. True, there is Auschwitz and Belsen—but we rational men are not implicated in that unpleasant interlude.

But are the monsters gone? Are we not implicated in the interlude? Of course not; we are men who respect Sovereign Reason.

In any case, the truth of what Lawrence had to say can be formulated more exactly and less offensively, but he could not be expected to make this new formulation, since *Sein und Zeit* and *L'être et le néant* did not make their impact on Anglo-American culture until a decade and a half after his death, after the second war. Lacking the terminology that existentialism has put at our disposal, he had to put his quarrel in terms of mind against the blood, reason against instinct, logic and scientific proof against the solar plexus, and he stuck to the solar plexus. What was required was the linguistic tools to get below these categorial dichotomies. Lawrence was frequently irrational in the sense of the older dichotomy, but at his best what he wanted to say—and said brilliantly in dramatic terms—was that a life lived mainly for the sake of thought, ideas, reason, logic, is an inadequate life. And while this contention may be inadmissible to the philosopher or the scientist, who gives knowledge primacy and for whom experience *is* thought and little else, and while it must also be inadmissible to the Knight of Faith, for whom experience is the encounter with God and the rest is meaningless, and to the serious moralist, for whom experience is right action, it is neither a dangerous claim nor a silly one.

From a different point of view, what Lawrence intended by the philosophy of the blood was something that would get him closer to "life" than the sterile lucubrations of his intellectual friends were able to. He sought what Thoreau sought in the woods, when he wrote in *Walden,* in the second chapter:

I went to the woods because I wished to live deliberately, to front only the essential facts of life, and see if I could not learn what it had to teach, and not, when I came to die, discover I had not lived. I did not wish to live what was not life, living is so dear. . . . I wanted to live deep and suck out all the marrow of life, to live so sturdily and Spartan-like as to put to rout all that was not life. . . .[22]

It is a pity that Lawrence did not leave us a study of *Walden* in his *Studies of Classical American Literature.* Nor do I remember any reference to Thoreau by him. I am quite certain that that section of Chapter II of *Walden* in which Thoreau discussed what he lived for would have made sense to Lawrence.

The last remark I shall make in defense of Lawrence's philosophy of the blood is that it is a philosophy that no naturalist has good ground to reject. For in the final analysis what Lawrence is asserting is what naturalists—whether neutral monists or some other kind of naturalists—are committed to, namely, that man is fundamentally an expression of a cosmic energy or something of the sort, that is the source not only of himself but of everything that is. Disregard the offensive language, so easily associated with Auschwitz, and you cannot fail to see that Lawrence's appeal to the blood springs out of a sense, strong in him, that men are the expressions or products of something that transcends them and connects them with the rest of the universe, connects them with a humble

insect and a galaxy. Lawrence did not go on to assert, with contemporary naturalism, that man and all his acts and works, can be
understood adequately by applying to them the methods of the
sciences. Towards the ultimate source of man he managed to retain an attitude of awe and piety that philosophical naturalists lack.
But what he shares with them is at least as important as what
distinguished him from them.

But this defense of the philosophy of the blood does not exhaust
all that must be said about it. It must be owned, first, that Lawrence seems seriously to have believed that the blood gave *knowledge*, and the knowledge that it gave was superior to that given
by reason. And of course it does give knowledge—it is not silly to
speak of the knowledge of the body or of the knowledge of insects
or of the heliotropic knowledge of the flower, however Jaques
Loeb may explain these knowledges. But to go further and to assert that the criterion of knowledge is the quality of the feeling it
gives us is one of those oversimplifications we frequently encounter in Lawrence (and others—in poets and theologians and
mystics, more often than in anyone else) which is the source of unnecessary confusion. Those who speak in this manner are indifferent to a serious ambiguity in the word. To say that knowledge of
the blood is superior to knowledge of the mind is to say that one
mode of experience is superior to another. This is a meaningful
judgment on which there is no likelihood of agreement. But it is
also an ambiguous one, and the ambiguity obfuscates the important
difference between a subjective experience and an objective one.
The former may be dominated by the felt quality of belief, irrespective of its possessing or lacking an external object in relation to
which it can be called adequate or true. The latter has such an object and by reference to it we may decide with more or less confidence whether the judgment that expresses the experience is true
or not. What Lawrence often meant by "knowledge" was the subjective feeling of belief that some propositions gave him, whether
or not these propositions had an object against which their adequacy could be checked. What he objecetd to in evolution, in the

well known story told us by Aldous Huxley, was that the theory left him cold.[23] He had a perfect right to be utterly indifferent to vast areas of knowledge or to all knowledge, for that matter, and so have we all. He did not have any interest, or very little, in theories or in scholarship. In "The Dragon of the Apocalypse" he writes: "We do not care, vitally, about theories of the Apocalypse: what the Apocalypse means. What we care about is the release of the imagination. A real release of the imagination renews our strength and our vitality, makes us feel stronger and happier. Scholastic works don't release the imagination: at best, they satisfy the intellect, and leave the body an unleavened lump." [24]

This statement is true Lawrence, nothing ersatz about it. Because *he* was not interested in theories of the *Apocalypse* or anything else—unless they were *his* theories—we are forbidden to care about them, and are ordered to seek the release of the imagination, as if the imagination was not released through scholarship as well as through the contemplation of the zodiacal cosmos.

Again, through his philosophy of the blood, Lawrence seems to have been seeking a "life" which was not only below knowledge in the narrow sense, but below any experience of any kind, whether dominantly aesthetic or moral or religious; he seems to have been trying to reach below all experience, to the flood of life itself, in its quickness and yet in its thickness and depth. Only by finding it can man, he was convinced, avoid the dessication the modern world condemns him to. But "life" that is not experience dominantly cognitive, moral, religious, or aesthetic, cannot be found, and it is indeed as much if not more of an abstraction than the shrivelled, conceptual irresponsibilities of the idea-mongers whom Lawrence despised.

The upshot of these comments, I take it, is that Lawrence's desperate search for a satisfactory religious solution of his problem is not one that we can, in justice to ourselves and to him, disregard. The metaphysical philosophy of blood is not altogether free from the charge Russell makes of it. But things are not quite so simple as Russell's charge would make them appear. If the human beasts who reared Auschwitz and Belsen were able to succeed as they did, their success must in part be traced to the uncompromising rationalism of men like Russell, the scientism of our age, the worship of that old eighteenth-century whore, Sovereign Reason, at the cost of the whole man.

It is primarily inadequate language that leads to these false claims to the primacy of the blood or the sovereignty of reason. When better language will become available, we shall be able to see more easily what now is seen with some difficulty, namely that none of the faculties that the old language distinguished and separated can function without the help of the others. But we shall also see—and this is more important and much more difficult to state with lucidity in the older language—that these divisive faculties have their roots deep in the flood of being and no one of them can claim unqualified sovereignty over the others. But we must also recognize that in spite of the mutual interdependence between the aspects of the functioning personality there are different types of men, although a science of typology is at present little more than a program.

I do not intend to suggest, however, that the problem is a purely linguistic one. It is a substantive question, a question as to the adequate and accurate analysis of the diverse functions of the personality, and an analysis that does justice to what we know of man from any source whatever and not merely from a scientific source. It is a question of a genuine empiricism and not the shriveled empiricism of the scientistic attitude.

[6]

If we ask, as we tend to do in an age that emphasizes genetic factors, why a man as sensitive as Lawrence was inimical to the mode of love that philosophers generally consider its highest manifestation, the answer is that Lawrence himself furnished us with the key to the problem. In his "Autobiographical Sketch," speaking of how his parents, had they been alive at the time of its writing, would have thought him successful, he comments:

But something is wrong, either with me or with the world, or with both of us. I have gone far and met many people, of all sorts and all conditions, and many whom I have genuinely liked and esteemed.

People, *personally*, have nearly always been friendly. Of critics we will not speak, they are different fauna from people. And I have *wanted* to feel truly friendly with some, at least, of my fellow-men.

Yet I have never quite succeeded. Whether I get on *in* the world is a question; but I certainly don't get on very well *with* the world. And whether I am a worldly success or not I really don't know. But I feel, somehow, not much of a human success.

By which I mean that I don't feel there is any very cordial or fundamental contact between me and society, or me and other people. There is a breach. And my contact is with something that is non-human, non-vocal.[25]

This pathetic statement is an amplification of a statement made in a letter to Trigant Burrow dated 13 July, 1927: "What ails me is the absolute frustration of my primeval societal instinct." [26] Both statements are, of course, oversimplifications: his misanthropy, the frustration of his social instinct, his rejection of the Son, his need to dominate, his self-assigned superiority—the roots of all these are deep in his illness.

Whatever the explanation of the frustration of his social instinct, the fact itself leads at once to Lawrence's tragedy—and not only the tragedy of the man but that of the artist also. For it is no doubt this radical alienation that denies his vision of the world the love (in the sense of agape) that would have placed his work at the level which, with his gifts, it could have easily attained. His work is the product of high talent, and it is overburdened with beauty. His novels probe aspects of human experience no other novelist of his age except Proust dares examine. But the world he forges is incomplete, it is not a fully human world. Lawrence, because of his incapacity to love, remained throughout his life a marginal man. His

own explanation of the distance between himself and the people he
knows is utterly inadequate. He tells us that the answer, as far as he
can see, "has something to do with class. Class makes a gulf, across
which all the best human flow is lost." [27] This was undoubtedly true
of Lawrence and back of his oversensitiveness to class differences
it does not take a Freud to see his mother's rejection of his father's
class. But class never stood in the way of a man in whose heart there
is charity, never prevented a man of the working class from reaching across the gulf and embracing his fellow human beings, wherever they were found—witness Dreiser. The answer has not
merely something to do with class; it also and more fundamentally
has to do, one cannot avoid saying it, with a radical deficiency of
his personality.

But it is not only a question of Lawrence's indifference to charity, his denial of the claims of human brotherhood, that we must
consider. Lawrence's error is not merely an ethical error. It is also
a metaphysical error. It does not merely deny that human beings
are bound by bonds that give them, irrespective of their differences, a common humanity. It also denies God the ethical dimen-
sion. In this respect Lawrence happens to side with the moderns
whom he so deeply loathes because their conception of the cosmos denies man the possibility of making full, complete, connection with it. Lawrence does not assert with the dominant schools
of philosophy that the cosmos is utterly value-free. If he did, he
would not write of the Indian dances as he did, nor would he insist
on our need to draw strength from the cosmos. But he denies the
cosmos a distinctively ethical value; the values that he attributes
to it are values that have been tried by history, and by themselves, outside ethical control, have been found wanting in
strength, vitality, and power. These are not values that without the
aid of ethical forces can make a human community. What they
produce is that peculiar form of chaos, that organized form of
human frustration and maiming that the despotic consciousness
calls "order." Had Lawrence been able to appreciate the ethical
aspect of God he would have noticed the role that the distinctively

ethical values play in human existence. The result is an evil component in Lawrence's desideratum. His values are devisive, for in
addition to vitality—which for all I know they may bring—they
also bring arrogance, self-glorification, and the tendency to deny
the validity of the life of those around us.

I do not mean to suggest that Lawrence apprehended in theory
the implications of his position or ever considered seriously its possible practical results. He was neither interested in doing so nor was
he equipped to do so. Lawrence was driven urgently by a constellation of needs which expressed themselves to him now in one
guise, now in another—by his desire for vital experience and by
his sense that our world does not attempt to satisfy that desire,
by his deep piety for the cosmos and his realization that our attitude towards it denies us its fertility and vitality, by his search for
authentic, tender sexual relations and his conviction that every
force in our world is dead set on making sexual experience brittle
and hard and cerebral. He gives expression to these needs, now
dramatically, now discursively. But he never considered them in
relation to the complex exigencies of a civilization from which he
was deeply alienated. The result is a hesitation between the alternative solutions of his personal predicament, which neither separately
nor together can be accepted as solutions of our historical dilemma
as he seems to have intended them: I refer to the solution offered in
Women in Love and *Lady Chatterley* on the one hand and that offered in *Kangaroo* and *The Plumed Serpent* on the other. Each is
rehearsed dramatically in novels of greater or lesser aesthetic
purity and put forth in quasi-philosophic, discursive essays. Each
embodies deep and true insights. But each is partial, incomplete, inadequate, heretical.

But it would be unfair to Lawrence, and to my grasp of his value,
such as it is, were I to end this chapter with this adverse judgment.
When the worst the critic must say about Lawrence the man and
the writer has been said, there is still much left, as I have tried
to show already and hope to show again. And what is left is
more than enough to give him a distinguished place among the

great poets of the English language. He dealt with important subjects, at his best with absolute probity, with complete authenticity. If the basic responsibility of a poet, as Eliot and Tate have
argued, is towards the language of his people, Lawrence met his
responsibility without reproach. Because he met his responsibility
in such a superb manner he helped forge our sensibility. What he
may come to mean to the future it is for the future to decide.
We who live in his own day know that he succeeded as artist, as
few men of his generation did, and that as prophet he did not altogether fail. A greater compliment cannot be paid a poet.

CHAPTER FIVE

Lady Chatterley's Lover

IN THE letter to Bynner in which Lawrence declares "the leader-*cum*-follower" idea "a back number," he writes: "But still, *in a way*, one has to fight." [1] Similar expressions occur a number of times, after the writing of the Mexican novel. In a letter to a Miss Pearn (who Nehls tells us was an employee of Curtis Brown [2]) Lawrence writes that he was in a quandary about *Lady Chatterley*, and he adds: "It's what the world would call improper. But you know it's not really improper—I always labour at the same thing, to make the sex relation valid and precious, instead of shameful." [3] And in *Lady Chatterley* itself we find the following statement:

. . . And here lies the vast importance of the novel, properly handled. It can inform and lead into new places the flow of our sympathetic consciousness, and it can lead our sympathy away in recoil from things gone dead. Therefore, the novel, properly handled, can reveal the most secret places of life: for it is the *passional* secret places of life, above all, that the tide of sensitive awareness needs to ebb and flow, cleansing and refreshing.

But the novel, like gossip, can also excite spurious sympathies and recoils, mechanical and deadening to the psyche. The novel can glorify the most corrupt feelings, so long as they are *conventionally* "pure." Then the novel, like gossip, becomes at last vicious, and, like gossip, all the more vicious because it is always ostensibly on the side of the angels.—CHAPTER IX

In one sense Lawrence was never confused about his reason for writing. With him it was either art for his, Lawrence's, own sake, or art for the sake of the world's health. In a letter to T.D.D. dated 7 July, 1914 he writes: "You asked me once what my message was. I haven't got any general message, because I believe a general message is a general means of side-tracking one's own personal difficulties." [4] It is interesting to note that Lawrence is not shocked or offended when asked for his message; the question did not seem to him an improper one. Perhaps the reason he does not find the question improper is that the only alternative then conceivable was *the theory* of art for art's sake which, as it was then and is even today interpreted, condemns the artist to the creation of anaemic and humanly irrelevant works. It is of slight importance here, but it is interesting to note, that by the time he wrote T.D.D. he had already become fully aware of the nature of one of the messages he wanted to convey to his readers. He wanted to teach them the proper attitude towards sex.

If this is the case, we are confronted with a number of questions. The first, put in Lawrence's own terms is, Did he handle the novel properly? This is a purely critical question, demanding a well defined notion of what a novel is, considered strictly as art, and of what art can and cannot do. The second is, What were Lawrence's ideas about sex? This question refers to the substance of the novel. The third is, How true is Lawrence's philosophy of love? And the last is, Is *Lady Chatterley* an obscene book? The first question, however, calls for a definition of terms, for in a sense a novel may be well made, but if it is obscene it is not art, in the rigorous sense in which I employ the term.

[2]

The answer to the first question is that in many respects *Lady Chatterley* appears to be, on a superficial glance, a well made novel.

It does not have the aesthetic blemishes that are to be found in *Aaron's Rod, Kangaroo,* and *The Plumed Serpent.* I do not include *The Lost Girl* in this group because this novel, which like *Lady Chatterley* may be said in a sense to be a well made novel, is not, in another sense, part of the corpus.

Lady Chatterley is not a thinly disguised record of events in the wandering life of Lawrence and Frieda, an account of his travels and a record of his conversations and fights with his wife, of his pressing and unsatisfied yearnings and frustrations. In *Lady Chatterley* there is some invention. What is actual autobiographical experience has been subjected to creative transformation, and one is not painfully aware of Lawrence and his wife in any of the scenes of the book. This is an important point particularly because of the unconventional scenes: not even those who defend his unconventional descriptions of the sexual act could fail to be embarrassed if they were aware, while they read, that they were peeping into Lawrence's own bedroom. Not as rich in vignettes as the Mexican novel, it contains a number of scenes one remembers with pleasure —Mellors tending the birds, for instance, or the brilliant sketch of the nurse, Mrs. Bolton, which justifies Mr. Leavis' coupling of Lawrence's name with that of Dickens. For these reasons and others of a similar nature Mr. Hough is right when he says that *Lady Chatterley* "is more successful as a novel . . . than as the sexual tract that it is often taken to be." [5] The observation can be accepted because Mr. Hough distinguishes, as one should, between the intention of the author and that of the book. And yet, the novel suffers from a number of fundamental defects which prevent me from putting it, as it has been put by one of his critics, among his best novels.

The first of these is that the organic unity of the novel is superficial, and on a careful look the book falls apart into two stories whose proper relationship has been bungled. The account of Clifford's development from the time he moved into Wragby to the time Connie left him, seems to be, on superficial consideration, and after analysis one sees it ought to remain, an ancillary part of the story since its purpose is to give coherence and validity to Connie's affair with the gamekeeper and to her final decision to leave her husband. But when we step back from the canvas in order to grasp it as a whole we discover to our astonishment that the story of Clifford does not keep its subordinate place. The story of Connie and Mellors, considered as art, whatever may be said about it from the standpoint of taste and of morality, is a good story. But Clifford and even Mrs. Bolton successfully steal the show for long periods of time.

The reason for the split of the novel into two stories is not one about which the student of Lawrence's life and character need cavil in prolonged perplexity. Lawrence hated the Cliffords of the world so bitterly, so implacably, that when he could get at them, he forgot every other objective, he forgot his central cause, his fight or labor for the phallic consciousness, as he put it, and he took off after the objects of his hatred until he cornered them and tore their living souls out of them. The reasons for his hatred leave room for differences of opinion. As to the fact itself there is none; the evidence we could gather even from his novels alone is irrefragable.

The sketch of Clifford is done without pity or understanding. No mitigation is permitted to soften the defects of the man. The word "compassion," so fashionable since the last war, is one the critic of Lawrence may forget, for Lawrence's hatred of the Cliffords of the world drained all compassion from his heart. Clifford not only loses his physical manhood in the trenches and comes home a wheel-chair cripple, but he is psychologically impotent. He is a mere willful and cerebral individual, a purely vectorial will guided by a fine mind that has no connection with the rest of his body. Lawrence sets out to show this in detail. That he had already shown it in *Women in Love, Aaron's Rod, St. Mawr*, and in a number of short stories, was no reason to keep the obsessive hater from doing it again. And the result of his attempt is twofold. First, it shifts the novel's center of gravity. The novel becomes, for whole chapters, not the story of Lady Chatterley and her gamekeeper lover, but the story of the villain, Clifford, and the woman who acts as his surrogate wife-mother, Mrs. Bolton, his nurse.

The second reason I cannot put this novel among his best is that Lawrence fails to make his case against Clifford. A hastily sketched Clifford, a less villainous villain, a man less conspicuously the embodiment of all Lawrence hated and less conspicuously the negation of all Lawrence loved, would have gotten by with the reader. But not Clifford. One scrutinizes him carefully and comes away unconvinced. In spite of Lawrence's effort to make us hate him, we can, with the data gathered from the book, make a defense of him. I am talking about what is or is not acceptable or convincing as judged in the context of the story itself, in terms of its own presuppositions. Clifford is *intended* as an odious character and nothing is spared to let us see how odious he is. But when we look at Clifford in the context of the story, he is no worse than anyone else in it. Why is he odious? Compare him to Connie, to her sister Hilda, and to the gamekeeper. For all his defects, Clifford is really no worse than they are. Clifford shows no consideration for others. But then neither does Mellors or Connie. In fact they are, the three of them, and Mrs. Bolton also, what in American we call "plain stinkers." And the worst of it is that when one brings the novel into critical focus one becomes aware that Lawrence does not realize that Connie and her lover are just as much stinkers as Clifford. And this from the prophet who would lead us to salvation.

In the chair episode Clifford treats Mellors without consideration. But then Connie's concern for the gamekeeper is not the concern of an employer for her servant; it is the concern of a woman for the man she loves, and if at this point it should be objected that Connie does not yet *love* Mellors, then it is the concern of the woman for the man from whom she is deriving deep sexual gratification. The gamekeeper, a miner's son, is more of a man than poor crippled Clifford, in a sexual sense. He is also more alive, perhaps more tender, at least in bed; he is more capable of passion and certainly less cerebral than Clifford. He is also emotionally self-sufficient, whereas Clifford, the astute, practical man, is al-

most an idiot—as we are told in these very words—when left to
his own emotional resources. Again, Mellors is also the first man
who ever was kind to the woman in Connie—not to her persona,
as we may put it in Jungian terms, or to Constance Reid or to
Lady Chatterley, but to the female in her. For Lawrence, a man
who was hypersensitive about social gradations, wants us to believe that Mellors had no interest whatever in Connie's social
status. It was to the female in Connie that he was tender. Indeed,
Lawrence would have us believe that as their affair progressed,
Mellors came to worship religiously the female in Connie.
These may be good reasons—if, with Lawrence, one does not
take seriously the binding nature of the marriage vows—for leaving Clifford to the sublimated wife-mother ministrations of Mrs.
Bolton. But they are not good reasons for our hating Clifford. Nor
can we hate him because, having lost his manhood in the trenches,
he is utterly dependent on Connie before Mrs. Bolton takes over.
His mutilation is cause for pity. It may constitute an argument
against war, but it is no ground for despising the men who, when
called to the service of their country, answered the call honor-
ably. In an effort to make the best of the situation, Clifford tries to
convince himself and his wife that what is important, what matters
most, is to carry on the best they can, accomplishing the things he
can accomplish, and living the pathetic picture of the good life he
tries to get Connie to accept, the integrated life of habit and trust
and intimacy without sex. But what would Lawrence or anyone
do, had he been mutilated and paralyzed as Clifford was?

In fact, Clifford is really a decent fellow. Considering his background and ingrained class prejudices, Clifford did not behave
meanly towards Connie. True, he was forced to yield or he risked
losing her. But he yielded with spontaneity and grace. When the
desirability of Connie's having an affair with another man and even
a child was pointed out to him, Clifford agreed and gave her a
practically free hand. The one condition he laid down he could
not have insisted on with more taste and grace: he merely affirmed
his faith that Connie, who had picked him for a husband, would
not pick a man for a lover whom he, Clifford, would find unac-

ceptable. If Clifford defined "unworthy of Connie" or "unacceptable to Clifford" as a man of whom Clifford would not approve,
this is no reason for our hating him. We cannot see how Clifford would have conceived of worthiness or acceptability except
in terms of his own values and standards.

It is true that Clifford is a snob. But if this is a good reason for
Lawrence's wanting us to hate him, he should also have wanted us
to hate Connie and her lover on the same grounds. For Connie and
Mellors are snobs after *their* kind. There is such a thing as inverted snobbishness; the boast that one *does not* belong to the
effete or anaemic upper classes but to the healthy, vital people. And
Connie is no more of an equalitarian than her plebeian lover. Clifford is a great one for social distinctions and finds himself, outside
members of his own class, alien and shy. Lawrence tries to make us
see the trait as a defect, but he does not realize that by painting
Connie and Mellors as misanthropic, violently hating the whole
human race, he is painting two persons who are morally at least on
the same plane with Clifford.

The import of these considerations is that if the novel is not the
sexual tract that it is usually taken to be—and to this question I
shall turn later—it is undeniably an anti-Clifford tract. Whatever
our response to Lawrence's effort to make us hate Clifford, he succeeds in engaging us in his own feud. We are not allowed to be
spectators, we are forced to become moral judges. And the upshot is that there is no difference between what Lawrence is doing in *Lady Chatterley* and what he accuses "old Leo" of doing in
Anna Karenina.[6] Grant, for the sake of the argument, that Lawrence is right about Tolstoy, is he not himself a propagandist? He
is doing propaganda in favor of an ideology different from that of
Tolstoy; but what makes a propagandist is not the substance of
the ideology he advocates but the fact that he advocates it.

[3]

We must now turn to the second question raised by *Lady Chatterley*, What is Lawrence's erotic message? I shall hastily go

over those doctrines of which his critics have given adequate account in order to consider with some care those aspects of his teaching that have been ignored or overlooked.

It has generally been recognized that Lawrence advised us to acknowledge the basic role that sex plays in human experience. He bemoaned the lack of spontaneity with which we approach sex, the hypocrisy and the prudishness. He thought we ought to make sex "a blood relationship" but instead we make it a cerebral or a willful one.

Were this all that Lawrence has to say on the subject of sex, the only comment it would deserve today is that, however revolutionary it might have been when he started his crusade, his recommendation is at this late date old, old hat. At certain levels of society, at any rate, it would be hard to find today traces of the Victorian prudishness with which he had to contend in the second and the beginning of the third decades of the century. But Lawrence would have us approach sex in a religious attitude, and this part of his program contemporary man seems incapable of understanding. Lawrence would also have us believe that women tend to absorb men, tend to drown them in their possessiveness, whereas according to him the proper relationship is one in which each person remains himself, each in his or her full integrity, while united in love. Lawrence intends this as a generalization, but to me it appears to be false, and I suspect it arises from a complex attitude of his which did not lack morbidity. It is not true that each and every woman tends to drown her man; and in any case what Lawrence would substitute for what he took to be the loss of the self by the man is, when looked at carefully, a kind of erotic solipsism in which no account seems to be taken of the tenderness and the interdependence between two persons in love.[7] True, Lawrence tells us in *Lady Chatterley* that Mellors was tender to the woman in Connie. But the editorial comment is not fully borne out by the drama and it is clearly denied in other presentations of the love relationship, as I shall show in the sequel.

But there is more. When we read Lawrence closely, we discover that his "love ethic" is neither clear nor straightforward, and involves a component that, within the range of my reading, has not been discussed but has been either covered up or overlooked. This is to say, the critics who have found a "love ethic" in Lawrence have managed the feat by selection. One component that critics have not overlooked is the homosexual—it had to be taken into consideration since it is too prominent an aspect to leave unnoticed. But there is another important aspect of Lawrence's erotic doctrine that has been overlooked and that cannot be labeled as easily. Since a label will in this case be of great utility, I shall call it what sexologists call it, "love play." I refer to activity engaged in by his fictional characters during the sexual act.

In order to give the best account of Lawrence's ideas about sex I shall return to *The Plumed Serpent,* before considering one aspect of the relationship that is presented in *Lady Chatterley.* In the Mexican novel Lawrence makes strenuous efforts to present dramatically what he took to be the proper relationship between a man and a woman in love. He conveys his opinions by means of a contrast between what Kate, before she learned better, had taken to be a satisfactory sexual relationship with her former husband and what she finally came to learn from Teresa, Ramon's second wife, and from Cipriano, her own lover. It is Teresa's relationship with Ramon that is put forth as the norm. We are told that Kate

. . . realized how all her old love had been frictional, charged with the fire of irritation and the spasms of frictional voluptuousness.

Cipriano, curiously, by refusing to share any of this with her, made it become external to her. Her strange seething feminine will and desire subsided in her and swept away, leaving her soft and powerfully potent, like the hot springs of water that gushed up so noiseless, so soft, yet so powerful, with a sort of secret potency. She realized, almost with wonder, the death in her of the Aphrodite of the foam: the seething, frictional, ecstatic Aphrodite.—CHAPTER XXVI

To accept this death in her of the Aphrodite of the foam is not easy:

Yet Kate herself had convinced herself of one thing, finally: that the clue to all living and to all moving-on into new living lay in the vivid blood-relation between man and woman. A man and a woman in this togetherness were the clue to all present living and future possibility. Out of this clue of togetherness between a man and a woman, the whole of the new life arose. It was the quick of the whole.—CHAPTER XXV

Kate gains this knowledge from Teresa. The latter has given herself entirely, in complete submission, to her husband. Teresa feared Kate as a woman of the world but

as an intrinsic woman, not at all. Trenched inside her own fierce and proud little soul, Teresa looked on Kate as on one of those women of the outside world, who make a very splendid show, but who are not so sure of the real secret of womanhood, and the innermost power. All Kate's handsome, ruthless female power was second-rate to Teresa, compared with her own quiet, deep passion of connection with Ramon.
—CHAPTER XXV

In the end, however, Kate learns her lesson and accepts Cipriano on his terms. The last line of the book is at once a plea and the expression of a deep wish: "You won't let me go!" Kate says to Cipriano.

When we ponder the problem we find ourselves faced with a bewildering number of closely related problems which are difficult to unravel and to examine. If we take the novel to be, not the didactic treatise that is plainly *its* intention (just as it is the author's intention), but a genuinely artistic presentation, it is open to criticism on the same grounds that *Aaron's Rod* is open to criticism. The reader is left puzzled by the distinction Lawrence seeks to draw between Teresa's submissive acceptance of a blood relationship with Ramon and Kate's response to her former husband, Joachim. Teresa may be right in accepting her man as she does, but the terms in which her acceptance is *presented* are inadequate to convey to us how she accepts him and how Kate used to accept, or respond to, Joachim. The passages just quoted hint at something, but the hint is never fully presented, and the contrast between the right and the wrong response remains most puzzling where it should have been made clearest by dramatic presentation. How did Teresa feel, what did she undergo, to make her experience with Ramon superior to that of Kate with Joachim? She submitted. But while submitting, what did she experience?

In *Sons and Lovers* and in *The Rainbow*, for instance, Lawrence came as close to full success in presenting the felt quality of experience as it is possible to do. To do so he had to strain the language. But at whatever cost, I am of the opinion that he succeeded. In the Mexican novel, however, the felt quality of Teresa's experience is referred to by abstract means, and its superiority is not conveyed. We have to take Lawrence's word for it that Teresa's experience with Ramon was superior to Kate's with Joachim.

But *The Plumed Serpent* is not art in the narrow sense in which I have been using the term. Its intention coincides with the intention of the author: it is a didactic treatise superficially novelized, and one of its central purposes is to teach us Lawrence's "love ethic." For this reason it must be examined in its own terms. We must ask, on what grounds does Lawrence teach that the submissive relationship of Teresa to Ramon is better than Kate's relationship to Joachim. Lawrence asserts that a woman's satisfaction consists in giving satisfaction to her husband. She should not seek what Kate, when living with Joachim, used to call *her* satisfaction (the italics are found in the text). Or putting the matter as clearly as possible, Lawrence is saying that a woman is wrong if she seeks as intense an orgasm as possible. This is the "frictional" love "charged with the fire of irritation," and it is wrong. We remember at this point that it is not the first time that Lawrence has written on this subject. The source of the early misunderstanding between Ursula and Rupert in *Women in Love* lies in Ursula's inability to accept the kind of love Rupert offers her. And in *Kangaroo* Harriet has a number of formidable battles with Lovat because of the latter's demands.

If a woman should not seek sexual satisfaction in the sexual act, what sort of satisfaction should she expect? Conceivably, a type of masochistic woman may find in submission a satisfaction she could not find in any other manner. But Lawrence does not write about Teresa as if she were an exception: she is presented as the norm.

Why was Kate wrong and why is Teresa right? We are told that Kate's satisfaction is not the deepest satisfaction that a woman can have. And this assertion does not seem reasonable to me. After all, Lawrence is discussing sex, something that, as he would be the first to point out, is rooted in physiological processes. It is the very heart of his doctrine, and in this respect it is obviously right doctrine, that a sexual act is a physical act. Human beings are able to add to the physical act much else and are thus able to raise sex above the level of the merely animal. But if eros is not based on physiology it is not eros. I do not put forth this statement because it is a great discovery of mine or of Lawrence or of anyone else. Lawrence "fought" (it is his own term and he applies it to the Mexican novel) for the recognition of the physiological basis of love. But it was not he who discovered it. If my history is not in error it was discovered in the Garden by Eve.

How shall we understand the nature of the sexual act? From the physiological standpoint, the process consists of a period of increasing tension followed by a climactic release brought about by the sexual union. It is the climactic release that brings about the satisfaction, the rush of pleasure—although the term "pleasure" is hardly adequate to the profound experience that the Elizabethans called "death." Obviously, the more intense the tension and the more complete the release of tension, the deeper the satisfaction. If this is not the case, what, then, is the case? From what we know of human beings we must expect a wide range of variations, not only between one person and another, but between one satisfaction and another by the same person.

If these general considerations are acceptable, it is difficult to see how Lawrence accounts for the difference between a man's response and a woman's in the sexual act. Whatever the physical and psychological differences, from the physiological standpoint, the account of the process of tension and release is the same for men and women. Why should the woman not have an orgasm; why should she be satisfied with giving satisfaction to her husband? The prescription does not make sense. It could make sense if the account of the act at the physical level were different for the male and the female. But of this difference Lawrence gives us no inkling. He just lays it down that a woman ought not to seek *her* satisfaction; she ought to find it, as Teresa finds it, in submission to her husband. But what sort of submission? In *Lady Chatterley* we shall find the nature of the submission in the kind of "love play" Connie allows her man.

As a didactic recommendation, Lawrence's erotic doctrine is open to another criticism. It does not occur to Lawrence that there may be different types of personalities, and that we cannot assume without careful examination that a complex drive such as sex can function identically for different types. An ethic of satisfaction, as contrasted with an ethic of duty, cannot ignore the problem which arises out of the differences there may be among types. Satisfaction has its source in the specific nature of the individual and if there are differences of types, the general physiological account I have just given is probably too simple to enable us to say that all men and women do in fact react similarly in the sexual act. Inquiry into the differences and how they affect the specific nature of the satisfaction is called for. This is not a subject on which we can at the moment be dogmatic. We do not know that what satisfied Ramon and Teresa satisfies Cipriano and Kate. An ethic of duty involves no problem. Such an ethic asks human beings to live up to certain standards, and differences that a characterologist may find among them are not thought to have anything to do with their duty. There are qualifications, of course, but these are obvious. In the Christian ethic, thus, it is the duty of a man and a woman to be continent outside marriage, but I would not be surprised if casuists recognize that there are certain circumstances in which reasons of state overrule, for a prince, the obligation expressed in the commandment. But aside from these exceptions identical conduct is expected of all men, and a man who runs in the face of the enemy, for instance, cannot offer as an excuse that he is typologically a coward.

But Lawrence's way is that of the reformer; his own conduct and his own desiderata are the norm, they define the ideal. A deviation from *his* style of life is wrong. Either you—whoever you may be, whatever your heredity and upbringing may have been, whatever your aims and commitments—manage your sexual life the way I, David Herbert Lawrence, by the grace of God and my own fiat appointed teacher of mankind, manage mine, or you are wrong, and nothing can alter that fact. Never mind the fact that I, David Herbert Lawrence, am a sick man trying desperately to shed my illness in book after book unsuccessfully. Never mind the fact that I, David Herbert Lawrence, have suspected at times that I am a bit dotty.[8] Never mind the fact that my mother mangled my development. It still remains an incontrovertible fact that I, David Herbert Lawrence, am, by the grace of God and my own fiat, the standard. You are not like me, you say? Obviously not—and that is what makes you wrong, utterly wrong, hopelessly wrong. Why can't you accept a bit of healthy, individual authority? Why can't you see what is so thoroughly self-evident?

That this formulation does justice to the attitude of the reformer in Lawrence we know from several sources. Let me mention three obvious ones. We have several accounts such as Knud Merrild's of Lawrence's implicit assumption of superior knowledge in respect to matters in which he was patently incompetent—the scene of the sawing of the tree, for instance. We have many expressions of his assumption of superiority in the autobiographical passages in his stories and novels. For instance, the passage in *Aaron's Rod* to which I have already alluded, in which Lilly, after rubbing Aaron with oil, sits down to reflect, while Aaron sleeps, why the mob can't submit to a bit of healthy individual authority. But if the evidence from the novels should be declared inadmissible, on the ground that no single character in a novel expresses the novelist's views (for them we have to go to the whole novel), we find the same idea in Lawrence's letters and essays. I shall confine myself to only one instance: a letter of 23 April, 1913, in which he states: "I do write because I want folk—English folk—to alter and have more sense." [9]

[4]

We have examined the love ethic advocated in *The Plumed Serpent*. What shall we say of that preached in *Lady Chatterley?*

In a letter dated 24 August, 1928, Lawrence writes David Garnett that David's father had once said that he would "welcome a description of the whole act." Lawrence claims to David Garnett that this is what he has accomplished in *Lady Chatterley*.[10] But the claim can easily be shown to require qualification. And as this is done a great deal can be revealed about the nature of Lawrence's "love ethic." Put bluntly, the fact is that not even in *Lady Chatterley* did Lawrence dare to make explicit what in earlier books he had suggested periphrastically. In *The Rainbow* and in *Women in Love* there are accounts of the nature of the love relationship between men and women, in which it is obvious that language is being used to suggest meanings the author does not dare state as explicitly as he does those aspects of the sexual act which in *Lady Chatterley* are described in four letter words. *Lady Chatterley* makes clear, although still in periphrastic terms, what is intended by them. Mellors indulges in embellishments that we shall continue to call "play," of which the specific nature cannot be misconstrued. I refer to two passages. One is the account of the night spent by Connie at Mellors' cottage—the night before she was to leave on her trip to Venice. Another is brought out by indirection when Forbes discusses the charges brought up against Mellors by his wife, Bertha Coutts. Of the night spent by Connie at Mellors' cottage we read:

It was a night of sensual passion, in which she was a little startled and almost unwilling: yet pierced again with piercing thrills of sensuality, different, sharper, more terrible than the thrills of tenderness, but, at the moment, more desirable. Though a little frightened, she let him have his way, and the reckless, shameless sensuality shook her to her foundations, stripped her to the very last, and made a different woman of her. It was not really love. It was not voluptuousness. It was sensuality sharp and searing as fire, burning the soul to tinder.

Burning out the shames, the deepest, oldest shames, in the most secret places. . . .

She had often wondered what Abelard meant, when he said that in their year of love he and Heloïse had passed through all the stages and refinements of passion.

The same thing a thousand years ago: ten thousand years ago! The same on the Greek vases, everywhere! The refinements of passion, the extravagances of sensuality!

. . . .

And what a reckless devil the man was! Really like a devil! One had to be strong to bear him. But it took some getting at, the core of the physical jungle, the last and deepest recess of organic shame.—CHAPTER XVI

Whatever Abelard may have meant, the Greek vases give us the meaning with sufficient clarity. But to relieve the reader of a lingering doubt, Lawrence introduces the charges of Bertha Coutts against her gamekeeper husband. In one of Clifford's letters to Connie in Venice, Clifford gives an account, in very proper language, of the details Linley and the doctor gave him of "all those incidents of her conjugal life," that Bertha Coutts aired in the village. One of them, we are told, is that Mellors used Bertha, as Benvenuto Cellini says, "in the Italian way . . ." (Chapter XVII). Duncan Forbes, the artist who consents to assume parental responsibility for Connie's unborn child, interprets for the reader to whom the Cellini reference may be cryptic, exactly what is involved. In a conversation with Connie, he defends a husband's right to make love to his wife any way he pleases.

Oh, said Forbes, you'll see, they'll never rest till they've pulled the man down and done him in . . . if he's a man who stands up for his own sex, then they'll do him in. It's the one thing they won't let you be, straight and open in your sex. You can be as dirty as you like. In fact the more dirt you do on sex, the better they like it. But if you believe in your own sex, and won't have it done dirt to: they'll down you. It's the one insane taboo left: sex as a natural and vital thing. . . . And what's he done after all? If he's made love to his wife all ends on, hasn't he a right to? . . . You have to snivel and feel sinful or awful about your sex, before you're allowed to have any. . . .—CHAPTER XVII

If one does not know what is meant by the "Italian way," the last few lines of this passage ought to relieve him of his ignorance. This is "the love ethic" of Lawrence—practices that Lawrence and his admirers argue are essential to burn out "the deepest, oldest shames, in the most secret places." Besides pointing out what is involved in accepting them as an operative ethic no comment is necessary.

Not only have those critics who admire Lawrence's love ethic ignored or overlooked all that it involves but they have not observed how radical is the transvaluation of values that he advocates. They take the love ethic and overlook the fact that his doctrine includes a social and economic revolution. It was not Lawrence's intention to have men and women worship at the altar of the Eros of the sacred mysteries while living the kind of life we now live. In *The Plumed Serpent* Lawrence had seriously urged a return to pre-industrial society—handicrafts, home production, the abandonment of clocks (as if the Mexicans ever had learned respect for chronometers), and a general simplification of our machine system of production. In *Lady Chatterley* something of the same program is put forth.

Why, if men had red, fine legs, that alone would change them in a month. They'd begin to be men again, to be men! An' the women could dress as they liked. Because if once the men walked with legs close bright scarlet, and buttocks nice and showing scarlet under a little white jacket: then the women 'ud begin to be women. It's because th'

men *aren't* men, that th' women have to be.—An' in time pull down
Tevershall and build a few beautiful buildings, that would hold us all.
An' clean the country up again. An' not have many children, because
the world is overcrowded.—CHAPTER XV

We are back to the ersatz savages of *The Plumed Serpent* with
a slight improvement. This is the Lawrentian wisdom, offered us
for our salvation in all seriousness.

In order to avoid misunderstanding, I want to make a clarification, and to reiterate what I am saying and what I am not saying. I
do not hold that Lawrence's erotic ideology is altogether wrong.
What I am saying is that it requires a much more careful scrutiny
than it has received from Lawrence's admirers. As Father Tiverton
has pointed out, there is an important insight to be salvaged from
Lawrence's erotic ideology.[11] But it is one thing to ask, What is the
indispensable legacy of wisdom he left us? and quite another to assume, as some of his critics do, that what he had to teach in matters
of sex is all-wise, all-healthy, and urgently needed by us, and that
any attempt to examine his ideology bespeaks a man a moron. The
Lawrentian *oeuvre* is not Holy Writ.

But the central question here is not the admissibility of Lawrence's "love ethic"—a problem which mature individuals ought
to decide for themselves, if they are interested in it. The central
question is that Lawrence employs the novel to teach us a "love
ethic." And by so doing he abandons the task of the artist and
undertakes that of the propagandist.

[5]

As for the admissibility of Lawrence's philosophy of love, the
first thing that must be stated is that we ought to take him seriously
when he insists on the quasi-divine nature of sex, although it is
precisely this aspect of his doctrine that modern men—and particularly those who deem themselves liberated and advanced—are
most likely to reject. Students of religion have long known what

many world religions have recognized, namely the intimate connection between religion and sex. Lawrence's conception of religion should not be taken, therefore, as aberrant. Referring to the community and its power, in a chapter entitled "The Covenant" (in his *Religion in Essence and Manifestation*) van der Leeuw writes as follows:

> The second division of powerfulness occurs with respect to *sex*. Man and woman have different charismata: to woman man is sacred, and conversely. This is conditioned by the awe, or even the reverence, with which they regard each other, just as by the mutual disinclination subsisting between the sexes. . . . *We* [in our culture, he means] connect religious ideas with neither the profound lack of understanding between man and woman, nor with the marvel of their mutual discovery; to us both avoidance and community are equally mundane conceptions. But wrongly so. . . .[12]

Mircea Eliade confirms van der Leeuw's observation in his *Patterns of Comparative Religion*. He writes:

> What I propose is by no means always easy. To the Western mind, which almost automatically relates all ideas of the sacred of religion, and even of magic to certain historical forms of Judaeo-Christian religious life, alien hierophanies must appear largely as aberrations. Even for those disposed to consider certain aspects of exotic—and particularly of Oriental—religions quite sympathetically, it is hard to understand the sacred value attached to stones, say, or the mystique of eroticism.[13]

A few pages later he tells us:

> Indeed one of the major differences separating the people of the early cultures from people today is precisely the utter incapacity of the latter to live their organic life (particularly as regards sex and nutrition) as a sacrament. Psychoanalysis and historical materialism have taken as surest confirmation of their theses the important part played by sexuality and nutrition among peoples still at the ethnological stage. What they have missed, however, is how utterly different from their

modern meaning are the value and even the function of eroticism and of nutrition among those peoples. For the modern they are simply physiological acts, whereas for primitive man they were sacraments, ceremonies by means of which he communicated with the *force* which stood for Life itself. . . . [This] force and this life are simply expressions of ultimate reality, and such elementary actions for the primitive become a rite which will assist man to approach reality, to, as it were, wedge himself into Being, by setting himself free from merely automatic actions (without sense or meaning), from change, from the profane, from nothingness.[14]

Why religious consciousness has so frequently attributed sacred character to sex is a problem on which writers are perhaps bound to disagree. The most obvious explanation would seem to be that men turn with piety and gratitude to those aspects of their experience whence vitality flows. Sex is not the only source of vitality, but it is a powerful drive and a naturally fit symbol for all vitality.

But once sex is recognized for the powerful force it is, man sees the need to regulate it without damaging it or weakening it. He has found only one way to control it successfully and that is to give it a sacramental character. If he allows it to go unregulated it will wreak havoc in society. Lawrence both saw this fact and did not see it. He was intensely opposed to promiscuity and to the taking of sex as "fun." He would not have sex vulgarized or degraded. He would sacramentalize it—turn it into the Eros of the sacred mysteries. But he did not see that to make it sacred is to make it taboo. We have long known that the term "taboo" comes from the Polynesian "tabu" which means "to forbid" and which can be applied to any kind of prohibition whatever. Frazer, who was one of the first to study taboos, took them to be systems of superstitions found the world over. But he was careful to emphasize their role in maintaining the institutions of society. Further, the word referred not only to the sacred but to the unclean. And this was taken to be a confusion in the mind of the primitive, for we have no trouble distinguishing between the holy or the sacred and the unclean. For the believer, the host is holy or sacred, and for most of us what Celia does is unclean, even if it is a function we all perform. But is the primitive confused or have we lost something he still possesses? What the primitive does is to recognize the all-important element the two phenomena share, both the sacred and the unclean are dangerous. Thus, those who set out to make sex clean rob it of its sacred character and of its dangerous nature. Make it sacred, worship the ithyphallic God, and you cast on it a dangerous aura that for all practical purposes denies that sex is clean. Lawrence could have it one way, either sacred but not clean or clean but not sacred, hence shallow—and easily and properly turned to "fun." Not even Lawrence could have it both ways.

After what I have just said the reader should not feel that I disparage Lawrence's philosophy of love when I call it "archaic." It was this archaic attitude towards sex that led him to his strong objection to the separation of the various activities of man, their being turned into autonomous processes, unrelated to one another; and even more, to the usurpation of primacy by mind and by will: a mind that was unrelated to the rest of man, and a will that was despotic. That Lawrence knew these evils in his own person, that he was victimized by his own despotic will and was given to the kind of intellectualism that he derided in others, does not nullify his indictment. His anti-intellectualism, his appeal to the blood, his rejection of science (because he could not feel its hypotheses in the solar plexus), his blasts against money and the machine, his pathetic longing for pure experience, which of course he himself could never achieve, or if he did achieve it, he could not enjoy it for long—these have their source in his yearning for integration and for a sacramental attitude towards living. He was utterly right when he wrote to Edward Garnett in 1914, "But primarily I am a passionately religious man, and my novels must be written from the depth of my religious experience." [15] That in terms of T. S. Eliot's orthodoxy he was a heretic, that in his longing to give sex a sacramental nature he was archaic, this and much more may be true. But it does not make Lawrence either a fool or a madman.

Indeed I would argue that it is his desire to approach all of life in a sacramental attitude, however archaic this approach may be considered today, that gives Lawrence's vision a positive value.

We have long known—Dilthey pointed it out but we do not need his authority, for it is by now common knowledge—that with the secularization of our culture, the activities of man become progressively autonomous, and that the claim of redemptive and revealed religions to synthesize human existence by reigning over the soul in primacy is challenged by these activities. Civilization brings about progressive differentiation. And if this is not a historical generalization valid for all cultures, it holds for ours: work becomes profane; art, science, and philosophy each go their way; and religion, which earlier ruled the whole of man's life, is now forced to compete for man's soul with activities that have become autonomous and profane, and must resign itself to be satisfied with a small part of man's energy. One of the meanings the religion of the blood had for Lawrence, the sacramental approach to life, the preservation of the mystery of existence which modern man is blind to or ignores, has at its root the need for integration. But unfortunately Lawrence was not consistent in his longing for integration and in his desire to put on all activity the sacramental sign. There is no human good unmixed with evil. In Lawrence the positive value was mixed with much that can hardly be accepted.

[6]

We turn next to the controversial question of whether *Lady Chatterley* is an obscene book. In the well-known essay on "Pornography and Obscenity" Lawrence defends his interest in sex on several grounds. One of his defenses is that

Half the great poems, pictures, music, stories of the whole world are great by virtue of the beauty of their sex appeal. Titian or Renoir, the *Song of Solomon* or *Jane Eyre*, Mozart or *Annie Laurie*, the loveliness is all interwoven with sex appeal, sex stimulus. Call it what you will . . . Sex is a very powerful, beneficial and necessary stimulus in human life and we are all grateful when we feel its warm, natural flow through us, like a form of sunshine.[16]

Lawrence also employs an argument from relativism. He writes:

. . . The word *obscene:* nobody knows what it means. Suppose it were derived from *Obscena:* that which might not be represented on the stage: how much further are you? None! What is obscene to Tom is not obscene to Lucy or Joe, and really the meaning of a word has to wait for majorities to decide it.[17]

But of course for Lawrence, it is obviously absurd to let the majority decide. He continues:

We have to leave everything to the majority, everything to the majority, everything to the mob, the mob, the mob. They know what is obscene and what isn't, they do. If the lower ten million doesn't know better than the upper ten men, then there's something wrong with mathematics. Take a vote on it! Show hands and prove it by count! *Vox populi, vox dei. Odi profanum vulgus. Profanum vulgus.*[18]

Still another argument employed by Lawrence is the argument from intention:

One essay on pornography, I remember, comes to the conclusion that pornography in art is that which is calculated to arouse sexual desire, or sexual excitement. And stress is laid on the fact, whether the author or artist *intended* to arouse sexual feelings. It is the old vexed question of intention, become so dull today, when we know how strong and influential our unconscious intentions are.[19]

Lawrence's contempt for the mob I think we can entirely disregard. *Vox populi* may not be *vox dei,* but anyone who sets out to teach the mob should not forget that the mob is likely to snap back in anger. Let us turn to the question of intention. It is indeed a vexed question, but if we judge by the amount of attention it is still receiving in the late fifties, thirty years after Lawrence wrote

Lady Chatterley, it cannot be said to be a dull question. But more importantly, it is not the author's intention that is in question but the book's intention. The author's intention, if we mean his conscious intention, is often easy to discover from his own statements of it. But as we have already seen, Lawrence knew clearly that it does not always coincide with the intention of the book. It is not easy to discover the intention of the book, and even when it is, there is still room for honest and widely inconsistent differences of opinion. Nevertheless, the intention of the book can be decided, if only roughly, and in *Lady Chatterley* the decision as to its intention is easier than in most cases. It is also clear that it coincides with Lawrence's intention and with the effect that it has on many of its readers.

The effect that *Lady Chatterley* has on many of its readers is a question of fact to be decided by empirical methods at the disposal of sociologists. But as for Lawrence's intention, he cannot claim that *Lady Chatterley* is intended to stimulate the reader erotically and claim also that the book is not obscene in an aesthetic sense. But it ought to be noted clearly that I have just used the term "obscene" as an aesthetic category and not as a moral one. As an aesthetic category it refers to the fact or alleged fact that the book cannot be read by a person in an attitude of intransitive attention, or in Bullough's terms, with the proper aesthetic distance. Lawrence did not intend the book to be read in that manner. He wrote that the reader is grateful, "we are all grateful," when art makes us feel the natural flow of sex stimulus. How he decided on this question of fact he does not tell us; but obviously the evidence is against him for if his decision were true he would not encounter two kinds of adverse critics: those who take issue against *Lady Chatterley* on moral grounds and those who take issue on aesthetic grounds. Nor would he have suffered from the censor morons. Nor would the custom authorities have prohibited the import of the Italian and Parisian editions.

The assertion that the great art of the world is great by virtue of the beauty of its sex appeal is a confusing half-truth. If what Lawrence is saying were true without qualification, there would be no distinction between art and experience outside the realm of art—a distinction that the reader of Lawrence's best novels is able to draw without difficulty, although it is not one which aestheticians find easy to define. It is, of course, an obvious truth that sex is an important element in art, and that its importance arises from the fact that it is a powerful stimulus, pervading, as we post-Freudians have learned, the whole of human experience. But this obvious truth requires careful qualification when applied to art. Sex and almost all other aspects of human experience may be both *matter for* art and the *informed substance* of art. These terms, it will be remembered, come from Bradley's essay on "Poetry for Poetry's Sake," and I hold the distinction to be of radical importance for the clarification of our problem. By means of it we are able to see clearly that something happens to the experience that goes into art—the matter for art—before it becomes the substance of art. What happens is a transubstantiation and transformation such that the finished object is able to hold us in an act of wrapt, intransitive attention. The change is of course the result of the creative process, and is complete in so far as the artist is able to bring creative energy into its consummation and is not distracted by any other motive than that of creating an object that elicits the aesthetic response.

I put it in this way in order to indicate that we are dealing here with a question of degree. If it could be said, as sometimes it is said, that a complete experience of wrapt, intransitive attention is something that has never happened and can never happen, I reply that I have adduced elsewhere evidence that it does happen, although it is a rare experience and an ephemeral one. But even if it does not happen in its absolutely pure state, it is a conceptual necessity to define it in this way in order to make clear that it is a goal which the aesthetic experience seeks to reach even if it always falls short of it. It is a criterion that enables us to judge aesthetic achievement. If the artist, because he lacks skill or because he is distracted by other motivations than the aesthetic, fails

to turn the matter of experience into the informed substance of
art, the product may be valuable, but it is not art.

I imagine that the majority of those who condemn Lawrence
for the description of the whole sexual act find the book morally
reprehensible. And those who praise him and condemn the censor-
morons find it an object of merit. But what we must notice is that
the quarrel is not an aesthetic one. It has nothing to do with art.
In art sex is involved, of course. But it does not function as sex
functions outside art, it does not elicit either our moral or our
erotic response. There is of course a great deal of room here for
varieties of response and it must be admitted that we are talking
about a vague and somewhat mythical "normal" person who is not
neurotically prudish, who is not obsessed with sex or sex-starved,
and who knows how to respond to art. To the sex-starved under-
graduate a Renoir is a stimulus and for him it must be admitted the
Renoir is obscene. But for the normal person it is not, although
for him the interest in the substance of the picture is no doubt
ultimately to be traced, among other factors, to the fact that we
are hetero-sexual animals. There is no question that it is extremely
difficult to define the difference between art and sexual stimuli.
But to overlook the difference or to deny it is to condemn a problem urgently in need of clarification to perpetual confusion. Art
has a function different from the arousal of sexual desire. Its function is unique and indispensable for the achievement and mainte-
nance of our full humanity. Its unique function Lawrence and his
defenders do not seem to be aware of, although Lawrence himself
was one of the great artists of his generation and possibly of all
English literature. But one can be an artist and even a great one
and not know, at the theoretical plane, what is art.

Another aspect of the problem of obscenity is the employment
of improper language. Lawrence undertook a campaign to erase
the distinction between proper language and obscene words,
which he sometimes called "taboo words." In his Introduction to
the unexpurgated edition of *Pansies*, which is easily available to us
in Mr. Moore's collection *Sex Literature and Censorship*, Law-

rence writes: "I am abused most of all for using the so-called 'obscene' words. . . . Myself, I am mystified at this horror over a mere word, a plain simple word that stands for a plain simple thing. . . ." [20] Later in the same essay we read:

There is a poem of Swift's which should make us pause. It is written to Celia, his Celia—and every verse ends with the mad, maddened refrain: "But—Celia, Celia, Celia, shits!" Now that, stated baldly, is so ridiculous it is almost funny. . . . Such thoughts poisoned his mind. And why, in heaven's name? The *fact* cannot have troubled him, since it applied to himself and to all of us. It was not the fact that Celia shits which so deranged him, it was the *thought*.[21]

For our purpose there is no need to consider whether Lawrence had understood or even read Swift.[22] Lawrence's statement is of interest because it makes sense only on the assumption that certain acts that we must perform in order to remain alive, are not revolting when we see them performed by others or when we read or think about others performing them. This assumption is ambiguous. It may mean either that that which one must do one does not in fact find revolting when done by others, or that one ought not to find it revolting. But as a statement of fact, the assumption is just plainly false. And as a prescriptive statement all I can say is that it seems to me nonsensical. Thus, in private we belch and perform other acts, which we may or may not consider revolting when we ourselves perform them. Some of them may even produce the pleasure which is the concomitant of relief from tension. But one thing is the private act and another the public, and one is the performance of it by ourselves, taken distributively, and another the observation of the same act when performed by others. In what novel of the First World War did I long ago read that one of the difficulties in the field was that men had to learn to perform physiological functions in public? One can learn, no doubt, but the acquired attitude does not increase the refinement. We know that human life can be lived minimally, but I take it that most of us do not find it desirable to live so. I am not speaking universally. If Lawrence's assumption is a matter of fact, not of prescription, allowance must be made for varieties of behavior among cultures and for differences of personality, of taste and of character. Thus, we control many physiological needs besides that of belching, that certain Brazilian Indians living in communal huts do not control.

At this point the reader may object that my discussion misses the point. Lawrence is not saying that it is better to sleep in a Brazilian communal hut than to sleep in our own bedrooms and to use our own toilet facilities. What he is saying is that the revulsion toward the so-called taboo words is something we ought to get over. My retort is that a good deal of nonsense has been written on this subject and most of it thoroughly pernicious. Thus one of the early critics of Lawrence wrote that in *Lady Chatterley*, Lawrence "was to say all that the inarticulate daren't say, and good old English four-letter words were to come into their own." I would have imagined that the inarticulate had always been quite articulate in the use of the good old English four-letter words. Isn't it precisely the possession of a limited four-letter-word vocabulary that makes a man inarticulate? In Spanish-America, in my childhood, we used to speak of "a mule driver's vocabulary," and we know about the vocabulary in use among the privates and sergeants of the Marine Corps. Highly charged with taboo words, these vocabularies are, it would seem, extremely poverty-stricken. The fully articulate man is not at a loss for four-letter words, but he knows how and when to use them. And in addition he has other words, of more letters than four, which he knows how and when to use. But what is the four-letter words' "own," into which they are said by the critic to have come? Ages before Lawrence, and in other cultures besides ours, and for good reasons, four-letter words have been performing their proper and their important function. They are indispensable for the expression of anger, curses, and contempt. To give them the same right of circulation that we give non-taboo words is to impoverish the language, for these words are a sort of *corps d'élite* which we fall back on in certain crises. The language has already been impoverished by the loss of words formerly considered taboo that are now to be found in general circulation in certain sections of society. Words like "bastard" and "son of a bitch" I have seen in print in a well-known weekly of formidable national circulation. And if we are going to put into circulation Swift's word and those Mellors employs when engaged in his erotic play with Connie, we shall have to invent others to take their place. What shall I exclaim when I hit my thumb with the hammer, if the word that Swift employs in reference to Celia is put into general circulation and loses its taboo character? And further, assume that we put all the taboo words into general circulation, are we to erase the distinction between topics of conversation that we now consider proper and those we consider improper? And are we to allow any subject anywhere at any time— for instance, are we to speak of the events taking place at the Indian's communal hut, in our dining room? Obviously the matter cannot be disposed of by calling Lawrence's critics "morons." [23]

A relatively minor matter connected with Lawrence's treatment of sex is his bad taste. In *Lady Chatterley* the bad taste displays itself in the description of practices which are presented with the author's approval and without his being aware of the impression they create on the reader. In the privacy of the bedroom, a woman may entwine forget-me-nots in the pubic hair of her man—if this is one of the ways they want to play erotically (Chapter XV). In the warmth, or better, in the fever of erotic passion and in the glow of tenderness and piety towards the other that erotic satisfaction generates, such play gets by without seeming ridiculous or in bad taste to those who indulge in it. But to advocate it seriously in public as an essential part of the sexual act is to confess an utter insensitivity to the difference between the private fevered context and the public.

CHAPTER SIX

Lawrence
Imitates
Lawrence

IN THE second section of the last chapter, I pointed out that there were other defects from which *Lady Chatterley* suffers besides those examined in that section. One of those from which the book suffers, and one Lawrence committed several times, is that of self-imitation. Lawrence ran out of matter and attempted to repeat his previous triumphs, and the result failed sadly to come up to the level of his highest achievements. In three works which I am going to examine in this chapter, we find characters that are imitations of older, previously presented characters: in *Lady Chatterley*, in *St. Mawr*, and in *The Daughters of the Vicar*. I put these works in this order, although it is not the order of their composition, because I take it to be the order of their worth taken as wholes.

In the essay "A Propos of *Lady Chatterley's Lover*," written as an introduction to the Paris edition of the novel, and in answer to a criticism of friends that it would have been better to have left Clifford whole and potent, that the "symbolism" would have been better, Lawrence writes as follows:

As to whether the "symbolism" is intentional—I don't know. Certainly not in the beginning, when Clifford was created. When I created Clifford and Connie, I had no idea what they were or why they were. They just came, pretty much as they are. But the novel was written, from start to finish, three times. And when I read the first version, I recognized that the lameness of Clifford was symbolic of the paralysis, the deeper emotional or passional paralysis, of most men of his sort and class today.[1]

This is not the first time Lawrence has made this claim. We have already seen that he made the same claim in the Foreword to *Fantasia of the Unconscious*, dated 1921. In the paragraph that follows in the Foreword of *Fantasia* he takes back the claim and tells us, without awareness of the incoherence, that art is utterly dependent on philosophy. But this will not surprise the seasoned reader of Lawrence, for one of the things he learns early about Lawrence is that consistency is not one of his dominant virtues. Fortunately the statement's inaccuracy need not concern us. For it is not Lawrence's intention that is in question but the failure of the creative imagination that we discern in the product. Clifford is not a person in his own right but an illustration of a concept. Lawrence understood him fully in analytic terms before he dramatized him. Clifford is a puppet drawn to a formula. But because the original of Clifford is one of the principal characters of *Women in Love*, I shall return to this point in Chapter X.

With a few preliminary references, Clifford appears on the scene in 1920 when he, paralyzed forever, and his wife Connie return to their home, Wragby Hall. But Clifford is more than a victim of the war. He turns out to be a congenital cripple in spite of a talent that carries him to success in two spheres of activity. On returning he becomes a very successful writer, a kind of *Green Hat* Arlen, clever, superficial, entertaining, and vacuous. But soon he gives up writing and becomes interested in his mines, and he is as successful as a mine owner as he was as a writer. Under the management of his nurse, he becomes the dependent baby that all along he has been potentially. And the more he deliquesces inwardly the harder and more brilliant and successful he becomes outwardly. This is the story of Gerald with this difference: Whereas Gerald is not a man we are asked to hate, nor is he a formula, but a man whom we can contemplate in the aesthetic mode of response. Clifford, a character drawn to formula, is not a person whom we can contemplate. Pushed by Lawrence to take sides against Clifford we resist for we have come to see that Clifford is a mere name for a constellation of qualities Lawrence hated.

Nor is Clifford the only imitation of Gerald we come across in Lawrence's work. Lawrence sometimes made slight alterations in Gerald and fused him with another type that he had learned to dislike: the futile young men whom in *Aaron's Rod* we meet in Shottle House and in London. These people play with ideas, talk Bolshevism, repudiate society, are sexually promiscuous, and are essentially weak and empty. We find them not only in *Aaron's Rod* but in a number of the short stories. The following quotation is from *Aaron's Rod*, but it could have come from any one of several of the novels and stories written after *Women in Love*.

The party threw off their wraps and sank deep into this expensive comfort of modern bohemia. They needed the Bach to take away the bad taste that *Aida* had left in their mouths. They needed the whiskey and curaçao to rouse their spirits. They needed the profound comfort in which to sink away from the world.—CHAPTER VI

But in *Women in Love* and in *Aaron's Rod* Lawrence does a much more effective job of showing up this type than he does in *Lady Chatterley*. And the reason is that hating them less he is better able to expose them.

[2]

What I have said about Clifford applies to Rico, the arch-villain of *St. Mawr*—if a spiritual castrato can be called a villain. Unfortunately, before reading Mr. Leavis' article on this novelette I had thought that it was, if not one of Lawrence's worst, one very close to the worst. How it can be said to be excellent is to me—as it has been to other critics—incomprehensible. My judgment is based on the fact that I thought I discerned the failure of the English part of the story to cohere with the New Mexican part, and it was also based on the fact that I saw it as a rather poor and careless imitation of Lawrence by Lawrence. Lawrence's language, which sends Mr. Leavis into paroxysms of enthusiasm, seemed to me nothing but careless writing, and the creative energy that went into the composition of the story seemed to me definitely third-rate. In *Lady Chatterley's Lover*, at least on the surface, there appeared to be an organic coherence, and the story of the love affair between Connie and Mellors, for all the prurient immediacy of the love scenes, had been fused by the imagination. In *St. Mawr* no such qualities are exhibited. For a good one hundred and fifty pages of the two hundred and twenty-two which make up the Knopf edition of the novel, the story drips hatred of Rico and his friends. In spite of the fact that Lawrence had already castigated these people in other books, his irritation had not abated. It had indeed increased. And he had to jeer at them again. They are futile, they are weak, they are cerebral in a shallow fashion, they are false, they are incapable of passion, they are engaged in an endless and hopeless chase after good times, after fun, they are unutterably boring bores. But they do not bore Lawrence, they irritate him, they exasperate him into fury. And therefore there is in the scenes in which he castigates them no poetry whatever. And what is worse, he had done it before and done it better and more convincingly.

When Lawrence confines himself to the task of bringing the horse, St. Mawr, before the eyes of his readers, he achieves a vivid and powerful revelation. Man has always approached the horse with awe. Of course he approaches all animals with something of the same feeling—respect, fear, admiration, curiosity. Twenty thousand years ago, in rough numbers, man looked at the animals that he hunted more or less successfully and his imagination fulgurated into the miraculous art of the Spanish and the French caves. But man approaches the horse with a special feeling. He masters it and uses it. But it is always more than a mere instrument. The artist in Lawrence, the irrepressible poet that the sciolist guru never succeeded in downing for long, probably first felt the

full shock of the horse when he came close to it in Taos; hence
the sketch of St. Mawr, a horse that embodies Vitality itself, all
that is potent and wild and untameable and quivering with the
creative power of the cosmos. There is nothing fake about the
picture, nothing contrived. It is an authentic and deeply felt picture. It dropped from his imagination, instinct with the awe that
had touched it into life. Therefore it is a grievous pity that Lawrence was not satisfied to give us a sketch of a horse, as he was
satisfied on several other occasions to give us sketches of other animals. Had he been satisfied with a sketch, it would have compared
advantageously with the sketches of Rex and of Adolph, the pets
which the Lawrences had enjoyed for a brief period, with the
sketch of the pine tree which he gave us in "Pan in America," and
the description of the porcupine he killed which he did so brilliantly before he took off into the embarrassing, metaphysical
lucubrations in "Reflections on the Death of a Porcupine." Had
Lawrence been satisfied with a sketch of St. Mawr, there would
have been no reason to quarrel with any panegyric anyone chose
to write about him.

But Lawrence was not satisfied with being a poet and giving us a
sketch of a horse bursting with vitality and power. The horse
reminded him of the futile young men and women whom he had
known and for whom he felt deep contempt, and the aroused
feeling against them flooded his consciousness. The weaklings,
Rico Carrington and his friends, are men of means, fashionable,
well dressed, but revoltingly futile. They arouse Lawrence's inverted snobbery, since he could never forget he was a miner's son,
and they arouse his sense of superiority, since they are such futile
castrati. And so he had to concoct a story to tell us again what he
had already told us and was to tell us again. The result is not a
great artistic achievement. Indeed, Lawrence never succeeded
even in making one story of the incidents he put together in the
novelette, *St. Mawr*, and there is a great deal of careless writing
in it.

Lou Witt, an American girl in her early twenties, marries an

Australian artist called Rico, and becomes Lady Carrington. Lou and Rico take a house in Westminster and become fashionable, both socially and artistically—or almost so, for there is a flaw in them somewhere. And in their relations with each other there is also a flaw:

Some inscrutable bond held them together. But it was a strange vibration of the nerves, rather than of the blood. A nervous attachment, rather than a sexual love. A curious tension of the will, rather than a spontaneous passion. . . . This attachment of the will and of the nerves was destructive. . . . And soon, tacitly, the marriage became more like a friendship, Platonic. It was a marriage, but without sex. . . . And the lack of physical relation was a secret source of uneasiness and chagrin to both of them.[2]

The nervous attachment, the tension of the will rather than the spontaneous passion of the blood is, of course, what Kate in *The Plumed Serpent* had to learn was not complete fulfillment. Lawrence has made his point before and has to make it here again. But notice that these lines are a bit of pure conceptualization. The "philosophy" does not come from the drama. The story is dramatized philosophy. One of Lawrence's greatest admirers and a man who has performed prodigious feats of biographical research, Mr. Harry Moore, taking Lawrence at his word, has stated his conviction that Lawrence's essays and his "philosophy" (a term which Mr. Moore, with wisdom and mercy for the real thing, puts between quotation marks) always came after he had worked out his ideas in fiction and in poetry. As we have seen, Lawrence made this claim in both the Preface to *Fantasia of the Unconscious* and implicitly in the Introduction to the Paris edition of *Lady Chatterley's Lover*. But we have also seen that there are compelling reasons for accepting the claim only with careful and extended qualifications. If the arguments already advanced in favor of these qualifications were not fully convincing, it seems to me that we have here an example that ought to carry conviction. A hasty reading of those passages in *St. Mawr*, such as the one just quoted, is all that is needed to see that the opposite of what Mr. Moore claims about Lawrence's essays and "philosophy" is generally the case. The writer who employed the abstract terms found in the passage I have quoted was a man who analyzed the relationship between Lou and Rico by means of a "philosophy," or more exactly a "psychology," which had been arrived at prior to his drawing of the picture of Lou and Rico.

Indeed Lawrence did not *create* Lou and much less did he *create* Rico. The act of creating them had taken place long before. What he did was recreate them. All he did was give new names to old characters and put them in altered settings. For this reason the picture of these characters lacks what the sketch of the horse has. The characters did not touch his imagination. Lawrence has a "philosophy" (or a "psychology") and he concocts two young people and a relationship between them *to illustrate* his abstract ideas. The relationship is an obviously dramatized expression of a law he had formulated long ago. Wherever the law came from, the one place it could *not* have come from was the story, *St. Mawr*. And we know this, not only because we have often been presented with Lawrence's song and dance about the Ricos and their friends before, but because the texture of the story, the manner in which the characters are presented, show clearly to the man who wants to look, that these are puppets lacking the effulgence of the imagination. The abstract, analytic account of the non-sexual, Platonic marriage is a concocted event which is essential for the complete illustration of Lawrence's "philosophy." Here we are witnessing another puppet show. Or rather, it is the old stock company again, and we know each and every one of the actors. The man now playing Rico is the same man who played Clifford Chatterley in an earlier production—earlier in this study, that is, for in fact *St. Mawr* antedates *Lady Chatterley's Lover*, having been published in 1925. And Lou, playing now an American role, is Connie. Lou will not fall for Phoenix, the Indian who accompanied her and her mother to New Mexico and who drove up to the ranch, "Las Chivas." The groom is the man who played Mellors, and the roles could easily be confused, for although we know nothing of the groom's Kinseyan prowesses, like Mellors he has a good hand with horses and is capable of arousing in women the response that led Connie to her affair with the gamekeeper.

And the woman who plays Lou's mother—have we seen her before? Why yes, she's versatile, but she is usually cast in roles that are not essentially lovable. She played Doña Carlota in *The Plumed Serpent* and Mrs. Bolton in *Lady Chatterley*, and much earlier, she played Hermione. And the minor characters, the Mamby girls, the futile young men and women happy with their vacuity and their odious "fun" and their facile sex—why, they played in *Aaron's Rod* and in *Lady Chatterley* too. They were the people who visited Clifford at Wragby Hall. These same bit players had originally filled Hermione's week ends with intellectual conversation and at the time had put on an authentic performance. Considering that they were playing the same old parts, they did a creditable job in *Aaron's Rod*. This is the reason for the persistent sense of *déjà vu* which haunts us when we read *St. Mawr*.

But the animal, let me reiterate, is genuine. And genuine, too, is Lou's response to his power. There is an invisible life-giving force about him, by contrast with which the weariness and futility of Rico and his friends are mercilessly exposed. But the book as a story is not carried by its isolated virtues. And Mr. Leavis' immoderate, his abandoned, adoration of it, particularly his praise of Lawrence's command of language, cannot be accepted. Referring to the opening passages of *St. Mawr*, Mr. Leavis writes of its "freedom—something extraordinarily like careless ease." And after a long quotation he comments:

"St. Mawr," I suppose, would commonly be described as a long short story—a *nouvelle*, rather than a novel. Actually, that description, with its limiting effect, has a marked infelicity. It certainly doesn't suggest the nature or weight of the astonishing work of genius that Lawrence's "dramatic poem" is. "St. Mawr'" seems to me to present a creative and technical originality not less remarkable than that of *The Waste Land*, and to be, more unquestionably than that poem, completely achieved, a full and self-sufficient creation. It can hardly strike the admirer as anything but major.[3]

After further quotation from the opening pages of *St. Mawr*, Mr. Leavis continues:

The economy of those opening pages, establishing the present from which the drama starts, is very remarkable. For what looks like carelessness—the relaxed, idiomatic, and even slangy familiarity—is actually precision and vivid firsthandness. And we soon discover that there is no limit to the power of easy and inevitable transitions. For Lawrence writes out of the full living language with a flexibility and a creative freedom for which I can think of no parallel in modern times. His writing seems to have the careless ease of extraordinarily fluent and racy speech; but you see, if you stop to cast a critical eye back over the page, that everything is precisely and easily *right*—the slangy colloquialism, the flippant cliché given an emotional intensity, the "placing" sardonic touch, and, when it comes (as it so marvellously can at any moment), the free play of poetic imagery and imaginative evocation, sensuous and focally suggestive.[4]

[3]

We want to agree with Mr. Leavis wholeheartedly when he tells us that Lawrence did what he wanted to do with something like careless ease. But is this the criterion of art? The journalist writing for the daily papers the dreary stories of murders and rapes and accidents does what he wants to do, and without any effort whatever. And the Tin Pan Alley lyrics writer does what he wants to do, and the writer of singing commercials does what he wants to do, with something like careless ease. Simenon writes, *Time* informs us, a chapter a day, one novel per year, year in and year out. He does it with greater ease than Lawrence. He does not think about what he will write before he starts, and the stuff pours and pours—if *Time's* account is accurate, for I have not read him. But we question whether what these people are doing with such careless ease is art. Let me cite two illustrations of Lawrence's style in

St. Mawr, though, of course, it must be understood that they do not exhaust the kinds of defects that an even moderately critical reading will discover in the book. This is the first passage:

. . . The talk, the eating and drinking, the flirtation, the endless dancing: it all seemed far more bodiless and, in a strange way, wraithlike, than any fairy-story. She seemed to be eating Barmecide food, that had been conjured up out of thin air, by the power of words. She seemed to be talking to handsome young bare-faced unrealities, not men at all: as she slid about with them, in the perpetual dance, they too seemed to have been conjured up out of air, merely for this soaring, slithering dance-business. And she could not believe that, when the lights went out, they wouldn't melt back into thin air again, and complete nonentity. The strange nonentity of it all! [5]

This passage is far from indicating supreme power over language. It is flat and shopworn with its wraithlike images, its clichés of the fairy story and the young men conjured up out of thin air. It is merely flat and shopworn prose trying to convey to us the nonentity of it all, and succeeding in conveying only that the author wants us to dislike his characters as much as he does. When a writer of-it-alls us, even if that writer is David Herbert Lawrence himself, one remembers the admonition Lawrence wrote to Edward Marsh in 1913. Modifying it to fit my purposes, I can retort: "One should not say 'of it all' any more than one should say 'I knew not why.' It is as meaningless as 'yours truly' at the end of a letter." [6] The reader should remember that this is not the first time Lawrence has of-it-alled us. When he did it in his earlier novels we excused the inexperienced writer who was highly talented. But by the time he writes *St. Mawr* no such excuse can be adduced. And when he does it, it means no more than "yours truly" at the end of a letter.

But you in turn may retort, "The 'of-it-all' is Lou's and not Lawrence's, and so are the other worn-out images you criticize. You do not have the right to criticize Lawrence for what his characters do or say, for how they feel and talk and think." The point

raises an important issue, and one that deserves consideration. I offer three observations about it. The first is that it is not entirely
clear that the passage is a report by Lou of her feelings and her reactions *as she experienced them.* This is what the passage starts
out to be. But as we have already noted, Lawrence was no Henry
James; he was never one to have scruples about sudden shifts of
points of view. He is not in this passage doing what James so mas-
terfully did, employing the third-person mode in order to render
the affections and thoughts of his characters as if he were inside
them and at the same time peering over their shoulders. Lawrence
does not hold on to his point of view and in the paragraph from
which this passage was taken, Lawrence is describing from his
own point of view what *he* takes to be Lou's feelings towards her
set after her meeting the horse. My second remark is this: Let us
assume that Lawrence is indeed writing from Lou's point of view.
The problem then is to convey to us Lou's reactions. They are
what they are. But can he convey their inexactitude, their fuzzi-
ness, by using imprecise and fuzzy language? Lou's emotions trail
off into the imprecision, the haze which irritation and rejection
are apt to induce. Does the writer convey them by means of the
vague and weak puff of an "of-it-all"? I would have thought that
one point settled in critical theory by now was that in order to
convey an emotion on the part of a character the author did not
have to suffer himself the emotion or arouse it in the reader.
Vagueness is not conveyed by writing vaguely. It requires very
precise language, of great subtlety and freshness, to convey vagueness and not to create it in the reader's mind. The vague, weak
puff of an "of-it-all" is objectionable because it fails to delineate
with precision the general rejection to which Lou was led by St.
Mawr.

The third observation is this: Even if we should grant that
when an author presents a character's reactions from her point of
view, the way to do it is by a kind of "iconic" transcription into
language of the object to be conveyed; there are other "of-it-alls"
in *St. Mawr* that cannot be excused on this ground. I did not mark

them as I read. But quite accidentally I ran into two more, and these can hardly be said to be iconic transcriptions of Lou's reactions. These are plainly and incontrovertibly Lawrence's descriptions, from his point of view, of what he takes to be Lou's reactions. In Texas, we are told, "Lou was a bit scared at the emptiness of it all." And on the next page, again from his own point of view, Lawrence tells us that Lou wondered, considering Texas, "What, in heaven's name, was one to make of it all?" [7] This is not a question attributed by means of quotation marks to Lou, and neither in the American edition of this novel nor in the Heineman (1934) collection, entitled *The Tales of D. H. Lawrence*, do we find quotation marks.[8]

The second illustration of style follows:

At a gate all waited for Mrs. Witt. The fair young man fell in beside her, and talked hunting at her. He had hunted the fox over these hills, and was vigorously excited locating the spot where the hounds gave the first cry, etc.
"Really!" said Mrs. Witt. "*Really! Is that so!*"
If irony could have been condensed to prussic acid, the fair young man would have ended his life's history with his reminiscences.[9]

If one is determined to defend Mr. Leavis' panegyric at all costs, he could say that the "etc." is Lawrence's means of calling attention to the triviality and dullness of the young man who can get excited about "the spot where the hounds gave the first cry, etc." But if this method of presenting the young man's excitement is not enough, Mrs. Witt's "Really! *Really!* Is that so!" is. Lawrence, however, must hammer on, and adds an editorial calling attention to the annihilating nature of Mrs. Witt's irony. An artist would have exhibited Mrs. Witt's irony dramatically instead of telling us *about* it.

There is still another reason for disagreeing with Mr. Leavis' judgment. Rico, he tells us, "represents the irremediable defeat of all that St. Mawr stands for." [10] I fully agree to the fact that Rico *represents*, but I must add that Mr. Leavis' praise exposes rather cruelly the weakness of the pseudo-symbol. Rico *represents* forces and factors that Lawrence has in other books sought to *present* by incarnating them more or less successfully in adequate symbols.

But Mr. Leavis, while praising Lawrence too much in one respect, does not do full justice to him in another, and the failure can be traced to a confusion on Mr. Leavis' part, in turn related to his well-known disdain for theory. For he tells us St. Mawr "stands for" life and Rico's defeat "represents" defeat of life. That this is no mere slip can be gathered from the fact that later we are told that St. Mawr "represents deep forces of life that are thwarted in the modern world," while elsewhere we are told, when Mr. Leavis speaks of the "deep spontaneous life which is not at the beck and call of the conscious and willing mind," that "St. Mawr, the stallion, *is* that life." I agree with this last statement. Within the context of the story, St. Mawr *is* what he is, he does not *represent* anything abstract, whether deep forces of life or shallow ones, nor does he *stand for* anything. He embodies, incarnates, renders, *is* vitality and potency. This is why he is a genuine symbol while Rico and his friends are not. It is, rather, the other way around; the expression "deep forces of life" *represents* what St. Mawr *is* and Rico would thwart. But this does not hold for Rico. He is not a symbol in the same sense that the horse is. He is a pseudo-symbol, and he merely represents and stands for the life St. Mawr is or embodies.

I am forced to dwell on this point at such length because it is central to my criticism of Lawrence. In the *nouvelle, St. Mawr*, in the person of Rico, Lawrence represents abstractions which he had drawn from experience and borrowed from others and which are not adequate poetic symbols. The horse *is*, but the symbol suffers from the fact that it does not function in a universe with other self-sufficient symbols, and also from the fact that it functions in a context which is a mere conceptualized imitation of experiences which Lawrence had long ago revealed poetically.

A reason of a different order, but one of equal weight, for denying the attribution of excellence to *St. Mawr*, is its essential inchoateness. To justify this judgment all we need do is ask: What happens to St. Mawr, the fiery and powerful animal, and to his groom, Lewis? After the horse injures Rico and kicks one of the trivial young men in the face, Lou and Mrs. Witt save him from gelding by taking him to Texas, and there the mother, the daughter, and the author abandon him and his groom—just leave them behind to get rid of them. When the two women decide to leave Texas because Lou cannot put up with the emptiness of it all, we are told they "left St. Mawr and Lewis" (the groom) and went to New Mexico, where Lou bought a ranch called "Las Chivas." St. Mawr has served the author's purpose, he has exposed the triviality of Rico's world, his male potency has been preserved, but what else can one do with him? If the hero is a man, he marries the heroine, and if he is married and his wife is naughty he divorces her or, if he is a fool, he makes up with her. If the hero is a race horse, he wins the Derby and the writer brings the story to a genuine close, giving the reader a sense of finality. But when the hero is only a horse, true, a vital horse, but only a horse, what can one do with it in order to tie the threads and finish the story? This is not a difficult problem for a resourceful writer. The hero is entitled to finish his days in uxorious contentment. What then can be done with St. Mawr? He can meet a mare worthy of his vitality, not a futile one, but one that knows a horse when she sees one, and they can get happily married and live happily ever after. This is what St. Mawr did. It is not exactly true, therefore, that Lou and her mother just left St. Mawr in Texas; they did not abandon him. They left him to his happily married life.

And what then does Lou do? She goes off to New Mexico to reach a new understanding. She won't have anything to do with sex unless something touches her spirit, the very quick of her. She will stay alone and give herself only to the "unseen presences, serve only the other unseen presences." And she continues to think:

She understood now the meaning of the Vestal Virgins, the Virgins of the holy fire in the old temples. They were symbolic of herself, of woman weary of the embrace of incompetent men, weary, weary, weary of all that, turning to the unseen gods, the unseen spirits, the hidden fire, and devoting herself to that, and that alone. Receiving thence her pacification and her fulfillment.

Not these little, incompetent, childish, self-opinionated men! Not these to touch her.

. . . .

No, no! She had loved an American, and lived with him for a fortnight. She had had a long, intimate friendship with an Italian. Perhaps it was love on his part. And she had yielded to him. Then her love and marriage to Rico.

And what of it all? Nothing. It was almost nothing. It was as if only the outside of herself, her top layers, were human. This inveigled her into intimacies. As soon as the intimacy penetrated, or attempted to penetrate, inside her, it was a disaster. Just a humiliation and a breaking down.

Within these outer layers of herself lay the successive inner sanctuaries of herself. And these were inviolable. She accepted it.[11]

But in "Las Chivas" a virtually new story begins, for now it is not through mystic communion with the horse that Lou draws vitality and significance but from the land itself. There is here in America, for her, a wild spirit that wants her, that needs her, that craves for her, to which her sex is deep and sacred, a spirit deeper than hers which saves her from cheapness. She cannot tell her mother what this unnamed force is, but she knows that it hovers over the ranch, the landscape, and that it is more real than men, that it soothes her and holds her up. All these metaphysical abstractions—for I have followed the text almost verbatim—are to be found at the very end of the story, and without further ado Lawrence leaves us to our bewilderment and mystification, for his metaphysical report neither defines the spirit adequately nor presents it dramatically in an adequate symbol. It is obvious that the story is not finished although it has ended. The spirit has been pointed to, it has not been incarnated as it was in Bismark or in St. Mawr. And one is reminded of the painter somewhere in *Don Quixote* who painted excellent pictures by writing on the canvass: here stands a cow, on the side a tree, and behind, in the distance, mountains—or something to that effect. But Lawrence did succeed elsewhere in presenting adequately the wild spirit that, he tells us, wants, needs, Lou. He did it in the sketches in *Mornings in Mexico*, and in so far as it involved a strong component of masochism, in "The Woman Who Rode Away."

[4]

But the most glaring defect of *St. Mawr* is the obtrusive manner in which its author wags his didactic finger at the reader to make certain the reader does not miss the point of the lesson. We have already noticed the three-line comment through which he makes certain we realize that Mrs. Witt is contemptuous of the trivial young man. This, unfortunately, is not the only instance of the editorial intrusion. Thus, immediately after Rico is thrown by St. Mawr, Lou, on the way to the farm for help, has a vision of "evil." Had Lawrence employed this device successfully it could have been the dramatic means of recapitulating the preceding action and introducing the following events. But Lawrence has come upon too good a thing to allow it to function as an artistic device; here is a step ladder on which he can climb to harangue us. Lou's vision of evil is soon abandoned and the speech begins:

Man must destroy as he goes, as trees fall for trees to rise. The accumulation of life and things means rottenness. Life must destroy life, in the unfolding of creation. We save up life at the expense of the unfolding, till all is full of rottenness. Then at last, we make a break.

What's to be done? Generally speaking, nothing. The dead will have to bury their dead, while the earth stinks of corpses. The individual can but depart from the mass, and try to cleanse himself. Try to hold fast to the living thing, which destroys as it goes, but remains sweet. And in his soul fight, fight, fight to preserve that which is life in him from the ghastly kisses and poison-bites of the myriad evil ones. Retreat to the desert, and fight. But in his soul adhere to that which is life itself, creatively destroying as it goes: destroying the stiff old thing to let the new bud come through. The one passionate principle of creative being, which recognizes the natural good, and has a sword for the swarms of evil. Fights, fights, fights to protect itself. But with itself, is strong and at peace.[12]

Oh, the weariness of it all! We have read the same thing in letters, in essays, and in novels, so there is no reason to summarize the meaning of it all. One wishes Lawrence had given us a novel —but if wishes were horses we could mount St. Mawr and run away from the sermon, etc. As for the lesson itself, it may be a very important one, but a poet has another job to do than preach the dreary lessons Lawrence tries to preach. The poet's job is important because no one else can do it for him, while the preaching can be done by others who are usually better qualified to do it than are poets. Oh, the weariness, the dreariness, of it all!

[5]

Another imitation of Lawrence by Lawrence that deserves attention is found in the story, "The Daughters of the Vicar." Mr. Massy, the clergyman who marries Mary, is a gargoyle of a man, life-denying, dried-up, and without a single quality in his favor— for his small competence and his social standing are not qualities that would recommend him either to Lawrence or his reader. Because he lacks Gerald's talents, we may not readily recognize him for what he is, another expression of the Gerald-type. But when we ponder the contrast brought out by Lawrence between the attitudes towards "life" of the two daughters of the vicar, as expressed in the kinds of men they choose, we realize that here once more Lawrence is concerned with the contrast between the life-denying Clifford and the life-giving gamekeeper. The gamekeeper type is this time a socially inferior farmer with whom the vicar's daughter, Louisa, falls in love. Mr. Leavis writes about her that

The courage with which she adheres to this resolute election of love and life affects us as movingly noble and heroic. It is in the fullest sense moral courage that we witness. . . . It is courage to live, and the way in which "life" here . . . gets its concrete definition is illustrated by the contrast between the vicarage and the cottage.[18]

This is of course what, by loading the dice, Lawrence made sure we would not miss. However, had he refrained from loading the dice, it would not have been possible for him to define "life" by the contrast between the vicarage and the cottage. In "art," as distinct from "propaganda," the dramatic clashes of will and of value do not carry on their face, as Mr. Leavis seems to believe, their own self-certification as to their place in the moral hierarchy. Each has its own "necessity" in the context, as defined by character and situation. It is we, as readers, who make the decision, if we do, that Louisa's values are preferable to her sister's. But ours is a *moral* choice, made possible by the introduction of our own criteria into a situation which, if aesthetically revealed, has no dominating moral criterion, or what is the same, has as many moral criteria as there are constellations of values in conflict. For this reason "art," when it is genuine and not faked by the autocratic intellect or the willful moral conscience, and "life" itself, as we encounter it in our own experience, are inevitable sources of moral outrage to the moralist. They appear to him, with his narrow choices and exclusive criteria, inherently and ineradicably ambiguous.

Nor can we say, in the context of the story as we have it, that it takes immense nobility and heroic courage to reject an unpleasant "little abortion" whose "body was unthinkable," and who "lacks the full range of human feelings." But it would have taken courage had security been made more attractive, as it often is, and had social position brought with it the genuine advantages that, in many cases, it brings with it. An inwardly dead man who was superficially less repulsive would have tested Louisa's choice and challenged the artist in a manner that the little abortion cannot and does not. The result of the test could not have been an unambiguous moral triumph for the values Lawrence preferred. But the frustration of the moralist would have been more than repaid by the success of the artist, who, by allowing a conflict between two sets of values, each of which has its own authentic claims, would have given us a story with genuine tragic tension.

It is of interest to dwell, in general terms, on a point I have just touched on hastily in the preceding comment on "The Daughters of the Vicar" I refer to the fact that while the only genuinely realized version of the Gerald-type we have is that which Lawrence gave us in *Women in Love*, the versions of the gamekeeper-type, which are as numerous as those of the Gerald-type, are usually not open to the same criticism that I have advanced against the Gerald-type. There is here, it seems to me, an interesting psychoanalytic problem—but one I shall only touch on in passing. The gamekeeper, in his potency, in his more intense and more fully realized manhood, is not only Lawrence, the Rupert Birkin of *Women in Love*, but is also his father, the miner, who was physically attractive to the woman D. H. Lawrence loved, his mother. Was this the way Lawrence made up for the cruelty with which he treated his father in life and in *Sons and Lovers*? In any case, the gamekeeper, in his numerous disguises as a groom, as a gypsy, as an Italian, as a Hungarian count, as a Mexican general of pure Indian blood, as a collier, as a young soldier returning from Salonika, as a writer called Somers—and these do not exhaust the list —is usually conceived dramatically. He is not reduced, or at least not as thoroughly reduced, to a formula as Gerald was, subsequent to his creation. This is no less true of the Connies and the Lous Lawrence puts into his stories—Anna and Ursula, Harriet, Kate, Teresa, and the others. And the reason neither the gamekeeper nor Ursula is produced by formula is, perhaps, that Lawrence retains the fascination and interest of a genuine novelist towards these people while after presenting Gerald, Lawrence reduces him to a mere sign to which he reacts in the manner of a conditioned reflex.

[6]

The plagiarism of Lawrence by Lawrence is not confined to the recurrent use of the same characters. In one case at least he employs a second time a pseudo-symbol that he had used earlier with greater dramatic effect.[14] The episodes in question are those of the mare in *Women in Love*, and those of the motor-chair in *Lady Chatterley*. If the reader does not remember the mare episode, he will find it discussed on page 240. I shall put the chair scene in a few words, for in the text it reads with the kind of obscene immediacy Lawrence all too frequently achieved. The chair episode is an account of a time when Connie and her crippled husband went into the wood on Sunday, Clifford in his motor-chair. On the way back the chair had to make a steep climb and after starting, balked weakly. Immediately Clifford became petulant and unreasonable, trying several times to start the chair but doing more harm than good. Finally he is forced to call on the gamekeeper. Clifford takes his irritation out on Mellors in a shameful and inexcusable manner. At lunch Connie cannot contain her feeling and reproaches her husband for his "abominably inconsiderate" treatment of the gamekeeper. The scene is short and intense and is intended, of course, to show up the insensitive industrialist and aristocrat. There is nothing implausible about it nor, considered by itself, anything wrong with it, except for the fact that its bitter intensity spills over the page and roils the reader's own emotions in a most unpleasant manner, leaving him angry not only at Clifford's shameful conduct but at the man who records it in a way that brings the reader into the writer's private grudges against his characters.

The contrast between the two episodes is of interest for several reasons. It is obvious that the chair episode is a copy of the mare episode. I am not saying, of course, that Lawrence consciously copies the one episode from the other, any more than I have suggested that Clifford is consciously copied from Gerald. It is his preoccupation with the brutality and with the essential weakness of the type, in spite of its specious strength, that keeps him coming back to the same theme. But it is interesting to see how, in the later attempt to deal with the Gerald-type, the ability to present it is weakened, the anger is more intense and the indictment is more furiously drawn. In the earlier episode, Lawrence wants to present the ruthless use Gerald makes of men, animals, and things, irrespective of any intrinsic worth they may have. All things, even Gerald himself, are instruments to his ends. The mare scene illustrates Gerald's will and his philosophy. Things, animals, and men are useless unless he can make them do his bidding. The mare episode is a pseudo-symbol because its meanings can be stated adequately in discursive terms. And so is the motor-chair episode.

But the justification Gerald had for teaching the mare to obey has been forgotten or altered by the time Lawrence wrote *Lady Chatterley*, and Clifford is no longer a man merely bent on dominion, weak inside although ostensibly strong, as Gerald was. He is a cripple who not only cannot control a motor-chair but who is a gratuitously brutal man, abusing the gamekeeper simply because he has to take out his frustration on some one and he cannot find any one else at the moment. There is more. Mellors, the servant, is the better man. And Clifford is totally blind, of course, to the difference in quality between his gamekeeper and himself. His higher rank utterly blinds him to the geuine difference in quality. In the earlier book the industrialist maintains control of the balking animal. His weakness is gradually exhibited by means of an adequate aesthetic presentation, and when he meets his end one does not hate him. In the later book no credit is given to Clifford for his genuine capacities. We are asked to see Clifford as wholly without redeeming virtues. Lawrence is not only falling back on a pseudo-symbol he has already used, but he is considerably more obvious about his intentions. The writer's intentions, however, do not coincide with the book's: the novelist remains the dribbling liar we have already seen him to be.

PART TWO

The Triumph of Art

CHAPTER SEVEN

Sons
and
Lovers

IT IS generally agreed that *Sons and Lovers* is one of Lawrence's best novels. I take it to be one of his best three and perhaps one of the best novels written in the English language in the first half of our century. It also happens to be his most popular work, if we judge by the place it has in the curriculum of English departments in American colleges. Mr. Cerf has told us that in 1928 Douglas' *South Wind* and *Sons and Lovers* were the two best sellers in the Modern Library Series.[1] Whatever functions it may have performed for the writer, on the whole experience here has been digested and presented in response to artistic exigencies: it does not fight for phallic reality, nor does it work to free the language from taboos, nor does it seek to realize any of the other extra-aesthetic ends that from time to time Lawrence proclaimed to be the purpose of his work. From the book itself we cannot infer that he attempted anything else than to write an artistically satisfactory book. The work has faults, of course. But after these are taken into account even a most exacting reader will probably be hard put to disagree with Lawrence's own estimate of it in a letter to Edward Garnett: "I tell you I have written a great book. . . . Read my novel, it is a great novel." [2] If we remember the relaxed manner in which we paste the label "great" on any achievement that is distinctly above the mediocre, there can be no serious objection to Lawrence's estimate of his own achievement.

173

Because *Sons and Lovers* is one of Lawrence's best novels, a study of his art may be expected to include a thorough and perhaps even an extended examination of it. And indeed critical works on Lawrence usually devote to it the attention which its quality deserves. But I am going to treat it from a restricted point of view. I have two reasons for my decision, either of which, by itself, justifies it in my opinion. The first is that, frankly, I have little to say about it that has not already been said. The second is that while, along with everybody else, I recognize its superior quality, it does not properly belong, in my estimation, with Lawrence's mature work. I do not mean it is immature; it is not like his first two novels, the work of a talented, promising apprentice. I mean that it is not Lawrence at his fullest and ripest. It does not embody the substance of his vision, as we find it, whether successfully or unsuccessfully, embodied in later works. And for that reason it cannot be put in the class with *The Rainbow* and *Women in Love*. Middleton Murry has told us that in the all-too-brief period between his leaving Jessie Chambers, the "Miriam" of *Sons and Lovers*, and the outbreak of the war, Lawrence was a happy man. It was during this all-too-brief period of happiness that he wrote *Sons and Lovers*, and that he conceived *The Sisters* out of which he wrote his two great novels, *The Rainbow*, published in 1915, and *Women in Love*, finished in 1916, although not published until 1920 in a private edition and 1921 publicly. These books, we know from both external and internal evidence, were not written by the baffled, essentially frustrated, psychologically ill, caged man who wrote *Aaron's Rod* and the Australian and Mexican novels.

Sons and Lovers may seem to the traditionalist a better novel than either *The Rainbow* or *Women in Love*. It keeps closer to the classical form of the novel than the other two works. It has a story whose development can be graphed. Beginning with the marriage of the miner and Gertrude, it goes on chronologically to an account of Paul's childhood and of the way in which, after the death of his older brother, the Oedipal relationship between Paul and his mother came to full and explicit expression. The story of the slowly developing love between Paul and Miriam follows, and it is in turn followed by Paul's effort to find in Clara what he deeply yearned for and Miriam could not give him—"the immensity of passion," physical passion. After this account follow the chapters on the death of his mother, his surrender of Clara to her husband, and his final turning to the city, not giving in, and not towards the darkness to follow his mother. These episodes serve simply to wind up the book and enable the novelist to write "The End."

It is well known that *Sons and Lovers* is an autobiographical novel, and Lawrence himself so considered it. It is known that the Miriam of the story is Jessie Chambers Wood and that a good many scenes are direct transcripts from Lawrence's own life. No one will of course want to deny that many literary artists exploit their own experience as matter for the composition of their works. But it is too often forgotten that a literary work is not a picture taken by a photographic camera and that to the degree that the artist is creative, what he has taken from experience is thrown into the furnace of his mind, where often, at depths far beyond the reach of consciousness, it loses its identity and gains new form, new significance, and a capacity for resonance that is altogether lacking before the act of composition. *Sons and Lovers* is a novel that should serve as a good test of this claim.

Sons and Lovers is not a mere transcription of events in Lawrence's life up to the death of his mother. From his remembered experience Lawrence had first to make a selection. He did not attempt to put into the book everything that he remembered as happening to him or his family and friends. Some episodes he discarded. But even the notion of "selecting" episodes is not adequate to describe what Lawrence did. No doubt, in a rough way, Lawrence performed such a selection. As he was thinking of his novel, he decided to give accounts of quarrels between his mother and his father, he also decided to include the incident of his giving Jessie a ride in the swing on his sweetheart's farm, the account of his life in the factory, probably including the occasion on which a girl gave him a present on his birthday. He also decided that one theme he had to explore in full was his gradual realization that the sweetheart of his childhood could offer him only the spiritual love of a nun and not the kind of passion for which he, as he grew older, came more and more clearly and insistently to crave. It may be assumed for our purposes that these and many other remembered experiences he "selected" from his actual life. But the material thus selected was subjected, for various reasons, to the creative process. Let one illustration suffice. Jessie Chambers Wood tells us that "The Clara of the second half of the story was a clever adaptation of elements from three people, and her creation arose as a complement to Lawrence's mood of failure and defeat. The events related had no foundation in fact, whatever their psychological significance." [3] It should be obvious that we cannot take the novel as an historical record or imitation of the facts of his life.

What Lawrence was trying to do in *Sons and Lovers*—besides writing a book that would give him the rewards of authorship and other purely external ends—was to achieve a grasp of his experience in its context. This called for his producing a coherent picture of his life and of the life of his family in terms of those factors that he took to have been important in their development. Central to the picture there had to be an account of two conflicts: the first, that between his father on the one hand and his mother and the children on the other; the second, the triangular conflict between his mother, his sweetheart, and himself. There also had to be an account of the discovery of his talent and its growth. The selected episodes had, finally, to be fitted into a harmonious whole. The whole, however, could not be clearly envisaged until it was more or less complete, and it could not be completed until the component parts had been fitted together. But fitting remembered experiences into a whole that meets the demands of the artist is not like fitting the parts of a jig-saw puzzle. In selecting the latter we are guided by determinate form and often by color. But the remembered experiences lack this form and while they do possess a kind of emotional tone that corresponds to the color of the jig-saw piece, the specificity of this tone is not fully determinate and perceptible in itself, nor is it fixed, and in any case it must be altered in order to comply with the demands to which the artist responds as he finishes the whole.

This means that the artist has to recreate each remembered experience as he creates the whole into which they are to be fitted. While working—whether "in his head" or on paper, with the aid of outlines—he finds himself more or less torn by his desire to use his experiences as he remembers them on the one hand and by his self-acknowledged responsibility to the emerging whole on the other. To the extent that he is an artist this is, for him, a difficult problem, for his concern with the whole puts the integrity of each individual experience in jeopardy and the loyalty to each experience threatens the harmony of the whole. Hence it is not a question of "carpentry work," of planing this board here and cutting that one down to size, of sandpapering and chiseling standard stock, guided as he works by a finished sketch or blue print with sizes clearly indicated. The sketch has to be conceived, and it has to be kept relatively fluid until the moment when the whole emerges, when the artist knows that at last he has the thing right and that what remains are minor details which are easily handled. Allowing, as we must, for the wide range of variation of habits of composition among writers, it is only after the whole has emerged that the labor of the file begins. But allowance must also be made for varieties of facility of composition. It is not true that the long laboured, the long gestated, work is always the best, the deepest and the most perfect. Nor is it true that that which comes easily and gets put down quickly is the least perfect and most shallow.

Even the earliest selection of remembered experience involves a creative evaluation as to its suitability to the whole and the whole's capacity to give room to the intended substance without danger to itself. The selection of remembered experience is *creative* because the artist does not fall back on a pre-determined standard by which he judges the acceptability of a given experience as a judge in a county fair judges the quality of the competing cows. For the artist, for some time, often almost to the very end, all is uncertainty, a feeling of walking blindly in an unknown dark alley, a matter of hunches which are frequently misleading; a process of false starts and sudden comings to unexpected and unpleasant stops beyond which there seems to be, and for a time there may be, no advancing.

This is far from being the whole of the account of the process by which an artist writes an "autobiographical" novel. So far I have only considered the purely aesthetic exigencies that control what goes into the whole and the whole that emerges as a result. The artist has other concerns besides the purely aesthetic. The respect he has for the integrity of his remembered experiences is more than an *aesthetic* respect. He is not a mere or a pure artist who leaves his other values outside the door when he enters his study. He is a man, which is to say, a moral person, with commitments of one kind or another, loyalties and anti-loyalties, prejudices, espousals, loves, and hatreds. And if he can (and often he tries to) put these out of his mind on entering his study, all he manages to do is push them down into the dark cellar of his subconscious, from where they manage to regain operative control, although in false face. If the writer is an artist, the artistic exigency seeks to control the moral demands in terms of the emerging whole. But if he wants a picture of his experience, a comprehensive whole, the artist cannot disregard the values the experience involves—values he realizes, values he eschews, values that outside his work room he hates and loves, that threaten him or allure him. And because these conflicts are present whenever the artist is at work and because, however perceptive and honest he may be, one can seldom if ever clearly know what he values, it often happens that the work gives him the lie and proves him to be the dribbling liar he often is.

When we compare what Lawrence told us in *Sons and Lovers*

about the relationship between Paul and Miriam and his mother to what Jessie Chambers Wood tells us and consider these two accounts in the light of Lawrence's reversal of attitude towards his father in later life, we have a case that is almost made to order to show how a novel which in a genuine sense is "autobiographical," is, in another, nothing of the kind. The tensions, moral and aesthetic, that go into its making and the creative process involved should dispose once for all of those theories that hold that art is an imitation of life.

This is not the occasion to go further into this question. Let it be enough now to indicate in passing that the alternative to imitation is creation, in the serious sense of the term, for the theories of "expression" with which I am acquainted are either theories of imitation or of creation, although the object of imitation in the former is often taken to be—as T. S. Eliot took it, in his conception of "the objective correlative"—a preformed inward experience that exists independently of the informing of it in language.

In the next chapter I intend to carry the discussion further, in terms of a notion I shall put forth under the name of "the constitutive symbol." Here, what I would emphasize is that Jessie Chambers Wood was not wrong when she was hurt by the account Lawrence gave of their relationship in *Sons and Lovers*. Although she tried not to, she could not help taking this novel as the account of their love affair, and as such the novel was a mendacious and a radically disloyal book. It belied what there had been between them: her devotion, her help, her encouragement. She saw it as an effort to conceal Lawrence's final submission to his mother's will. She was utterly right in writing that she "could not appeal to Lawrence for justice as between his treatment of Mrs. Morel and Miriam." [4] And it would be wanton cruelty on the critic's part to tell her that her complaint was beside the point since Lawrence was writing a novel and not a history. For Mrs. Wood, *Sons and Lovers* could not be anything but history, and thus taken it was false, unjust, and a very cruel book.

[2]

It is well known that *Sons and Lovers* attempts to elucidate the triangular relationship between Paul, his mother, and Miriam. If Paul's interest in literature and in painting comes into the picture, it is not because Lawrence, like Joyce, is centrally interested in giving us the portrait of the development of an artist. And if the relationship between the parents is accented, it is in order to give us the background out of which the triangular relationship grew. Lawrence wants to show how Paul and his mother were forced to come together because Gertrude's husband, the uncouth, drinking, bullying miner, was no husband to her nor was he, properly speaking, a father to his children.

Lawrence's gift as a writer, the living quality of his scenes, enable him almost to get away with his intention and to write off the father and the sweetheart. But he did not altogether succeed in doing so. And the novel shows the novelist to be not only a dribbling liar but in some respects, and in spite of his magnificent capacity to see, almost altogether blind. In *Sons and Lovers* Lawrence's intention and the intention of the novel are disparate. But I should add that in this case, the disparity does not constitute an artistic defect: it merely gives the novel qualities that Lawrence did not see were there, and that, within my knowledge, have not been generally noticed.

For Lawrence wants us to believe that both Paul's father and his sweetheart were at fault, and that his mother, Gertrude Morel, was a superior person, who rose above her miserable world by virtue of superiority of class and personal endowment, a loving mother and a wife made unhappy by an uncouth, drinking, irresponsible husband. But in terms of the evidence to be found in the novel, was this actually the case? There is no question that Morel was not the right man for Gertrude, but was Gertrude the right wife for the miner?

Take the early scene in which Mrs. Morel comes downstairs to find William shorn of "the twining wisp of hair clustering around his head." Mrs. Morel is furious and with gripped, lifted fists, comes forward. Morel shrinks back. "I could kill you, I could!" she says. She cries and later she tells her husband she has been silly. But we are told that "she knew, and Morel knew, that the act had caused something momentous to take place in her soul. She remembered the scene all her life, as one in which she had suffered the most intensely." And Lawrence goes on in the next paragraph: "This act of masculine clumsiness was the spear through the side of her love for Morel. Before, while she had striven against him bitterly, she had fretted after him, as if he had gone astray from her. Now she ceased to fret for his love: he was an outsider to her. This made life much more bearable (Chapter I). But this is belied by her reaction when she saw William's head shorn. She "looked down at the jagged, close-clipped head of her child. . . . 'Oh— my boy!' she faltered." But before he cut his son's curls Morel was already an outsider. And because without asking her the man had clipped her boy's curls, she would remember the scene all her life. All one can say, confronted with the writer's statement, is that whether he knew it or not, he was giving us a vivid and living picture of a woman who had an unusual capacity to nurse a slight injury and had a powerful capacity for resentment. But does the writer know what he is presenting us with? Since the novel gives the writer the lie, the answer must be that he does and he does not. And we are here faced, not with a contradiction, but with a psychological conflict.

In any case, Paul's mother-sweetheart is a hard woman, a willful, unbending woman, and Paul is a myopic, love-blinded boy and young man. She would reform the miner she married, she would bring him up to her level of manners and gentility, and when it becomes clear to her that her husband cannot be reformed and when the physical attraction that brought them together subsides, she begins a relentless, ruthless war against him, setting the children against their father. The reason for her attitude is that he bullied them and drank: "The sense of his sitting in all his pit-dirt, drinking after a long day's work . . . made Mrs. Morel unable to bear herself. From her the feeling was transmitted to the other children. She never suffered alone any more: the children suffered with her" (Chapter IV). But Mrs. Morel was more than a willful, unbending woman. Paul, in the entanglement of an Oedipal relationship, could not see it, and Lawrence gives no indication that he sees it, but Mrs. Morel was not a good mother to Paul and while Lawrence did in fact try to hand Paul's mother "the laurels of victory," as Jessie Chambers points out, and while Miriam was indeed defeated and cast off, the price was high. We do not know what happens to Paul when he reaches the city towards which he turns at the end of the book. But we know that the struggle has turned him already into a cruel man and has damaged his capacity for normal sexual relations.

With cruelty goes pathos. For the reader who reads it with care the book is instinct with desolating pathos, when he considers the illusions in which Mrs. Morel and her children live. The belief in the mother's superiority because she comes from a class just a notch higher than her husband, the belief that theirs is a home superior to their neighbors' because, living in a corner house, they pay a few more pennies for it than their neighbors do, the belief that they have better taste and superior education (which they do have, but which makes them pitiful snobs)—the hollowness of their values is pathetic. And Lawrence does not see their pathos. Neither through irony nor by any other means does he give us an indication that he sees through Gertrude Morel and her children. He is utterly lucid about the miner's faults. But about Paul's and his mother's false values he is blind.

How do we know about Paul's cruelty? We know from his treatment of his sweetheart. It is true that there is an important extenuating circumstance. The love between Paul and Miriam developed so slowly and so unconsciously, that by the time Paul realized clearly that Miriam could not satisfy his sexual needs, the involvement between them could only be severed by brutal surgery; there was no other way. When Miriam was twenty-one,

Paul wrote to her that she was a nun and reproached her because in all their relations the body did not enter. After this letter was sent we are told that Paul, then twenty-three, was still a virgin, and that this was the end of the first phase of Paul's love-affair with Miriam. One can hardly blame Paul for discovering that what he needed was, in Miriam's words, "a sort of baptism of fire in passion" (Chapter XII). But while it is not necessary to take the attitude of a judge, and while in any case passing moral judgments on characters in books is an act of supererogation which interferes with the revelation the artist seeks to make, we cannot overlook the fact that Paul was cruel and that he knew it. Lawrence tells us that Paul "fought against his mother almost as he fought against Miriam" (Chapter IX). But this statement we may disregard, for the evidence of the novel gives it the lie. He did not fight against his mother; he grew in bondage and until her death in bondage he remained. And while his mother did not fear Clara and did not interfere with his affair with her, she resented Miriam bitterly and she did not interfere when her son-lover was unspeakably cruel towards his sweetheart. His cruelty was part of the fruits of her victory.

We know that the struggle damaged Paul's capacity for normal sexual relations from the account of Paul's affair with Clara Dawes. For a brief moment the affair appeared to be satisfactory. On one occasion at least it led to an experience the depth and amplitude of which was what Paul had yearned for and Miriam had not been able to provide. But the affair soon peters out and Paul ends up by virtually making Clara return to her husband. What is wrong between Paul and Clara? The book does not reveal the cause and therefore we cannot answer the question. But the fact that the book does not reveal it is itself significant. For a time Clara gives Paul what Miriam could not give him, the complete erotic satisfaction he had long craved. While the peewits scream in the field, they come together in an embrace of love and both seem to achieve complete fulfillment. "They had met, and included in their meeting the thrust of the manifold grass-stems, the

cry of the peewit and the wheel of the stars" (Chapter XIII).
Which is to say that the universe has been involved in their love,
and this is as it should be. And not more than three lines later we
are told, "And after such an evening they both were very still,
having known the immensity of passion." But if they *both* had
known the immensity of passion, why had the passion, as we are
told only a little over a dozen pages later, "failed her often"?
And what prevents them from reaching again the height of that
one time when the peewits had called? And why does Paul finally
hand Clara back to Dawes? Surely this is a question in which we
are legitimately interested and to which we need an answer. The
failure to give an answer leaves us in the dark about the relationship between Clara and Paul. What went wrong between them?
For a man who has had a sexual experience with a woman as complete and deep as that which Paul had with Clara, and who had
wanted just that kind of experience, would not give the woman
up as easily as Paul did. But the point I wish to make is not that
Paul handed Clara back to her husband, but that the action is not
grounded in anything that happens to them. We are left here with
an unanswered question that the story itself gives rise to, not one
we introduced from the outside.

This is not the only piece of evidence we have of Paul's incapacity for the complete sexual experience for which he craves.
There is something else in the account of the affair between Paul
and Clara that we must examine. On the occasion already mentioned we are told that the experience constituted for both a complete and deep consummation. But why then did the experience
fail to be the first cause of the ripening of the bond between
them? The universe was involved in their affair the evening the
peewits were screaming in the field. This is as it should be: they
are part of the earth, and at the moment of love-death, the earth
and the stars are part of their experience. After the evening Paul
and Clara are still, having known "the immensity of passion." But
the experience does not lead to tenderness between them. The
fierceness, the wildness, the naked hunger are appeased and we

are told that "in the morning Paul had considerable peace and was happy in himself." This sentence suggests a kind of emotional solipsism which neither Paul nor Clara broke out of during their liaison. Even at the time he was most completely satisfied by her, Paul's mode of being is that of aloneness. Sexual completion is no bridge thrown across from one self to the other, to bring them together in tenderness, mutual dependence, and understanding. The morning after the evening when the peewits screamed in the field, we are told that "the intensity of passion began to burn him again," and of Clara we are told that she "was mad with desire of him" (Chapter XIII). But each seems to be, for the other, a mere means to an end, and when the end is achieved, it is enjoyed in isolation.

A similar impediment arises in the relations between Tom and Lydia, Will and Anna, and Ursula and Skrebensky in *The Rainbow* and between Ursula and Rupert Birkin and Gudrun and Gerald in *Women in Love*. There is no positive evidence for this judgment, except for an explicit statement in the case of Ursula in *The Rainbow*, to which I shall refer shortly. The basis for the judgment consists in the fact that Lawrence does not indicate that the relationships of the couples mentioned develop into tender intimacy, into the kind of piety a man and a woman feel towards each other when they owe each other their supreme moments of complete fulfillment. The reference to Ursula is presented to us in the account of the evening on which, perhaps for the first time, she had a sexual experience with Skrebensky. Lawrence writes:

Then he turned and kissed her, and she waited for him. The pain to her was the pain she wanted, the agony was the agony she wanted. She was caught up, entangled in the powerful vibration of the night. The man, what was he?—a dark, powerful vibration that encompassed her. She passed away as on a dark wind, far, far away, into the pristine darkness of paradise, into the original immortality. She entered the dark fields of immortality.

When she rose, she felt strangely free, strong. She was not ashamed, —why should she be? He was walking beside her, the man who had

been with her. She had taken him, they had been together. Whither
they had gone, she did not know. But it was as if she had received another nature. She belonged to the eternal, changeless place into which
they had leapt together. . . .

     . . . .

This curious separate strength, that existed in darkness and pride of
night, never forsook her. She had never been more herself. It could not
occur to her that anybody, not even the young man of the world,
Skrebensky, should have anything at all to do with her permanent self.
As for her temporal, social self, she let it look after itself.

Her whole soul was implicated with Skrebensky—not the young
man of the world, but the undifferentiated man he was. She was perfectly sure of herself, perfectly strong, stronger than all the world.
The world was not strong—she was strong. The world existed only in
a secondary sense:—she existed supremely.—CHAPTER XV

The sentences that give us a clear insight into the relationship
between Ursula and Skrebensky are easily enough detected in
these passages: "The man, what was he?—a powerful vibration
that encompassed her." "She belonged to the eternal, changeless
place into which they had leapt together." "It could not occur to
her that anybody, not even the young man of the world, Skeben-
sky, should have anything at all to do with her permanent self."
Her soul was implicated with her lover, but her soul was implicated not with a person, but with "the undifferentiated man he
was." And notice how much in the next sentence the emphasis is
upon her aloneness, her isolated self: "She was perfectly sure of
herself, perfectly strong, stronger than all the world. . . . She existed supremely." And the lover, what did he mean to her? He was
an undifferentiated man, which is to say, that any man qua man
would do, and not this particular one who is a person and for
whom there is no duplicate and for whom there can be no substitute. Is this not the same as to say that the role he plays in the
relationship is that of means to the end of her satisfaction and no
more?

But at this point it is necessary to make explicit the intention of my remarks. I am not advancing a moral criticism of the relations between Ursula and Skrebensky or between Paul and Clara, nor a moral criticism of Lawrence's conception of love as found in these books. What I am trying to do is to make as clear and as unmistakable as I can what the nature of the relationship was as he presented it. There was a time when to say of a woman that she was a redhead was to say something derogatory of her; but the statement may be intended also as the expression of a value-free fact. And it is in this latter sense that I intend my remarks: this is the way these people feel, and to ask of them to feel in any other way or to criticize Lawrence for making them feel as they do would be as irrelevant as criticizing Shakespeare from the standpoint of certain marriage laws of certain states in the Union or of Germany under Hitler, because in *Othello* he presented us with a clear case of miscegenation. It is only when Lawrence is interpreted as offering us a "love ethic" or as offering us insights into "life" which we cannot do without, that the counter-criticism is relevant: "Let us examine carefully what Lawrence is actually presenting." As a presentation, we must take it or leave it. This is the way these people are—in *Sons and Lovers* and in *The Rainbow*, and elsewhere for that matter, for that is in the end what Birkin's conception of love adds up to and that is what Kate finally learns to accept in *The Plumed Serpent*. Lawrence's dramatic persons are erotic solipsists, they never break out of the isolation of their selves, no bond of tenderness or need for the other develops. And if what Lawrence is offering us is an ethic, we have a right, in fact, a duty, to criticize it after carefully examining what it involves.

Let me reiterate that I am not suggesting that the same kind of evidence that can be adduced concerning Ursula and Skrebensky can be adduced concerning her parents and grandparents, or concerning the two couples of *Women in Love*. While the evidence as to the nature of the relationship between Paul and Clara and Ursula and Skrebensky is positive, for the other couples it is circumstantial, it consists only in the fact that Lawrence does not tell

us that the inward, emotional isolation of each of the couples has
been breached. This is not the whole of the matter, as we shall see
when we examine the love Birkin offers Ursula in *Women in Love*.
But about that other aspect, later.

[3]

There is a sense, one which has been generally acknowledged,
in which *Sons and Lovers* constitutes indisputably a great triumph
of Lawrence's art. But there can be no serious harm in bringing it
forth again.

Lawrence will keep a place in the history of English literature
because he was first and last and all the time *a writer*. When I
speak of Lawrence *the writer*, I mean the term in the sense in
which Allen Tate means it when he applies it to Flaubert. In his
brilliant essay, "Techniques of Fiction," [5] Mr. Tate reminds us of
Henry James's constant admonition, " 'Don't state,' says James,
time and again—'render! Don't tell us what is happening, let it
happen.' " This is what Flaubert does in a small scene quoted by
Mr. Tate from *Madame Bovary*. This Jamesian "rendering" is
what I call "a presentation," something the artist is capable of
achieving, and something which, when achieved, is the evidence
we need in order to know a writer is back of it. And this is a
power of which Lawrence gave evidence in almost everything he
wrote. By the time he wrote *Sons and Lovers* his power as writer
was fully developed. The earlier novels are over-written. From
Sons and Lovers on Lawrence demonstrated fully and constantly
that he was a great writer.

To prove my point—a point, I acknowledge, that almost no one
at this date would require proof of—let me cite a passage picked
almost at random but not quite. I came across it only recently
looking for something else in *Sons and Lovers*, and since it reminded me of Mr. Tate's essay, I tucked it away in my mind as a
masterful scene. Fanny, the hunchback, greets Paul in the factory
on his twenty-first birthday. As he was changing his coat, he
heard a voice behind him:

"Paul, Paul, I want you," she said.

It was Fanny, the hunchback, standing at the top of her stairs, her face radiant with a secret. Paul looked at her in astonishment.

"I want you," she said.

He stood, at a loss.

"Come on," she coaxed. "Come before you begin of the letters."

He went down the half-dozen steps into her dry, narrow, "finishing-off" room. Fanny walked before him: her black bodice was short—the waist was under her armpits—and her green-black cashmere skirt seemed very long, as she strode with big strides before the young man, himself so graceful. She went to her seat at the narrow end of the room, where the window opened on to chimney-pots. Paul watched her thin hands and her flat red wrists as she excitedly twitched her white apron, which was spread on the bench in front of her. She hesitated.

"You didn't think we'd forgot you?" she asked, reproachful.

"Why?" he asked. He had forgotten his birthday himself.

"'Why,' he says! 'Why!' Why, look here!" She pointed to the calendar, and he saw, surrounding the big black number "21," hundreds of little crosses in blacklead.

"Oh, kisses for my birthday," he laughed. "How did you know?"

"Yes, you want to know, don't you?" Fanny mocked, hugely delighted. "There's one from everybody—except Lady Clara—and two from some. But I shan't tell you how many *I* put."

"Oh, I know, you're spooney," he said.

"There you *are* mistaken!" she cried indignant. "I could never be so soft." Her voice was strong and contralto.

"You always pretend to be such a hard-hearted hussy," he laughed. "And you know you're as sentimental—"

"I'd rather be called sentimental than frozen meat," Fanny blurted. Paul knew she referred to Clara, and he smiled.

"Do you say such nasty things about me?" he laughed.

"No, my duck," the hunchback woman answered, lavishly tender. She was thirty-nine. "No, my duck, because you don't think yourself a fine figure in marble and us nothing but dirt. I'm as good as you, aren't I, Paul?" and the question delighted her.

"Why, we're not better than one another, are we?" he replied.

"But I'm as good as you, aren't I, Paul?" she persisted daringly.

"Of course you are. If it comes to goodness, you're better."

She was rather afraid of the situation. She might get hysterical.

"I thought I'd get here before the others—won't they say I'm deep! Now shut your eyes—" she said.

"And open your mouth, and see what God sends you," he continued, suiting action to words, and expecting a piece of chocolate. He heard the rustle of the apron and a faint click of metal. "I'm going to look," he said.

He opened his eyes. Fanny, her long cheeks flushed, her blue eyes shining, was gazing at him. There was a little bundle of paint-tubes on the bench before him. He turned pale.

"No, Fanny," he said quickly.

"From us all," she answered hastily.

"No, but—"

"Are they the right sort?" she asked, rocking herself with delight.

"Jove! they're the best in the catalogue."

"But they're the right sorts?" she cried.

"They're off the little list I'd made to get when my ship came in." He bit his lip.

Fanny was overcome with emotion. She must turn the conversation.

"They was all on thorns to do it; they all paid their shares, all except the Queen of Sheba."

The Queen of Sheba was Clara.

"And wouldn't she join?" Paul asked.

"She didn't get the chance; we never told her; we wasn't going to have *her* bossing *this* show. We didn't *want* her to join."

Paul laughed at the woman. He was much moved. At last he must go. She was very close to him. Suddenly she flung her arms around his neck and kissed him vehemently.

"I can give you a kiss today," she said apologetically. "You've looked so white, it's made my heart ache."

Paul kissed her, and left her. Her arms were so pitifully thin that his heart ached also.—CHAPTER X

For the reader the scene builds up to the kisses with increasing tension, contributed by the threatening squall of barely repressed hysteria on Fanny's part, by her love yearning unexpressed but clearly visible in her words, her tenderness, her jealousy of Clara, and her deep sense of inferiority which she makes Paul deny. After giving us her age we *see* the hunchback, with the skirt waist under her armpits, we *see* the thin hands and the flat red wrists, we take her excitement in directly. We need not be told that Fanny is in love with Paul. We gather the knowledge from her behavior: her eagerness to show Paul that she stole a march on the other girls, her indication by denial that there is more than one cross of hers on the calendar, and her pathetic insistence that she is as good as Lady Clara—pathetic, of course, not only because Lady Clara gives herself airs of social superiority over Fanny and the other girls and they resent it, but because she is superior to Fanny as a woman, since she is not deformed. I find in the scene a deep pathos. And one that the writer intensifies at the end with a superb touch: Paul's heart breaks not because of her deformity but because of the thinness of her arms.

I do not believe that there is a novel or a story by Lawrence, whatever its defects, that lacks a picture or a scene done with the masterfulness that, for me, this one has. Who has read *Aaron's Rod*, for instance, and forgotten the sketch of the two young Englishmen, and the insecurity, never mentioned by Lawrence directly, aroused in Aaron by their self-possession and their obvious social superiority? And who can forget the scene in which young Paul Morel goes for his father's wages in *Sons and Lovers?*

But I shall soon be gushing with unseemly abandon about a quality of Lawrence that no one, I imagine, would fail to recognize today, and that was recognized from the very beginning of his career.

[4]

There are times, however, when Lawrence's mastery over language, as evinced in his power of immediacy, betrays him. At such times Lawrence is *obscene*, in the primitive sense of the word: for he brings into the scene things that should be left out, and that should be left out for a very good reason. Shakespeare is obscene in *Lear*—oh, the pity that such a grave fault is found in

such a great play!—when he brings onto the stage the eye-pluck-
ing episode. Obscenities of this sort arouse the spectator of the
scene, breaking the delicate poise, pushing him into the scene itself, and forcing him to engage as partisan in the action. Paradoxi-
cally, then, it is Lawrence's power of language that betrays him.
He gets carried away by the description and the excessive
immediacy pole-vaults us into the thick of the action. He forces us
to respond to the emotions of the scene or to resist them, in any
case forcing us to lose the poise by which an act of aesthesis is possible. If the purpose of reading Lawrence—or any author who
claims the stature of artist—were to indulge in an emotional binge,
these scenes, flawed with excess of immediacy, would be the highest peak of his achievement. But I cannot believe that this is the
purpose of reading poetry. And if it were, it would not give art
the status it has because outside itself there is no substitute for art.
Emotional binges we can indulge in by many other means.

These abstract statements will probably not carry the force that
a concrete illustration can carry. In *Sons and Lovers* there is an account of a quarrel between Walter Morel and his wife which is
done with great force, indeed with an excess of emotion that embarrasses the reader. It's an ugly scene, in which Lawrence does
Walter Morel in, obviously in the attempt to show that Paul's
mother was the victim of the miner and his faults. Walter Morel
left The Nelson in a jolly mood but before he arrived home he
grew irritable. As a result, a quarrel follows. The scene is short,
not over a page and a half in length, and it is pure drama, pure
presentation. This is superb mastery of language, the result is pure
immediacy. But there is another result: the reader cannot help entering into the quarrel and the complex emotions aroused by the
quarrel leave him embarrassed and confused. However, the reader
is not so utterly confused that he overlooks the fact that Lawrence
himself is on the side of the young wife against the drunken husband and this injects the suspicion in him that Lawrence here is
not merely presenting a quarrel but is doing more, he is probably
justifying a private grudge of his own.

He entered just as Mrs. Morel was pouring the infusion of herbs out of the saucepan. Swaying slightly, he lurched against the table. The boiling liquor pitched. Mrs. Morel started back.

"Good gracious," she cried, "coming home in his drunkness!"

"Comin' home in his what?" he snarled, his hat over his eye.

Suddenly her blood rose in a jet.

"Say you're *not* drunk!" she flashed.

She had put down her saucepan, and was stirring the sugar into the beer. He dropped his two hands heavily on the table, and thrust his face forward at her.

"Say you're not drunk," he repeated. "Why, nobody but a nasty little bitch like you 'ud 'ave such a thought."

He thrust his face forward at her.

"There's money to bezzle with, if there's money for nothing else."

"I've not spent a two-shillin' bit this day," he said.

"You don't get as drunk as a lord on nothing," she replied. "And," she cried, flashing into sudden fury, "if you've been sponging on your beloved Jerry, why, let him look after his children, for they need it."

"It's a lie, it's a lie. Shut your face, woman."

They were now at battle-pitch. Each forgot everything save the hatred of the other and the battle between them. She was fiery and furious as he. They went on till he called her a liar.

"No," she cried, starting up, scarce able to breathe. "Don't call me that—you, the most despicable liar that ever walked in shoe-leather." She forced the last words out of suffocated lungs.

"You're a liar!" he yelled, banging the table with his fist. "You're a liar, you're a liar."—CHAPTER I

The ugly quarrel goes on and the reader is not spared its overpowering immediacy. But I shall stop here because I do not want my reader involved in the Morels' quarrel. If the sample I have given is not convincing, let him turn to the book and read the scene in full. It will shake him, I fear, as it shook the miner and his wife. But what is the point of dragging the reader into the quarrel? The point is the need to prove that the hatred that the wife finally developed for her husband and that she transferred to her children is fully justified. But why should the reader be made a partisan in this quarrel? He did not pick up the novel in order to exercise his gifts as judge, and particularly as judge of a quarrel between a man and his wife. He need not be wise in order to know that the right is very seldom, if ever, altogether on the side of one and the wrong altogether on the side of the other.

In point of fact, this is the case in *Sons and Lovers.* The novel gives the lie to the dribbling liar who is the novelist and gives us evidence that Mrs. Morel, having married below her precious and ever so superior social level, soon had to face the fact that she had made a horrible mistake. The matter is not quite as simple, of course, for two reasons: it is obvious that for a time the sexual flame that was kindled in Mrs. Morel by her miner husband kept her from facing the truth, and it is also clear that at the very beginning, at any rate, Morel had tried to live up to the factitious standards which his wife set for him—he took the pledge and in general tried to raise himself from the level on which he had always lived. But I shan't pursue this question. For the point that must be made is, I hope, already adequately made, namely that the experience of being dragged into the quarrel is anything but pleasant and it induces in the reader ugly and frustrated emotions which he could very well do without.

This ugly scene is followed by a very different one—one of those Aldington called "nympholeptic." In *Sons and Lovers* the ecstasy is aroused in Mrs. Morel, after she calms down, by the sight of "the tall white lilies reeling in the moonlight, and the air charged with their perfume as with a presence." The scene is as powerfully presented as the nympholeptic scenes in *The Trespasser*, and later in *The Rainbow*. But its power would have been greater if our response to it had not demanded that we push off violently the feeling aroused by the ugly fight.

This is not the only scene in *Sons and Lovers* open to the criticism of obscenity because of excessive immediacy. The brutal fight between Clara's husband, Baxter Dawes, and Paul, is another in which the excess of hatred embarrasses and roils the reader's emotion (Chapter XIII). The objection to the account of this

fight may be put from a shifted point of view, in different terms:
It is as if Lawrence were, as he wrote, living over an experience
he had actually undergone, and living it over as he underwent it,
without the benefit of aesthetic transformation; living it over,
rather than recollecting it in tranquillity. The description of the
fight with Dawes takes less than a thousand words; but they are
not words one is reading but an action one is participating in and
the experience is exhausting and extremely unpleasant. It is always unpleasant to be dragged into a fight—even if one has a personal stake in it. But to be dragged into a fight in a novel is not
only unpleasant but offensive.

Another feature of the description of Paul's fight with Dawes
adds to the reader's embarrassment, although it is not related to
the problem of excess of immediacy. The reader cannot help feeling that the writer is distinctly on the side of Paul Morel and is
justifying his defeat and is trying to picture him as a formidable
antagonist. But the fact is that Paul is not a formidable antagonist
and Lawrence has not altogether been able to conceal that Paul is
afraid of Baxter Dawes. Indeed no hero of Lawrence drawn from
autobiographical matter gives one convincing evidence of physical courage. On the contrary one gets the impression, a very definite if elusive impression, that they are all cowards. Whether Lawrence was a physical coward or not is not here in question. That
he was a physical bully, we know. The story Knud Merrild tells
about the beating Lawrence gave the dog is enough evidence.
But whatever the case, his heroes are not "men" in the sense in
which a marine sergeant or a Spanish-American would use the
term.

[5]

Excess of immediacy is to be found in many of Lawrence's
works. It turns what might have been one of his best short stories,
"The Prussian Officer," into a very poor one. This story exhibits
many kinds of excellence, to which Lawrence's critics have not
been blind, but it is also open to a number of seriously damaging

criticisms, not all of which have been noted. Only recently, long
after this work had been completed, Mr. Kingsley Widmer, apro-
pos of this same story, had some wise things to say about Lawrence's perverseness and nihilism.[6] In view of what Lawrence en-
thusiasts say about the health of his work, these aspects of his
work deserve serious attention. What I am concerned with here is
the excess of immediacy that seems to me almost entirely to deny
positive quality to the story. From the time the Captain notices
the young orderly's scar on his left thumb to the time when the
youth assaults the officer, leaving the dying Captain twitching and
jerking, one is submerged in a heavy, acrid atmosphere of intense
emotion and counter-emotion, confused by the intensity of the
passion. One is forced to hate and pity the Captain, caught in a
sadistic and homosexual passion for the orderly that he cannot acknowledge, and one pities the victim, the youth, anxious about his
fate.

But what does the youth think or feel? The officer's emotional
involvement is communicated to us in a brutally direct way; we
see the officer from the inside, so to speak; but about the youth we
learn very little. And here is a puzzle that would seem inconceivable if one had not experienced it. The story is told as much from
the standpoint of the youth as from that of the Captain, and yet
the youth remains strangely out of reach for us. We are told that
he is afraid of really meeting the Captain, and as the story opens
we are told about his marching and his pain, and just before he
throws himself at the officer and kills him, we are told that a flash
of flame went through the younger soldier. Of course, after the
Captain is killed it is only the actions and feelings of the orderly
that concern the writer. But in spite of this fact, we are engulfed
in the emotional flood of the Captain, and the orderly's reactions
we deduce rather than feel as we do the older man's.

For one reader at least, the total impact of the story is confusing and unpleasant, and not merely because of the homosexual
component that is probably the germinal source of interest for

Lawrence in the story, but because of the unspeakable, the obscene, sadism in which one is forced by the writer to participate.
It matters little that the villainous captain, with his pure cruelty
and pure arrogance and pure corruption of sexuality, in the end
gets killed and that the youth mercifully dies, thus being spared a
trial and an execution. What does matter is that we have been
dragged into an intense, acrid, unpleasant emotional imbroglio for
which the writer provides no relief. There is something seriously
wrong in an age called "the age of criticism," in which the "symbolism" of the tale is carefully analyzed, and the excess of immediacy is overlooked. What is, one asks, the advantage or the profit
to one in this involvement, what is the gain in wisdom or in seren-
ity—surely not catharsis of these corrosive emotions aroused in
one by the story, for catharsis is known by the effects, and the effect of the reading of this tale is pure irritation and disgust—with
the writer, the captain, and oneself.

In *The Rainbow* we find several instances of excess of immediacy spoiling an otherwise almost perfect work of art. I shall refer
to only one more. In Lawrence's account of Ursula's excruciating
experience at the school, one is forced to participate in a scene of
pure hatred (Chapter XIII).

Another aspect of the criticism I am making may engender misunderstanding. It is not a question of the legitimacy of hatred as
matter for poetry, it is only a question of the manner in which it
is treated and the effects that are achieved. I say this because, as
already noted, at least one aesthetician has argued that all art
comes from love, and this is patent nonsense. And also because in
our society only the arousal of sexual passion is considered obscene. The Greeks knew better; the arousal of any passion, the
breaking of the delicate equipoise to which Bullough referred as
"aesthetic distance," is obscene. In the scenes to which I had referred—and they do not exhaust the number which can be found
in Lawrence—we are forced to take sides and, in retrospect, we
resent the fact that the taking of sides is unpleasant.

[6]

And yet, when all these factors are taken into account, as they must be by the critic, the fact remains that Lawrence was a great writer and that *Sons and Lovers*, the first of his three great novels, is a superbly written book. He was a great *artist*, but he was also a great *writer*, which is to say, a master of language. As an artist he frequently fails, as I have attempted to show in the preceding chapters. He does not compose with care, he pads, he often lacks inventiveness, he copies himself, he dramatizes concepts, and under the very poor excuse of bringing health where unhealthy prudishness reigns, he is obscene. Even as a writer, he fails occasionally. He is often extremely careless. At such times his prose loses its power of immediacy. In *St. Mawr*, as we have seen, he does not seem to have even tried to achieve his best. It is sloppy work, and can only be praised by a critic determined to find positive quality at all costs and everywhere in his idol. Sometimes Lawrence allows a cuteness to creep into his prose, that spoils the effect he is seeking to create. The opening pages of "Reflections on the Death of a Porcupine" give evidence of this cuteness, which spoils an otherwise luminously etched portrait of the animal in the moonlight. Lawrence has been criticized for the monotony of his prose; others have objected to its repetitiousness. Some of these animadversions are unimportant and some irrelevant. The repetitiousness is there, but to consider it a fault is to fail to notice what he achieves by means of it. He has also been criticized for attempting the impossible by seeking to give us the felt quality of an experience by direct presentation in words. The truth is that when he makes such attempts he sometimes falls into incoherence, straining the language and piling metaphor on image, with disastrous results. But at his best, the quality of experience as felt is conveyed by Lawrence successfully. We have seen that he actually presents Fanny's experience, her tender and anxious response to Paul, her desperate need to get close to him, and her jealousy of "the Queen of Sheba." And we shall see in our examination of *The Rainbow* and of *Women in Love* how, by means of the constitutive symbol, he manages to present what would otherwise remain outside the reach of the writer's power to present. So that when the worst is said against him, it must be acknowledged that Lawrence was a superb artist and writer. He had his faults. But his triumphs more than make up for them.

CHAPTER EIGHT

The
Rainbow

THE RAINBOW is, prima facie, the history of three generations of Brangwens, for Alfred, the earliest ancestor of the family mentioned by name, does not come into the narrative. But as the reader makes his way into the book, a question arises: Is Lawrence interested in giving an account of three generations of Brangwens, or is he perhaps interested in something else? A consideration of the book forces on us a qualified answer: there is ample evidence that he is interested in the story of the Brangwens, but he is interested in more than that. The story is first set on a farm, The Marsh, in a clearly indicated geographical location. And Ilkiston, Cossethay, and even Poland, from which Lydia Lensky comes, are described in relatively realistic terms. Lydia's life before coming to England is presented. Dates are given. The account of Anna's childhood is beautifully done, showing that Lawrence had not wasted his time when he read Dickens. Consider the scene in which little Anna is called "a little pole cat" by Marriott, "the gentlemen farmer from Ambergate," in The George Inn. Or take the brilliant sketch of the wedding scene in Chapter V and the light, humorous, yet firmly delineated touch with which it is brought off. Take the scene of Tom's drowning, or the quarrels of Ursula, her sisters and brother with Billy Pillins and his tribe, the account of Ursula's teaching experience at the Brinsley Street school, the family's move to Beldover, Ursula's college experience. Surely in view of such a sequence of objective and realistic scenes we cannot doubt that Lawrence properly belongs among realistic and perhaps among traditional novelists.

Not only are there realistic scenes in the novel but the form, to the casual glance, is there too. Lawrence, as it seems to the reader at first, had no difficult problem to solve in respect to form. The story is told chronologically and is brought to an adequate completion after Ursula breaks with Skrebensky, falls ill, and recuperates.

And yet, is it really the case that *The Rainbow* exemplifies the classical tradition as it was brought to its full development by Henry James? When the question is pressed, we cannot be as certain as we were before that the answer can be positive and unqualified. For plot, in the sense of a scheme or framework that unifies action, which in turn exhibits and arises from delineated character—this is not to be found in *The Rainbow* any more than it is to be found in *Women in Love*. This is not to say the book lacks form but that it lacks form in the traditional sense: character is not exhibited in action, nor does action arise from character. There is no interrelated series of episodes rising to a climax and reaching a resolution after which the novel ends. Indeed the "persons of the drama," such as we find them in Fielding, in Jane Austen, in George Eliot, and in Henry James are not to be found in *The Rainbow*. And surface proof of this contention is that the love experiences of Lydia, Anna, and Ursula are very much alike and only immediately after a fresh reading can we differentiate them. Indeed, in essence we cannot differentiate them at all. We know these women by name: one is a Pole and her child, born in England, is also a Pole. In the same superficial manner we know Tom Brangwen and Will. Tom is a farmer, working land the family has owned for two hundred years, while the other is vaguely a teacher and a quasi-artist. But we know none of these persons as we know Emma Woodhouse or Isabel Archer. Lawrence is obviously not interested in doing what Jane Austen and Henry James had done. I do not mean this in denigration of Lawrence's work. Surely one hundred years after the publication of *The Origin of Species* it is too late to apply irrelevant, because obsolete, criteria to art forms, which are as much in flux as anything ever was or is in history. What we must do is to discover the intention of the work itself, since that intention is realized in it. And this, as we know, is quite different from trying to discover what Lawrence himself took to be the intention of his own work.

What was Lawrence actually doing? Beyond his interest in the story of the Brangwens there is another, and if I am right, a more basic interest—that of presenting the phenomenology of pure experience, of experience qua experience. I know the phrase is a heavy one and there will be readers who will react to it as Lawrence might have done, jeering at what seems gobbledegook. But I know of no more exact way to characterize what Lawrence was actually doing. If the phrase must be withdrawn, however, his interest can be formulated in the following words: in *The Rainbow* Lawrence sought to present in language the felt quality of experience; he tried to convey by means of language the ebb and flow of the affective life, particularly the felt quality of erotic passion and of religious emotion—or at least of what he took to be religious emotion.

We have a statement by Lawrence that shows not only that it was the felt quality of experience that he was interested in but that he was fully aware that this was his central interest. He is writing in 1920 about verse, but his remarks apply to his own prose as they do to his own or Whitman's verse or to free verse in general. In the Introduction to *New Poems*, which Mr. Anthony Beal has made available to us, we read that "the poetry of that which is at hand" gives us the immediate, the instant, present. Lawrence writes:

Let me feel the heavy, silting, sucking mud, the spinning of sky winds. Let me feel them both in purest contact, the nakedness of sucking weight, nakedly passing radiance. . . . Give me the still, white seething, the incandescence and the coldness of the incarnate moment . . . the moment, the immediate present, the Now. . . .

Two pages later we read:

One realm we have never conquered: the pure present. One great mystery of time is *terra incognita* to us: the instant. The most superb mystery we have hardly recognized: the immediate instant self.

To the immediate instant self, he continues, the writer of verse "gives us the clue." [1] This, of course, is not altogether true. Before Lawrence, impressionist painting had succeeded in presenting us with the instant now of visual sensory qualities.

True, there are the objective, the realistic scenes in *The Rainbow*, already acknowledged, and these cannot be ignored. But we fail to grasp the book if we assume these represent its main intention. For what action is to be found in the book is not action that reveals character. There is no response of one character to another or to a situation in which the decisions are reached as men react normally and habitually to situations, in terms of values and moral principles. What we find beyond the surface, is the response of a center of consciousness (not a person) to a situation or to another center of consciousness, and the emphasis is on the felt quality of the affective experience.

This is best shown by concrete example. In the early days at the Marsh Farm, Tom Brangwen feels towards Lydia a mixture of erotic passions which range from awakening desire to urgent need to the intensity and ecstasy of fulfillment, to a violent, gloomy, wordless emotion "which is almost hate." Gradually the feeling changes and Tom and Lydia come together again "within one rushing hastening flame" of erotic need. The need is satisfied and there is nothing beyond. "They are together in an eternal embrace" which is followed by "a severance between them." We must remember that the snippets I can quote and the paraphrase I can provide, however close to Lawrence's text I may have been able to keep them, can only serve as mnemonic devices to help the reader recall the novel. When we read the account in its full context we see that Lawrence is bent on conveying the quality of affective experience; it is experience as such, experience disengaged from a substantial individual self, that we are presented with. A person endowed with character, as a person cannot help but be, individuated by fundamental moral commitments which are either served or betrayed, and about which the person may be right or wrong—such a substantial self does not enter into the picture. The following passage refers to Lydia and Tom:

And when he arrived home, there was no sign between them. He waited and waited till she came. And as he waited, his limbs seemed strong and splendid to him, his hands seemed like passionate servants to him, goodly, he felt a stupendous power in himself, of life, and of urgent, strong blood.

She was sure to come at last, and touch him. Then he burst into flame for her, and lost himself. They looked at each other, a deep laugh at the bottom of their eyes, and he went to take of her again, wholesale, mad to revel in the inexhaustible wealth of her, to bury himself in the depths of her in an inexhaustible exploration, she all the while revelling in that he revelled in her, tossed all her secrets aside and plunged to that which was secret to her as well, whilst she quivered with fear and the last anguish of delight.

What did it matter who they were, whether they knew each other or not?

The hour passed away again, there was severance between them, and rage and misery and bereavement for her, and deposition and toiling at the mill with slaves for him. But no matter. They had had their hour, and should it chime again, they were ready for it, ready to renew the game at the point where it was left off, on the edge of the outer darkness, when the secrets within the woman are game for the man, hunted doggedly, when the secrets of the woman are the man's adventure, and they both give themselves to the adventure.—CHAPTER II

But because their experience had been abstracted from their substantial selves, because it is not referred to persons who are defined in terms of character, and because attention is directed to the pure erotic experience, this situation does not essentially differ from the experience later undergone by Will and Anna during the first months of married life. During the honeymoon in their cottage by the church at Cossethay we are told about Will's relation to Anna:

One day, he was a bachelor, living with the world. The next day, he was with her, as remote from the world as if the two of them were buried, like a seed in darkness. Suddenly, like a chestnut falling out of a burr, he was shed naked and glistening on to a soft, fecund earth, leaving behind him the hard rind of worldly knowledge and experience. He heard it in the hucksters' cries, the noise of carts, the calling of children. And it was all like the hard, shed rind, discarded. Inside, in the softness and stillness of the room, was the naked kernel, that palpitated in silent activity, absorbed in reality. Inside the room was a great steadiness, a core of living eternity. Only far outside, at the rim, went on the noise and the destruction. Here at the centre the great wheel was motionless, centred upon itself. Here was a poised, unflawed stillness that was beyond time, because it remained the same, inexhaustible, unchanging, unexhausted.

As they lay close together, complete and beyond the touch of time or change, it was as if they were at the very centre of all the slow wheeling of space and the rapid agitation of life, deep, deep inside them all, at the centre where there is utter radiance, and eternal being, and the silence absorbed in praise: the steady core of all movements, the unawakened sleep of all wakefulness. They found themselves there, and they lay still, in each other's arms; for their moment they were at the heart of eternity, whilst time roared far off, forever far off, towards the rim.

Then gradually they were passed away from the supreme centre, down the circles of praise and joy and gladness, further and further out, towards the noise and the friction. But their hearts had burned and were tempered by the inner reality, they were unalterably glad.

Gradually they began to wake up, the noises outside became more real. They understood and answered the call outside.—CHAPTER VI

Nor does this experience differ from that of Ursula's intense erotic passion after she begins her liaison with Skrebensky:

. . . He kissed her, and she quivered as if she were being destroyed, shattered. The lighted vessel vibrated, and broke in her soul, the light fell, struggled, and went dark. She was all dark, will-less, having only the receptive will.

He kissed her, with his soft, enveloping kisses, and she responded to them completely, her mind, her soul gone out. Darkness cleaving to darkness, she hung close to him, pressed herself into [the] soft flow of his kiss, pressed herself down, down to the source and core of his kiss, herself covered and enveloped in the warm, fecund flow of his kiss, that travelled over her, flowed over her, covered her, flowed over the last fibre of her, so they were one stream, one dark fecundity, and she clung at the core of him, with her lips holding open the very bottommost source of him.

. . . .

They stood enjoying the unmitigated kiss, taking it, giving to it endlessly, and still it was not exhausted. Their veins fluttered, their blood ran together as one stream.

Till gradually a sleep, a heaviness settled on them, a drowse, and out of the drowse, a small light of consciousness woke up. Ursula became aware of the night around her, and water lapping and running full just near, the trees roaring and soughing in gusts of wind.—CHAPTER XV

If we did not know that these three quotations constitute accounts of the experience of three different couples, we could not, by reading them, say that they did. Only in one respect that I shall discuss in another context, can I find a difference between one of these couples and the other two. And the reason is that if we take character away, and the specific constellation of values commitment to which constitutes character (with whatever consistencies or inconsistencies these commitments may be maintained), and if we take action away as determined by character, and if we strip off all other components of the person and leave nothing else but the affective flow—whether it be erotic passion or hatred or boredom—the basis of distinction between one stream of affective life and another is withdrawn. One erotic need may be more or less intense than another, one hatred more implacable than another, one state of boredom more pervasive than another, but we cannot distinguish them as we distinguish Emma from Mrs. Elton or Mr. Knightly from Mr. Elton.

Among the erotic experiences of these three couples some distinctions can be noticed, but they are external and cannot be the basis for distinguishing the men and women who underwent them. The most obvious distinction is that the erotic passion of Tom and Lydia is not rendered as fully as that of Will and Anna. And while Lawrence conveys fully the inwardness of Ursula's affective life, and not merely her love passion, Ursula's lover, Skrebensky, is seen always from the outside. Again, somehow

Tom Brangwen comes off as more of a person than Will. But the
reason for this is that the account of Tom's activities is fuller,
his interests, background and relationships with others more detailed—which is to say that Tom appears to us as a person, while
Will remains relatively shadowy and indistinct, because in the
delineation of Tom the traditional means of characterization are
more fully employed. During Anna's childhood, whatever is going on, whatever we are appraised of, is rendered from Tom's
point of view and Lawrence maintains the standpoint with some
consistency. After Tom's death by drowning, the standpoint
shifts to Anna, Lydia recedes and is rarely exhibited as Ursula's
grandmother, and Will, Anna's husband, is not as fully defined as
his wife. The latter retains the center of attention until Ursula
begins to grow up and she gains it.

[2]

There are several occasions, then, in *The Rainbow* when Lawrence manages successfully to present the quality of experience
as felt. And the reason for his success is the use of a device that he
did not use in *Sons and Lovers* but does use in *Women in Love*
and in a number of the short stories. I propose to call this device
"the constitutive symbol." Before we can examine the successful
presentation of experience as such, we must consider the nature
of this symbol. But because such an examination will lead us into a
somewhat abstract disquisition, I shall not undertake it in this
chapter but shall take it up in the Appendix, saying here only
that a constitutive symbol is a symbol whose referend cannot be
fully exhausted by explication, because that to which it refers is
symbolized not only *through* it but *in* it. This is not true, as I have
already suggested, of what I shall call the pseudo-symbol or the
quasi-symbol, nor is it true of a metaphor. In the metaphor the
vehicle and the tenor can be exhibited and fully apprehended independently of each other, in spite of the "interanimation" to
which I. A. Richards has called attention.

There are at least two powerful constitutive symbols in *The Rainbow*, although more careful search will reveal a third. I refer to the scene in which Will and Anna stack the sheaves in the moonlight, the cathedral scene, and the scene towards the end of the book in which Ursula runs from the horse. Of the stacking of the sheaves we are told:

They went across the stubble to where the long rows of upreared shocks ended. Curiously populous that part of the field looked, where shocks rode erect; the rest was open and prostrate.

The air was all hoary silver. She looked around her. Trees stood vaguely at their distance, as if waiting like heralds, for the signal to approach. In this space of vague crystal her heart seemed like a bell ringing. She was afraid lest the sound should be heard.

"You take this row," she said to the youth, and passing on, she stooped in the next row of lying sheaves, grasping her hands in the tresses of the oats, lifting the heavy corn in either hand, carrying it, as it hung heavily against her, to the cleared space, where she set the two sheaves sharply down, bringing them together with a faint, keen clash. Her two bulks stood leaning together. He was coming, walking shadowily [*sic*] with the gossamer dusk, carrying his two sheaves. She waited near by. He set his sheaves with a keen, faint clash, next to her sheaves. They rode unsteadily. He tangled the tresses of corn. It hissed like a fountain. He looked up and laughed.

Then she turned away towards the moon, which seemed glowingly to uncover her bosom every time she faced it. He went to the vague emptiness of the field opposite, dutifully.

They stooped, grasped the wet, soft hair of the corn, lifted the heavy bundles, and returned. She was always first. She set down her sheaves, making a pent house with those others. He was coming shadowy across the stubble, carrying his bundles. She turned away, hearing only the sharp hiss of his mingling corn. She walked between the moon and his shadowy figure.

She took her new two sheaves and walked towards him, as he rose from stooping over the earth. He was coming out of the near distance. She set down her sheaves to make a new stook. They were unsure. Her hands fluttered. Yet she broke away, and turned to the moon, which laid bare her bosom, so she felt as if her bosom were heaving and panting with moonlight. And he had to put up her two sheaves, which had fallen down. He worked in silence. The rhythm of the work carried him away again, as she was coming near.

They worked together, coming and going, in a rhythm, which carried their feet and their bodies in tune. . . .

It seems to him as if they would never meet. The work goes on, the moon grows brighter and more clear, the corn glistens.

Till at last, they met at the shock, facing each other, sheaves in hand. And he was silvery with moonlight, with a moonlit, shadowy face that frightened her. She waited for him.

"Put yours down!" she said.

"No, it's your turn." His voice was twanging and insistent.

She set her sheaves against the shock. He saw her hands glisten among the spray of grain. And he dropped his sheaves and he trembled as he took her in his arms. He had overtaken her, and it was his privilege to kiss her. She was sweet and fresh with the night air, and sweet with the scent of grain. And the whole rhythm of him beat into his kisses, and still he pursued her, in his kisses, and still she was not quite overcome. He wondered over the moonlight on her nose! All the moonlight upon her, all the darkness within her! All the night in his arms, darkness and shine, he possessed of it all! All the night for him now, to unfold, to venture within, all the mystery to be entered, all the discovery to be made.

Trembling with keen triumph, his heart was white as a star as he drove his kisses nearer.

"My love!" she called, in a low voice, from afar. The low sound seemed to call to him from far off, under the moon, to him who was unaware. He stopped, quivered, and listened.

"My love," came again the low, plaintive call, like a bird unseen in the night.

He was afraid. His heart quivered and broke. He was stopped.

"Anna," he said, as if he answered her from a distance, unsure.

"My love."

And he drew near, and she drew near.

"Anna," he said, in wonder and birthpain of love.

"My love," she said, her voice growing rapturous. And they kissed on the mouth, in rapture and surprise, long, real kisses. The kiss lasted, there among the moonlight.—CHAPTER IV

What does the scene mean? Let me repeat that it is my contention that a successful presentation of a constitutive symbol cannot be exhaustively paraphrased. Ultimately the symbol means itself and what discursive analysis can give us does not take us very far. But surely no one can read the magnificent scene without realizing how the work in the gold of the moon-flood is a stately dance, hastening gradually in tempo until the young man and the young woman come together in the wonder and the birthpain of love. The moon, of course, is Anna's female goddess. Anna is dominant and the young man follows, seeks, and gains what he seeks when Anna chooses to yield. When the young man sets down the sheaves for the first time, the corn hisses like a fountain. Water is invoked, for water, the moon, and fertility are a usual symbolic combination involving the mystery of sex. The hair of the corn is wet. And it is Anna who begins to make a house of the sheaves. When they finally come together, the moonlight is on her, the darkness within—the mystery of her womanhood—and it is the dark mystery within that he has to discover, to enter, and to possess in full.

Although a digression, it is interesting to notice that in this passage Lawrence does not have to strain language to its breaking point, as he sometimes does, when he tries to convey the quality of experience as such. Contrast this passage with that in *Sons and Lovers* in which Paul and Clara come together and you will see how in the earlier one he failed and in the latter he succeeded.

[3]

While in *The Rainbow*, as I read it, Lawrence's interest centers on the quality of erotic experience as felt, a secondary but important interest lies in the quality of the religious experience of Lydia, and of Will and Anna. It is not difficult to put together the various accounts of religion Lawrence has given us in *The*

Rainbow, for in spite of the apparent conflict between Will and Anna, there is no essential difference in response among the accounts. About Anna we are told in Chapter IV that when she was seventeen she became an assiduous church-goer, but "the *language* meant nothing to her. It seemed false." Her religious feelings when not expressed, were passionately moving. Later, in Chapter VI, we are told that while she had never questioned any beliefs and from habit attended church regularly, she had ceased to come with anticipation, but a few days after her marriage she went to church expectant and delighted. But a little later a contrast is drawn—or seems to be drawn—between Anna's religious response and that of her husband. After accepting for a brief period in her high school days the injunctions of the minister, they palled quickly for Anna. Her soul wanted not social duty but something for herself (Chapter VI). She hated the ostensible church because it did not fulfill anything in her, whereas for Will the church had an irresistible attraction, for it was the source of "a dark nameless emotion, the emotion of all great mysteries of passion." But dogma, teaching, and sermon he simply disregarded. "The verity" for Will Brangwen "was his connection with Anna and his connection with the church, his real being lay in his dark emotional experience of the Infinite, of the Absolute."

Lawrence undertakes to give us an account of the dark emotional experience of the Infinite, and by the use of the constitutive symbol of Will's "beloved Lincoln Cathedral," he manages as successfully as such things can be managed, to convey to us the actual felt quality of the quasi-mystical experience Will underwent the first time he showed Anna the cathedral. I shall quote a number of passages, hoping that they will suffice to prove the point:

. . . In a little ecstasy he found himself in the porch, on the brink of the unrevealed. He looked up to the lovely unfolding of the stone. He was to pass within to the perfect womb.

. . . His soul leapt up into the gloom, into possession, it reeled, it swooned with a great escape, it quivered in the womb, in the hush and the gloom of fecundity, like seed of procreation in ecstasy.

. . . Here, the twilight was the very essence of life, the coloured darkness was the embryo of all light, and the day. Here, the very first dawn was breaking, the very last sunset sinking, and the immemorial darkness, whereof life's day would blossom and fall away again, re-echoed peace and profound immemorial silence.

Away from time, always outside of time! Between east and west, between dawn and sunset, the church lay like a seed in silence, dark before germination, silenced after death. Containing birth and death, potential with all the noise and transitation of life, the cathedral remained hushed, a great, involved seed, whereof the flower would be radiant life inconceivable, but whose beginning and whose end were the circle of silence. Spanned round with the rainbow, the jewelled gloom folded music upon silence, light upon darkness, fecundity upon death, as a seed folds leaf upon leaf and silence upon the root and the flower, hushing up the secret of all between its parts, the death out of which it fell, the life into which it has dropped, the immortality it involves, and the death it will embrace again.

Here in the church, "before" and "after" were folded together, all was contained in oneness. Brangwen came to his consummation. Out of the doors of the womb he had come, putting aside the wings of the womb, and proceeding into the light. Through daylight and day-after-day he had come, knowledge after knowledge, and experience after experience, remembering the darkness of the womb, having prescience of the darkness after death. Then between-while he had pushed open the doors of the cathedral, and entered the twilight of both darknesses, the hush of the two-fold silence, where dawn was sunset and the beginning and the end were one.

Here the stone leapt up from the plain of earth, leapt up in a manifold, clustered desire each time, up, away from the horizontal earth, through twilight and dusk and the whole range of desire, through the swerving, the declination, ah, to the ecstasy, the touch, to the meeting and the consummation, the meeting, the clasp, the close embrace, the neutrality, the perfect, swooning consummation, the timeless ecstasy.

There his soul remained, at the apex of the arch, clinched in the time-less ecstasy, consummated.

And there was no time nor life nor death, but only this, this timeless consummation, where the thrust from earth met the thrust from earth and the arch was locked on the keystone of ecstasy. This was all, this was everything. Till he came to himself in the world below. Then again he gathered himself together, in transit, every jet of him strained and leaped, leaped clear into the darkness above, to the fecundity and the unique mystery, to the touch, the clasp, the consummation, the climax of eternity, the apex of the arch.—CHAPTER VII

Anna is first impressed by her husband's response, but it finally makes her angry, and she catches "at little things, which saved her from being swept forward headlong in the tide of passion . . ." (Chapter VII). She turns on him jeering and ridiculing his feel-ing, until she finally destroys his passion.

Let me mention, hastily, that there is another reference to re-ligion later on, when we are told of the influence Winifred had on Ursula during their love affair; but it only adds up to the fact that the older woman showed her beloved how to strip religion of its dogma and "humanize it" (Chapter XII). The reference is brief and it tells us very little about the religious substance of *The Rainbow*.

Religion in this book is stripped from any relation to the life of the community. Particularly in the case of Will and Anna, the little church or the cathedral is one thing and the outside world another. Religion is not the basis for a moral scheme; the emphasis throughout is put on the subjectivity of the experience. True, for Lydia there is an external object which elicits her experience, but the object is a metaphysical something, abstract, a great abso-lute, a great mystery, conceived in just these terms. This is not the God of Abraham but the God of the philosophers. In the case of Anna and Will, in so far as we are told, there seems to be no ques-tion of God at all. In church and in the cathedral they undergo experiences that are satisfying to them, but these are aroused, not by the contemplation of God and a feeling of relationship to

Him, however conceived, as an object of religious devotion, but by the church, the building itself, the environment, the cathedral. To put it baldly, the stimulus does not seem to have mattered at all. What matters is the response itself, its depth and amplitude, its satisfying or fulfilling quality. In a sense Will and Anna carried Schleirmacher to an extreme logical conclusion. The inwardness of the experience is deep indeed. But it is solipsistic. Religiously speaking, Will and Anna are Leibnizian monads. And as a result, religion does not serve—and this is made explicit to us about Anna, but seems to hold for Will also—as a means of establishing a relationship with their fellow beings. In the sense of binding, and of establishing community and love towards their fellows, and hence of generating and sustaining a moral scheme, Anna rejects religion outright and Will rejects it implicitly.

Lawrence takes great pains to bring out the exact nature of the experience that Anna and Will undergo, marking the difference between them with precision. In order to be faithful to his account, it is best to give the passages in which this difference is made clear. About Anna we read:

. . . After a short time, she was not very much interested in being good. Her soul was in quest of something, which was not just being good, and doing one's best. No, she wanted something else: something that was not her ready-made duty. Everything seemed to be merely a matter of social duty, and never of her *self*. They talked about her soul, but somehow never managed to rouse or to implicate her soul. As yet her soul was not brought in at all. . . . She became hostile to the ostensible church, she hated it for not fulfilling anything in her. The Church told her to be good: very well, she had no idea of contradicting what it said. The Church talked about her soul, about the welfare of mankind, as if the saving of her soul lay in her performing certain acts conducive to the welfare of mankind. Well and good—it was so, then.

Nevertheless, as she sat in church her face had a pathos and poignancy. Was this what she had come to hear: how, by doing this thing and by not doing that, she could save her soul? She did not contradict it. But the pathos of her face gave the lie. There was something else

she wanted to hear, it was something else she asked for from the
Church. . . .

By contrast, Will's experience is rendered in these terms:

. . . Church had an irresistible attraction for him. And he paid no
more attention to that part of the service which was Church to her,
than if he had been an angel or a fabulous beast sitting there. He simply paid no heed to the sermon or to the meaning of the service. There
was something thick, dark, dense, powerful about him that irritated
her too deeply for her to speak of it. The Church teaching in itself
meant nothing to him. "And forgive us our trespasses as we forgive
them that trespass against us"—it simply did not touch him. It might
have been mere sounds, and it would have acted upon him in the
same way. He did not want things to be intelligible. And he did not
care about his trespasses, neither about the trespasses of his neighbour,
when he was in church. Leave that care for weekdays. When he was in
church, he took no more notice of his daily life. It was weekday stuff.
As for the welfare of mankind—he merely did not realize that there
was any such thing: except on weekdays, when he was good-natured
enough. In church, he wanted a dark, nameless emotion, the emotion
of all the great mysteries of passion.

He was not interested in the *thought* of himself or of her; oh, and
how that irritated her! He ignored the sermon, he ignored the greatness of mankind, he did not admit the immediate importance of mankind. He did not care about himself as a human being. He did not
attach any vital importance to his life in the drafting office, or his life
among men. That was just merely the margin to the text. The verity
was his connection with Anna and his connection with the Church,
his real being lay in his dark emotional experience of the Infinite, of
the Absolute. And the great mysterious, illuminated capitals to the
text, were his feelings with the Church.—CHAPTER VI

Whether the kind of dark emotional experience Lydia, Anna,
and Will sought and sometimes underwent in church can or cannot be properly called a religious experience is fortunately a question we need not explore *au fond*. All that we need say is that it
is the experience these people undergo and it is conceived by them

as that which for them is valid in religion. We might also observe that Lawrence seems to think of it as genuine religious experience. The imagery of this passage interrelates three aspects of human experience that we moderns are accustomed to distinguish and dissociate implicitly and without effort: sex, religion, and death. In Will's mind these aspects of life are so fused that it would be hopeless and inaccurate to try to disengage them and to indicate which of them serves as vehicle and which as tenor. Also, Will is outside the orthodox tradition of our civilization: Eros and Thanatos reign and between the prenatal darkness of germination and the darkness of death, the sexual union, the union of the arch, takes place without benefit of providential Father or of loving Son. The meeting of man and woman in the sexual union is impersonal because profoundly and ineradicably monadic, it is, in some sort of fashion, although involving a man and a woman, isolated for each.[2]

[6]

One consequence of Lawrence's effort to present the phenomenology of experience should be observed. I said above that *The Rainbow* seems to be firmly anchored in social reality, for the story begins at the Marsh Farm and its geographical location is clearly indicated. But this statement must now be qualified, and the qualification holds for the whole book, including the fine chapters in which Lawrence gives us Ursula's maturing reaction to her world, to college, and to her uncle's colliery. In spite of Lawrence's firm delineation of the external world and his brilliant rendering of the spirit of place, because he draws our main attention to the felt quality of experience, he fails to integrate the experience of his characters with their external world. Will and Ursula are English, and so is Anna in spite of her foreign ancestry. But these people are already contemporary, uprooted people, even though they do not know it. We are told about Will Brangwen that "for his own part, for his private being, Brangwen felt that the

whole of the man's world was exterior and extraneous to his own
real life with Anna" (Chapter VII). This feeling is experienced by
all of the persons who appear in the book: external reality is in
some sense epiphenomenal; they live their lives from within,
they have cut the nexus between themselves and their world, to
which they do not feel they belong and which they repudiate. Together they constitute a monad.

In pointing to the monadic nature of the men and women we
find in Lawrence's novels, I am not passing an adverse moral judgment against them or against the man who created them. But it is
necessary to understand what has been presented to us, for otherwise we fail to understand the contribution that Lawrence made
to our grasp of the modern world. That contribution begins with
The Rainbow, and continues, now in purely dramatic terms, now
in terms that are abstract, conceptual, until the end of his life. But
there is a radical difference between the dramatic presentation to
be found in *The Rainbow* and *Women in Love* and that which we
find elsewhere. In these two books, the criticism of her world is
made by Ursula; her reaction to the colliery and to her uncle who
serves the industrial monster are authentic parts of the novel, just
as is her reaction to her college education.

Ursula's reaction to the industrial world is recorded towards the
end of the chapter entitled "Shame":

Every man his own little side-show, his home, but the pit owns
every man. The women have what is left. What's left of this man, or
what is left of that—it doesn't matter altogether. The pit takes all that
really matters.

"It is the same everywhere," burst out Winifred. "It is the office, or
the shop, or the business that gets the man, the woman gets the bit
the shop can't digest. What is he at home, a man? He is a meaningless
lump—a standing machine, a machine out of work."

"They know they are sold," said Tom Brangwen. "That's where
it is. They know they are sold to their job. If a woman talks her throat
out, what difference can it make? The man's sold to his job. So the
women don't bother. They take what they can catch—and *vogue la
galère*."

"Aren't they very strict here?" asked Miss Inger.

"Oh, no. Mrs. Smith has two sisters who have just changed husbands. They're not very particular—neither are they very interested. They go dragging along what is left from the pits. They're not interested enough to be very immoral—it all amounts to the same thing, moral or immoral—just a question of pit-wages. The most moral duke in England makes two hundred thousand a year out of these pits. He keeps the morality end up."

. . . .

But her Uncle Tom and her mistress remained there among the horde, cynically reviling the monstrous state and yet adhering to it, like a man who reviles his mistress, yet who is in love with her. She knew her Uncle Tom perceived what was going on. But she knew moreover that in spite of his criticism and condemnation, he still wanted the great machine. His only happy moments, his only moments of pure freedom, were when he was serving the machine. Then, and then only, when the machine caught him up, was he free from the hatred of himself, could he act wholly, without cynicism and unreality.

His real mistress was the machine, and the real mistress of Winifred was the machine. She too, Winifred, worshipped the impure abstraction, the mechanisms of matter. There, there, in the machine, in service of the machine, was she free from the clog and degradation of human feeling. There in the monstrous mechanism that held all matter, living or dead, in its service, did she achieve her consummation and her perfect unison, her immortality.

Hatred sprang up in Ursula's heart. If she could she would smash the machine.—CHAPTER XII

Lawrence was not the writer who began the revolt against industrialism and the human degradation it brought about. But Ursula's reaction to the machine is genuine, utterly authentic, and as we find it expressed in *The Rainbow* it is an organic part of the novel. We can, of course, generalize from it, and we can also relate it to Lawrence's own passionate hatred of the machine and its evils —something which he knew at first hand. But in the novel itself the hatred is a thoroughly organic part of Ursula's experience, and those who feel sympathy for Ursula do so simply because their minds were made up before coming to the passages just quoted. A

Marxist would not react against the machine in the same manner and would consider Ursula's attitude romantic and reactionary. It is not the machine, he would say, that must be disowned, but the owners, who must be expropriated; and the most moral duke in England who makes two hundred thousand a year out of these pits must either be liquidated or brought around to accept "socialism." I make this obvious remark to press again a point that has already been made: when we have a genuine work of art before us, if we derive moral judgments from it, it is not the art that forces the judgments on us, but our own implicit choices and commitments. In the novel, Ursula's reaction to the pits is her own. If there are indications (and these cannot be denied) that Lawrence sided with Ursula against her uncle and her ex-lover, these are not sufficiently obtrusive to turn the novel into propaganda.

Equally valid within its context, and equally authentic and organic in the novel, are Ursula's reactions to college during her last two years. But here again a quotation conveys the matter much more clearly and efficiently than paraphrase. The impact, however, of the following passage will not be felt unless we bear in mind that when Ursula first began college, she approached the experience with high, idealistic, romantic expectations which for a while were not given the lie.

But during this year the glamour began to depart from college. The professors were not priests initiated into the deep mysteries of life and knowledge. After all, they were only middle-men handling wares they had become so accustomed to that they were oblivious of them. What was Latin?—So much dry goods of knowledge. What was the Latin class altogether but a sort of second-hand curio shop, where one bought curios and learned the market-value of curios; dull curios, too, on the whole. She was as bored by the Latin curiosities as she was by Chinese and Japanese curiosities in the antique shops. "Antiques"— the very word made her soul fall flat and dead.

The life went out of her studies, why, she did not know. But the whole thing seemed sham, spurious; spurious Gothic arches, spurious peace, spurious Latinity, spurious dignity of France, spurious naïveté of

Chaucer. It was a second-hand dealer's shop, and one bought an equip-
ment for an examination. This was only a little side-show to the fac-
tories of the town. Gradually the perception stole into her. This was
no religious retreat, no seclusion of pure learning. It was a little ap-
prentice-shop where one was further equipped for making money. The
college itself was a little, slovenly laboratory for the factory.

A harsh and ugly disillusion came over her again, the same darkness
and bitter gloom from which she was never safe now, the realization
of the permanent substratum of ugliness under everything.—CHAP-
TER XV

But Ursula's reaction is not a purely negative one. It does not
merely express a rejection of the unashamed utilitarian function
that the college actually performs under the guise of a pure dedication. It was not merely that "the religious virtue of knowledge
was become a flunkey to the goal of material success" (Chapter
XV). Her reaction springs from a need that was unfulfilled and
of which we are given a relatively clear account by Lawrence two
pages after the last quotation. Father Tiverton quotes the passage I have in mind, but as I read him he is not interested in what
to me seems to be its central significance. For Ursula's reaction
against the machine and the sham and the second-hand quality of
the goods bought at college springs from an unsatisfied religious
need—although, of course, in the sense in which Lawrence employs the term. Ursula is coming to the end of her college period
and reviews her experience. She recognizes the various phases
through which she has gone, and acknowledges that these are
phases through which she had passed. But she herself, what was
she? She did not know what she was. She knew she was pure rejection, pure refusal. But why the rejection, the refusal? Because
she had not yet found herself. And the reason she had not was that
men insisted that the world in which they lived was all light, a
bright area lit by man's completest consciousness in which everything was disclosed forever, but her soul "had acknowledged in a
great heave of terror only the outer darkness" (Chapter XV).
The lighted area, the ostensible world, was the world of men, of

science, of efficiency, of the machine; but she could see the darkness beyond the light, and she felt the foolishness of men who insisted on denying the darkness. "Beyond our light and our order
there is nothing," they said and would jeer at any one who would
dare throw a firebrand into the darkness. But why is the darkness beyond the light denied, and those who would acknowledge
it, why are they jeered at? Ursula had peered beyond the light and
had found in it "points of light, like the eyes of wild beasts,
gleaming, penetrating, vanishing."

Nevertheless the darkness wheeled round about, with grey shadow-
shapes of wild beasts, and also with dark shadow-shapes of the angels,
whom the light fenced out, as it fenced out the more familiar beasts of
darkness. And some, having for a moment seen the darkness, saw it
bristling with the tufts of the hyaena and the wolf; and some, having
given up their vanity of the light, having died in their own conceit, saw
the gleam in the eyes of the wolf and the hyaena, that it was the flash
of the sword of angels, flashing at the door to come in, that the angels
in the darkness were lordly and terrible and not to be denied, like the
flash of fangs.—CHAPTER XV

What does this mean? I take Lawrence to be referring to two
areas of darkness: within, the darkness of urges that are not admitted, and without, the cosmic darkness, the great mystery to
which our religious responses are ultimately addressed, when we
strip from them the local expression in belief, rite, and cult. Did
Lawrence ever clearly make a statement that would confirm my
interpretation? Not in the abstract terms in which I have put it.
But dramatically he did. His was an archaic mind, as I have already pointed out, which accepted what we moderns reject: the
intimate relationship between the mystery of sex and the mystery
of the cosmos.

Having reached the point where we are able to comprehend
Ursula's reaction to industry, to the machine, and to college, and
are aware of Ursula's acceptance of mystery, we are in a position
to grasp the complex achievement that *The Rainbow* represents.

It begins with an account of the Brangwens, who have lived "for generations on the Marsh Farm." As has been noticed by other critics, the quality of the writing of the first pages of the novel is Biblical, and the substance of the account is the quality of life in the country, in which men worked the earth and were fulfilled by their work, but in which the women wanted another life, "something that was not blood-intimacy." "About 1840 a canal was constructed across the meadows of the Marsh Farm, connecting the newly-opened collieries of the Erewash Valley." And the process is initiated that is finally to end with Ursula's revolt against the machine and college and with her inchoate longing to acknowledge the darkness beyond the social world. The contrast between the bucolic, slow, organic happiness that is enjoyed by the earlier Brangwens and the disruption and uprootedness of Ursula is as much the essence of the novel as is the account of the erotic experience of three generations of Brangwens and of the religious response of Anna and Will. Lawrence has given us a magnificent picture: the story unrolls as a long Chinese scroll unrolls, presenting not only the felt quality of experience but also the ground from which the emotional solipsism of his characters springs—the alienation from the soil. To the themes examined— the erotic and the religious—we must add then this other. *The Rainbow* presents the uprooting which took place during the period between 1840, when the canal was built, and ends with the recuperation of Ursula from her illness. The uprooting is the result of the loss by these people of the "blood-intimacy" which their dedication to the soil made possible. But in *The Rainbow* we do not find philosophy or sociology but drama. Whether the presentation can be formulated in general terms is, for the reader of the book interested in the novel, irrelevant.

CHAPTER NINE

The Form of
 Women in Love

IT IS an old story that Lawrence was, early in his career, forced to abandon the classical form of the novel. We remember his explosion in a letter of 1912: "They want me to have form: that means, they want me to have *their* pernicious, ossiferous skin-and-grief form, and I won't."[1] In much of his work Lawrence achieved neither pernicious nor ossiferous nor any other form. *Aaron's Rod, Kangaroo, The Plumed Serpent* are novels of major pretension that are padded, rambling works, poorly thought and poorly executed. But in *Women in Love* and in a few other of his major novels and in some of his short stories he succeeded in achieving a form appropriate to the substance of his poetry. Of course, his is not the kind of form that can be expressed in simple terms—as one expresses the rhyme scheme of a sonnet. And the reason, as we have seen, is that in the classical sense of the term there is no action or plot in his work. He was interested, mainly, in revealing the quality of experience as experienced and he came as close to success here as is possible. The revelation of experience is undertaken by Lawrence, not merely to give the reader the "feel" of it, but also to exhibit the values discovered and actualized by it. Were he not interested in both experience and its values his work would not be as important as it is for us. The form he achieves is grasped by us when we notice the progress of developing experience: the beginning and gathering of passion, its swelling to flood-strength, its leaping over the dyke or its baffled pounding against it. Because the form of action in the behavioral sense is easier to perceive than the structure of inward experience, a first reading of Lawrence and even a second or a third gives us little more than a chaos of incidents and scenes that, however brilliantly presented, seem to lack formal inter-relationships. But persistent search for the structure of the work is at last rewarded. Synoptically we grasp the pattern of an ordered whole. We notice the first signs of nascent desire turning into clearly directed urge and notice the passional urge seeking satisfaction and succeeding or arriving at frustration; we notice the pattern of attraction and repulsion, the harmony of wills or their clash, and back of these harmonies and conflicts we notice the values that these inward commotions seek to realize and succeed or fail in realizing. And strange as it might seem, since Lawrence is so frequently dismissed as anti-rational, we notice also the growth in wisdom on the part of his characters—or of what Lawrence takes to be wisdom—and the causes for the success or failure of that growth.

More concretely, although *Women in Love* is incredibly rich in detail and dense in substance, its organization is achieved by means that, formulated in abstract terms, appear to be relatively simple. Its form is given to it by the account of the genesis and development of two contrasting love affairs—that of Birkin and Ursula and that of Gerald and Gudrun. They begin at about the same time but from the beginning they display contrasting qualities which leads one of them to a catastrophic ending and the other to an apparent degree of maturity and fulfillment. There are, of course, between the two affairs, intimate and complex interrelationships. The women, for instance, are sisters, while the men are good friends. Every incident, conversation or scene can be shown to bear on and to support the development of one or both of the love affairs that constitute the novel's main theme. To trace these complex relationships in detail would be an enterprise demanding almost a book. All that I can hope to do now is to sketch the two major lines of development that define the form of *Women in Love*.

[2]

Let us begin with the older sister, Ursula, and her lover Birkin. The first time we find Ursula in conversation with Birkin is in Chapter III, the afternoon he visited her classroom in his capacity as school inspector. She had seen him at the wedding, earlier, and had been piqued, attracted and annoyed by him. But although the basis of a relationship is established in the classroom—under the aegis, as Kenneth Burke would put it, of the gynaceous and androgynous flowers—it is not until considerably later on, in Chapter XI, that they meet alone and that Birkin tells Ursula that his affair with Hermione is finally over. From this time on the development of their love affair runs its stormy course to the inconclusive last conversation with which the book ends. Ursula visits Birkin in his apartment at the mill house and Birkin attempts, but fails, to convey to her that the kind of love he wants and is ready to give is different from ordinary love. But the lovers gradually come to an understanding in spite of their quarrels, or perhaps because of them. Some of their fights are so intense and are reported with such immediacy that the reader is swept into the clash and forced to share in the burning emotions of the conflicting lovers. The proper intransitivity of attention is impossible and an aesthetic spectacle becomes a partisan emotional experience. The poet's power of revelation has betrayed him again, as it did earlier, and does later, into failure. These scenes are followed by moments of peace, of tenderness, of a fulfillment which strains the rich linguistic resources of the poet to convey. But for all its flaws, the account of the affair comes off, for one reader at least, with the quick vitality without which poetry turns into soggy journalese. Grasp synoptically the jagged line of development from the beginning of the affair to the heights of erotic satisfaction, down to the depths of hatred, take the relationship in its full span, and you will see how it is the genesis and fruition—such as they are—of their love that informs the substance of the novel.

But the love affair is more than an informing agent; it constitutes
the substance of the novel and, as it is conceived by both Birkin
and Lawrence, it constitutes one of its themes.

We are given the most important clue to this fact in the conversation between Gerald and Birkin, reported in the chapter
entitled "In the Train." Birkin introduces the subject by asking
Gerald, somewhat abruptly, what he lives for. Gerald, committed
to "the ethics of productivity," confesses that life does not center for him but is artificially held together by the social mechanism. Birkin agrees.

"I know," he said, "it just doen't centre. The old ideals are dead as
nails—nothing there. It seems to me there remains only this perfect
union with a woman—sort of ultimate marriage—and there isn't
anything else."
"And you mean if there isn't the woman, there's nothing?" said
Gerald.
"Pretty well that—seeing there's no God."
"Then we're hard put to it," said Gerald . . . —CHAPTER V

The importance of this passage cannot be over-emphasized and
I shall have to refer to it several times in the following discussion.
It gives us an early clue to the formal and substantive role that
love plays in the book. It is put forth by Birkin as a substitute for
God. In what sense Birkin's and Gerald's opinions are borne out
and what are the consequences, for each, of their quandaries, it
will be our chief business to consider later. At this point it is only
necessary to note that the love affair between Birkin and Ursula is
idiotic, in the original acceptation of the term. Of course they
live among friends and in their unconventional way accept the
conventions of their group. But they blandly refuse to reckon
with established social institutions and Birkin particularly exhibits
a strong streak of misanthropy whose fountainhead is not traced
in the novel. The fact that we remain in the dark as to the reason
for Birkin's hatred of his fellow men constitutes one of the defects
of the novel (as it does of many other novels and stories of Law-

rence). But let that pass. We are not told what source of income the couple has. Finally, I own, they do marry. But the ceremony is obviously external and unimportant both to the couple and to the novel, for it is only in passing that we are told that it took place. If there is something sacramental in the nature of their union (and the term is not as incongruous as it may seem to those who have not grasped the ethos of *Women in Love*), its sacred character does not come from the ceremonies and rites, the conventions and practices, with which society puts the seal of the sacred on the institution of marriage. It is to be found in the union itself, in the manner in which the lovers for all their difficulties and quarrels, come to respect, even to venerate "the Eros of the sacred mysteries."

But the *idiocy* of their union is not to be interpreted to mean that the lovers "shack up" in a love-nest with the blinds drawn and the doorbell disconnected—in the way in which Will and Anna do after their wedding in *The Rainbow*. Nor does it mean that the love affair can be grasped in its specific quality without reference to the relationships between the lovers and other persons. Indeed, in order to grasp the quality of their relationship Lawrence must give us an account of the collapse of the affair between Birkin and Hermione; and in turn, in order to make this account intelligible, he must give us a comprehensive idea of the personality of Hermione and her friends. He must also introduce us to the bohemian world of Halliday and his friends in London. Thus, the ramifications and dramatic entailments of one love affair are numerous, complex, dense.

With the appropriate changes in detail the same observation holds for the affair between Gerald and Gudrun. Its development is one of the two unifying principles of the novel. And in order to understand the reason for Gerald's failure in love, which constitutes the second major theme of the novel, Lawrence must give us a fairly complete account of Gerald's life, including such information about his past as is relevant, his attitude towards the world and his successful activities as a mine owner—for Law-

rence intends us to notice a connection between Gerald's nature
and the industrial world that he built and that in turn produced
him. To appreciate Gerald's ruthless efficiency, his management
of the mines must be contrasted to his father's, whose paternalism
was inefficient and finally proved impractical. And in turn to appreciate properly the specious nature of Gerald's success as manager, we must grasp the inadequacy of his attitude towards sex,
defined dramatically by the account of the night he spends with
Halliday's mistress. Lawrence wants us to see that the weakness of
the man is connected with his failure to venerate the Eros of the
sacred mysteries. And the point for us is not whether Lawrence's
account of Gerald's failure is or is not causally adequate; the
point is that Lawrence conceives of the Gerald-Gudrun affair in
this manner and uses it—successfully in my opinion—to bring
into harmonious unity the multiplicity of incident, the complexity
of episodes, the density of dramatic specification which constitutes *Women in Love*.

[3]

The assertion that the two love affairs organize or give form to
the substance of the novel may be tested by taking each of the
episodes or incidents that at first sight do not appear to be related
to the main themes and showing how it is in fact related. As already suggested, I shall take only some of the incidents that at
first sight may not appear to have any relation to the central
themes and show how they are related to them. Some of course
will be found to be more closely related to the love affair of Birkin
and Ursula than to that of Gerald and Gudrun. But the relations
will be found to obtain for each one of the incidents, however
remote the incident may appear at first sight. Let me begin by
showing how the drowning of Diana Crich and the young doctor
who attempted to save her are organically part of a harmonious
whole.

In order to grasp the connection we must remember Gerald's

sense of superiority, his unquestioned conviction that he can dominate men and nature. The conviction is not an altogether empty conceit, for his unquestionable success with the colliers only substantiated his belief and, for a time, ours. But for all his managerial talent and his indisputably masterful will, not only are there limits to his power but there is an inherent weakness in it, which we must be aware of if we are to accept the fact that two persons who do not at first sight seem to possess his strength, Gudrun and Loerke, can be the main agents of his catastrophic ending. Bearing this in mind, let us recall that, as Lawrence takes the trouble to inform us, Gerald is responsible for the water during the party which ended with the drowning. And while in neither a moral nor a legal sense can he be blamed for the drowning, dramatically he fails. For he made a desperate effort to save his sister and her friend. The industrial magnate who thinks of men as mere tools and who wants the pure fulfillment of his own will in the struggle with natural conditions, the highpriest of the false idol, the Machine, when he is responsible for the water at the party, a relatively minor responsibility, fails. And the failure draws clearly for us the limits of his power. There are a number of indications throughout the narrative of Gerald's prospective failure; but they would not be convincing or even significant for us if we had not taken the measure of his specious strength. Lawrence wants to tell us that Gerald's failure in his life, particularly in love, has its source in his dedication to the wrong God, the Machine. Whether his intention and the intention of the novel coincide is another question—one that will be considered later.

This is not the only connection of the drowning episode with the rest of the novel. A summary reference to other connections will give us a firmer sense of the closely woven texture of the composition. One of these is ironic and throws us back to Chapter IV, entitled "Diver," in which the sisters, out for a walk, see Gerald diving into the lake and swimming off. In the account the viewpoint shifts—as it does frequently with Lawrence—from the sisters to Gerald and back to the sisters. Watching him swim,

Gudrun envies his masculinity almost painfully. She desires the freedom, the liberty and mobility that enables him to do anything he wants, whereas she, a woman, is thoroughly restricted. But it is he who is in fact restricted because weak, and it is she who shows up his weakness and leads him to his death. And this is in part the irony of the situation.

The irony, however, is considerably more complex. The situation in which Gerald is envied by Gudrun for qualities and powers he in fact does not possess is symbolic (in an ordinary semiotic sense of the term). For obvious reasons, water has been thought of by many peoples throughout the world and throughout history as part of a complex which links vegetation, woman, the moon, with fecundity and life. But as it turns out, Gerald is not the source of creativity, fecundity, life; he is bound for destruction. His talents are the talents of destruction and evil, anti-human. Immediately after the sisters resume their walk, having looked at Gerald swimming, Ursula tells Gudrun that Gerald, who is making all sorts of modern improvements in Shortlands, the Criches' home, will "have to die soon, when there is nothing more to improve." And then Ursula tells her sister that Gerald killed his brother when "they were quite boys." This is not the only time that reference is made to Gerald's bearing the sign of Cain. There is a premonitory connection, then, between the drowning of his sister in the water-party chapter, and Gerald's end—for it is by water that Gerald dies. True, it is not the fluid element that kills him, but the vast abstraction of ice and snow up in the Alps; but it is water that kills him nevertheless. Thus we see that the drowning incident is intimately related to the substance of the novel, and not factitiously: the incident is no mere "plant" put there by Lawrence artificially, but is organically and deftly woven into the whole.

It is not altogether irrelevant at this point to dwell on the manner in which Lawrence employs water, and not only in *Women in Love*, but also in *The Rainbow:* not as a symbol of generation and life, but of destruction and death. Thus, the Brangwens' bucolic life is destroyed by the opening of the canal near their farm and we are told that it is the women of the Brangwen family who are different and reject the "blood intimacy" which was the essence of their farming life. And it is by drowning, when the canal breaks and floods the land, that Tom Brangwen dies. Am I being too ingenious? I do not think so. Consider that in *Women in Love*, when Birkin comes back from France after the lapis lazuli incident, the crisis comes to a head after his futile effort to break the image of the moon on the surface of the pond. It is almost as if for Lawrence the symbols of the water and the moon sometimes were reversed. Whether it be true of Lawrence the man or not, of *Women in Love* we can say that neither of the two principal male characters are men who accept love in its full span, as a means for the procreation of life. Neither Birkin's Eros of the sacred mysteries, nor Gerald's Eros of the jaunty "amours," leads to the family with its roots, its stability, and its fulfillment. There is never any question that the Gerald-Gudrun liaison may lead to marriage, the family, and the assumption of the responsibilities of man in society; and the marriage of Ursula and Birkin does not point towards a normal, if eventual and postponed, settled life.

[4]

The chair episode, Chapter XXVI, furnishes us with another test of the claim that the novel is closely organized. Ursula and Birkin go to a jumble market to look for furniture. First they notice a young woman who is pregnant and her young man looking at a mattress, and then they discover a chair that attracts them very much and they decide to buy it. But in the conversation that follows the purchase, Birkin tells Ursula that the fact is that he does not want things at all. The thought of a house and furniture is hateful to him and Ursula replies that it is hateful to her too. He makes an emphatic declaration that they will avoid having things of their own, but Ursula points out that they have just bought a chair. They decide they don't really want it, and give it to the young couple whom they had seen looking at the mattress. The significance of this episode is that it serves to reinforce the conversation they had at the inn where they put up after visiting Southwell Minster, in which Birkin tells Ursula that they have to drop their jobs and wander about for a bit.

The connection between the chair episode and the rest of the novel is obvious enough; it is, indeed, directly indicated in the text by Lawrence himself. But the relationship between Chapter XXVIII, entitled "In the Pompadour," and the rest of the story is not so obvious. The chapter contains the scene in which Halliday reads Birkin's ridiculous letter to his friends and Gudrun snatches it from him and leaves with Gerald in the taxi. What does this chapter tell us? While the scene is sharply etched, the relationship between its content and the rest of the story is not at all clear. Surely its central purpose cannot be to give us a picture of Halliday and his friends: for not only has Lawrence already give us an adequate picture of these people, but the incident is really concerned with Birkin. What then is its purpose? It completes, for us, the figure of Birkin. To see how it does, we must go back to the chapter entitled "An Island," Chapter XI, in which a conversation takes place between Ursula and Birkin and in which Birkin expresses his hatred of humanity, a subject on which he has already expressed himself twice before. As I have remarked already, the misanthropy is not elucidated; from the novel it is not possible to discover why Birkin hates mankind as he does. In any case there is no doubt about his feeling in the reader's mind: Birkin tells us he loathes himself as a human being, and believes that humanity is itself dry-rotten, that it is a tree of lies, less than the individual "because the individual is sometimes capable of truth." Ursula watches him rant and decides that she wants him for himself and that she hates the Salvator Mundi, the Sunday-school teacher, the prig of the stiffest kind that in part he is. We are given another picture of this Salvator Mundi aspect of Birkin in Chapter XIV, "Water-Party," in the scene in which Birkin, seemingly for no plausible reason, starts a harangue somewhat similar to that which Halliday is making fun of. He talks of "the other river," and speaks to Ursula of the flowers of dissolution, a progressive process which is the end of the world. Exactly what Birkin is telling Ursula I cannot make out clearly. But this much is clear: that it is this aspect of Birkin that Ursula has seen earlier and disliked because it is the Salvator Mundi side of Birkin. Ursula knows that Birkin "would behave in the same way, say the same things, give himself as completely to anybody who came along, anybody and everybody who liked to appeal to him." But we have only Ursula's word for it, and we do not see, until Halliday reads the letter, in precisely what manner Birkin would give himself away to people who would ridicule him for it and who, we have already been shown, are a rather shabby lot of bohemians. In Chapter XXVIII, "In the Pompadour," we see the degree to which Birkin was ready to expose himself. Gudrun had reason to be angry, for the letter made a fool of Birkin. But whatever her reaction, by the scene Lawrence showed this aspect of Birkin's nature without pity.

When we view the novel in this manner, I believe we must agree with Lawrence when he exploded against the "pernicious, ossiferous skin-and-grief form," which critics wanted him to have. For the traditional form of the novel he has substituted his own form, and one which answered adequately to the demands made by the substance of the novel, which is no longer defined by character and action, as I have tried to show in the discussion of *The Rainbow*. His best work does have form, but it is a form which is organic with the substance informed and not one copied from earlier work.

CHAPTER TEN

The Substance of Women in Love

WHILE THE two main themes, the development of which defines the organization of *Women in Love*, are the love affair of Birkin and Ursula and the liaison of Gerald and Gudrun, the substance of the novel cannot be adequately defined in terms of the love affairs alone. The novel is a very ambitious book whose substance consists of the elucidation of the theme of human destiny at a given moment in history in terms of the conditions in which the four main characters find themselves. If I am right, and I hope to validate my judgment in this chapter, Lawrence could have claimed much more than he did when, defending himself from a criticism, he wrote to Edward Garnett in a phrase already cited that he was "a passionately religious man," and that his novels had to be written from the depths of his religious experience.[1] In *Women in Love* religion, as ordinarily understood, does not enter: man's relation to God is not part of the substance of the novel; but Lawrence poses the problem of human destiny in view of the fact that his characters cannot believe in God, so that religion, by its failure, defines the central problem of the novel.

It is only when we put *Women in Love* in this perspective that we are able to see clearly the relation of Lawrence to the most profound and most challenging movement in contemporary philosophy in our Western world, atheistic existentialism. Nietzsche's exultant cry, "God is dead!" is one of Sartre's starting points. God's death forces the atheistic philosopher to face the problem of destiny in ultimate, radical, and desperate terms. And it was in these

terms that Lawrence faced the same problem. The philosophy of
love, the religion of the blood, the "leader-*cum*-follower" program
—all his ideas, solutions, insights, and messages, significant as they
are by themselves, achieve full significance only when we see them
as attempts to discover a way of life that would center, "seeing
there is no God." And it is only when we put Lawrence in this perspective that we are able to see fully what kind of novelist he was.
Most contemporary novelists are moralists—or immoralists as the
case may be. Witness Conrad and Gide. I do not mean that they
preach or have a message; I mean that the matter they seek to elucidate by transforming it into the substance of art is the stuff of
human relations. Only very few are, if I may so call them, "cos-
mologists," in the sense that their matter is man's relation to the
cosmos. This was the matter Dreiser sought to transform into the
substance of art, as I have indicated elsewhere. And this is the
"problem" that, in the last analysis, obsessed Lawerence. That he
"failed," in the sense that not one of his "answers" was acceptable
and viable, is a relatively minor consideration. He posed the problem; and this, in philosophy and in poetry, is all, or nearly all that
we can expect. An honest man today, whether for him God is
dead or living, knows, knows in his entrails, as Unamuno would
have put it, that there is no easy answer to his cosmic query, no
easy way out of his radical predicament.

And finally, from the critical standpoint, it is only when we make
explicit Lawrence's basic theme or problem that we are able to
appreciate in their full value the role played by some of the components in defining and elucidating that problem. Why are
Hermione's values false? Why must Gerald die? What is the importance of the discussion of the African figurine in Halliday's
flat? The answer is that neither Hermione's cerebral values nor
Gerald's ethics of productivity can serve as a substitute for God.
But the African way may serve, although Lawrence would have
us believe that Birkin finally rejects it. It is in a sort of "ultimate
marriage" that Birkin finds an adequate substitute for God. This,
at any rate, is what Lawrence would have us believe. What the

novel says is not the same thing. But while the novelist remains what we have already seen him to be, a dribbling liar, the novel does not suffer from his lies: for the truth of the novel is not in disruptive conflict with the lies of the novelist; it is to be found below them.

[2]

The repudiation of the ethics of productivity and of the machine, as embodied in the colliery, is not new in Lawrence's work. We found it in *The Rainbow*, conveyed powerfully by Ursula's reaction to her uncle and the colliery he manages. (In mentioning Ursula here, I am not suggesting that the two novels are continuous; I do not think they are, although we know they were carved from a single novel entitled *The Sisters*.) In *Women in Love* Lawrence offers us a more detailed account of the essential weakness of the man who serves the machine and the flaws of the ethics of productivity than he offered us in *The Rainbow*. Carefully he draws a contrast between Gerald and the older Crich, and between Gerald and Rupert. The father manages the mines paternalistically and inefficiently while Gerald is pure efficiency and "go." And Gerald's love life is shallow while Rupert's is deep in spite of the conflicts that thwart him. This contrast is brought out by dialogue, by actual description, and by means of a number of semiotic signs and constitutive symbols, all of which converge to give us a picture of Gerald. The power of the Industrial Magnate is a sham. He is killed by the woman and the German whom Gerald thinks of as a "little vermin."

As I have already mentioned in a different connection, in Chapter IV, "Diver," Gudrun sees Gerald dive and swim and envies him for his "freedom, liberty and mobility," and Ursula tells Gudrun about his improvements of Shortlands, his "go," and the way in which the miners hate him. In Chapter V, "In the Train," through the conversation between Birkin and Gerald, we are given a fairly clear account of Gerald's callousness, glistening through "the ethics of productivity." And we are also informed that he is satisfied to let his life be artificially held together by the social mechanism. In the semiotic sign or quasi-symbol of the mare scene, in Chapter IX, "Coal-Dust," we are given a picture of Gerald's ruthlessness. The Brangwen sisters are on the way home from school and the colliery train is rumbling near. They know Gerald only slightly at this time. Lawrence tells us:

Whilst the two girls waited, Gerald Crich trotted up on a red Arab mare. He rode well and softly, pleased with the delicate quivering of the creature between his knees. . . . The locomotive chuffed slowly between the banks, hidden. The mare did not like it. She began to wince away, as if hurt by the unknown noise. But Gerald pulled her back and held her head to the gate.—CHAPTER IX

I need not quote any more. The mare tries to bolt but Gerald forces her back. "The fool!" cried Ursula loudly. "Why doesn't he ride away till it's gone by?" The struggle goes on. "And she's bleeding! She's bleeding!" cries Ursula, while Gudrun looks and the world reels and passes into nothingness for her.

We have already seen that throughout his career Lawrence brooded long and deeply, almost obsessively, on the Gerald type and that he contrasted it with the type of the gamekeeper. In *The Rainbow* Gerald had a small part to play in the form of Tom Brangwen, Ursula's uncle. Sometimes he is metamorphosed into an emasculated Clifford Chatterley, and sometimes into an intellectual or a member of an artistic group such as the Bricknells and their friends in *Aaron's Rod*. He also appears, as we saw, as the effete rich young man, Rico. There is an important difference between Gerald and his imitations: the presentation of Gerald's deficiencies and limitations is achieved in dramatic terms. Whatever the sources of his conception (and the combination of Major Barber and Middleton Murry could not, on the surface, have appeared more incongruous and less promising than they evidently were) the result is a person grasped directly, not in terms of con-

cepts, a moving, responding, human being, whose industrial success, whose inward disorganization and failure in love are not the
product of a philosophy on the part of their creator, but a genuinely creative conception. Gerald is an industrialist moved by a
strong will to power, a man whose world does not center. Having
succeeded as a mine owner, he gets trapped in a love affair that
kills him. And we are made to see, in terms of the relationship between him and Gudrun, why he had to die and how he was
spiritually dead before he died physically.

Birkin, with whom Gerald is contrasted, is no less protean. He is
the gamekeeper in *Lady Chatterley*, sometimes he is a gypsy, a
southern Italian, a Mexican general of pure Indian blood, a Bohemian count, a groom, and once even a horse. The contrast in its
many allotropic manifestations is the expression of a kind of Mani-
chean conception of life in which the gamekeeper type is the fountain of life, potency, and tenderness; the Gerald type, often sexually impotent, is the bearer of corruption, causing destruction of
self and of others. One could say, it is Eros against Thanatos.

It is important to notice the difference between the two types.
The gamekeeper is always conceived in authentic dramatic terms;
he is created out of pure experience. But this is not the case with
the Gerald type. In *The Rainbow* Tom Brangwen, Ursula's uncle,
although not a fully developed personality, is as authentic as any
one in the book. And, with a qualification to be made next, this
holds for Gerald. However, the Gerald type soon becomes a
dramatized concept, an idea dressed up as a man, and sometimes—
as in the case of the clergyman, Mr. Massy, in "The Daughters of
the Vicar"—a mere caricature whose function in the story is to
serve as a foil and a cathartic stimulus for Lawrence's hatred.

The qualification that must be entered is that the business magnate aspect of Gerald is not conceived in an utterly dramatic manner. There is in him something of the dramatized idea, and that is
the reason we can apprehend this aspect of Gerald in terms of
semiotic symbols without remainder. The mare scene is not at all

a constitutive symbol and its meaning is given us discursively in Chapter XII, "Carpeting," and in XVII, "The Industrial Magnate." In the first of these two chapters the Brangwen sisters criticize Gerald for his cruelty to the mare, and Gerald defends himself on the ground that the mare must be taught to stand if it is to be of use to him. And in the second of these chapters, which contains a fairly complete account of the contrasting philosophies of industry held by the older owner, Thomas Crich, and his son, Gerald, the picture of both men is given discursively and conceptually. All the chapter does, therefore, is to fill out the details of what we already know about Gerald, and what we know about him is something Lawrence states fully by means of a combination of behavioral traits and a statement of Gerald's ideology. When he takes over the management of the mines from his father, Gerald abandons the benevolent paternalism with which the mines have been managed. He has conceived the idea of "the pure instrumentality of mankind," and what he wants is "the pure fulfillment of his own will in the struggle with the natural conditions. His will was now to take the coal out of the earth profitably." What "mattered was the great social productive machine." Gerald now had his life work, which was "to extend over the earth a great perfect system in which the will of man ran smoothly and unthwarted, timeless, a Godhead in process." I hope it can be noticed from the snippets I have quoted that the picture of Gerald, however behavioral, is essentially a conceptual one. We understand Gerald as we understand the Robber Barons or as we understand Don Juan. Don Juan may be different from Casanova, and Don Juan Tenorio may be different from Don Giovanni, but the difference lies on the surface and we conceive of them in essentially the same terms and these terms are more conceptual than dramatic.

An essential part of Lawrence's concept of Gerald the industrial magnate is the emptiness of the man, and this is also stated conceptually, although the discursive statement does not do justice to the dramatic presentation we also find in *Women in Love*. We are told that once Gerald succeeds in overhauling the system and in making the mines pay, he is up against the horror of his own vacuity:

But now he had succeeded—he had finally succeeded. And once or twice lately, when he was alone in the evening and had nothing to do, he had suddenly stood up in terror, not knowing what he was. And he went to the mirror and looked long and closely at his own face, at his own eyes, seeking for something. He was afraid, in mortal dry fear, but he knew not what of. . . . He was afraid that one day he would break down and be a purely meaningless bubble lapping round a darkness.

But his will yet held good, he was able to go away and read, and think about things.—CHAPTER XVII

His will holds good, after a fashion, until Gudrun and Loerke make a concerted and successful, if unconscious, effort to kill him.

But Gerald is more than a business magnate; he is also a friend and a lover, and these other sides of his personality are not dramatized illustrations of concepts. If we attempt to "reduce" them to abstract terms our effort is doomed to failure, as we realize when we turn from the semiotic or quasi-symbol of the mare to the scene in which Gudrun dances before the highland cattle and slaps Gerald's face (Chapter XIV, "Water-Party"), and to the scene presented in Chapter XVIII, "Rabbit." These are the two most important scenes in the novel for our grasp of Gerald's disastrous end and hence of Lawrence's authentic and pure poetic vision of the world.

At the party given by the Criches, Ursula and Gudrun had gone away from the crowd in Gerald's canoe. After a swim, Gudrun asked Ursula to sing because Gudrun wanted to dance. She begins to dance and notices a little cluster of Highland cattle among which there are some bullocks. Ursula is afraid, but Gudrun becomes possessed by "a strange passion to dance before the sturdy, handsome cattle." While she is dancing, Rupert Birkin and Gerald come looking for them and Gerald, with a loud shout, makes the cattle run off. He is angry because of the risk Gudrun is running, frightening the cattle, and asks Gudrun why she wants to drive them mad. They are nasty, he points out, when they turn. Gudrun mocks his fear. The rest of the incident must be given in Lawrence's own words:

"You think I'm afraid of you and your cattle, don't you?" she asked. His eyes narrowed dangerously. There was a faint domineering smile on his face.
"Why should I think that?" he said.
She was watching him all the time with her dark, dilated, inchoate eyes. She leaned forward and swung round her arm, catching him a blow on the face with the back of her hand.
"That's why," she said.
And she felt in her soul an unconquerable lust for deep brutality against him. . . .
He recoiled from the heavy blow across the face. He became deadly pale, and a dangerous flame darkened his eyes. . . .
"You have struck the first blow," he said at last, forcing the words from his lungs. . . .
"And I shall strike the last," she retorted involuntarily, with confident assurance.—CHAPTER XIV

Earlier in their acquaintance, Gerald had seen that Gudrun was "a dangerous, hostile spirit," and this understanding on his part had established the bond between them. This interchange takes place in Chapter X, "Sketch-Book," and we are told that in her tone of voice Gudrun made the understanding clear to Gerald: "They were of the same kind, he and she, a sort of diabolic freemasonry subsisted between them. Henceforth, she knew, she had power over him. Wherever they met, they would be secretly associated. And he would be helpless in the association with her. Her soul exulted." It is as if the relationship from the beginning were predestined to lead to his destruction. She did indeed strike the last blow.

The present scene, particularly if we read it entirely and in its context, is a very powerful scene and makes up a constitutive symbol. There is, however, one aspect of the scene that can be explicated, although ultimately, for me at least, both as regards the relationship between Gerald and Gudrun and as regards Birkin, there remains a fascinating but obscure something that teases but does not yield to any kind of clear grasp. What is more or less explicable about the scene is Gudrun's dancing before the cattle, among which there are some bullocks, her taunting them, defying them, and forcing them, or trying to force them, to break and run. For bulls are semiotic symbols throughout many cultures of male potency, of fruitfulness, but bullocks have lost that potency. Again, it is Gerald's bullocks Gudrun taunts with her dance, as if it were his male power she denied. But what remains beyond my grasp is this: Gudrun is presented in the book as a sexually normal woman. We shall see that she craves for refinements of perversion, but she does not repudiate the male qua male, as a homosexual woman would. Why then does she want to destroy the man? Why does she deny his power as man? That the man should fear the female is understandable, since it is a recurrent phenomenon throughout human history and its grounds are obvious: it is the man who invents the myth of the *vulva dentata*. That Gudrun should want to dominate the male is also understandable. But the scene, and the whole relationship, has another meaning: Gudrun sets out from the beginning to annihilate Gerald. The intention itself is clearly stated. But as to its motivation one is left wondering. Of course Gerald is bent on destroying himself. Having succeeded as an industrial magnate there is nothing left for him but death. But why should Gudrun want to destroy him?

That those aspects of Gerald's personality, the lover and the friend, are not mere dramatized illustrations of concepts and cannot be "reduced" to abstract terms can be realized by turning to those powerful scenes and incidents in which these aspects are presented. Take for instance, the scene in which the rabbit, Bismarck, unites Gerald and Gudrun in a demonic marriage, Chapter XVIII. It will be remembered that Gerald and Gudrun never actually "marry" in a conventional sense and they do not begin living together until later. But it is in the rabbit scene that their ritual union finally takes place. To be present at an obscenity is, of course, literally speaking, an impossibility, if we take the term in its primitive sense. But the very paradox of our witnessing that which is out of sight while we are spectators in front of the stage, emphasizes the fact intended objectively by the scene, namely that there is something beyond the ordinary, beyond the presentable in the mystic communion of Gerald and Gudrun of which the officiating priest is a kicking, angry rabbit, and the witness is a child. Bringing to a final ripening the relationship between Gerald and Gudrun, the symbolic episode of the rabbit recapitulates dramatically the understanding that they had reached earlier and throws light on the experience that is to follow.

At the time of the rabbit episode a considerable degree of understanding had already been arrived at between Gerald and Gudrun. The first time Gudrun saw Gerald at his sister's wedding (Chapter I), she had reacted strongly to his presence, wanting to be alone, to know the strange, sharp inoculation that had changed the whole temper of her blood. From there on we begin to realize gradually that the relationship is going to generate a destructive force the victim of which will be Gerald. But although the scenes in which the destructive action is presented are stages in the development of an understanding between the two and contribute to our grasp of the quality of their relationship, they do not fully give us that quality. And what is much more important, no adjective or combination of adjectives seems adequate to characterize the quality of the relationship. When it finally comes to its catastrophic ending, the inadequacy of such characterization is more obvious. To call the relationship antagonistic is completely inadequate, since until the very end there is a kind of love between the two of them. But it would be no less inadequate to call it ambivalent. In the final analysis it is ineffable in abstract terms, and nothing but the full synoptic grasp of the chapters in which it is dramatically defined will yield its complexity, its nuances, the ebb and flow of its passion, and its corrosive destructiveness. Gerald and Gudrun move towards one another to their fulfillment, and the union is disastrous for Gerald, although they do not engage in the frightfully intense fights that Birkin and Ursula engage in. Gudrun's early slapping of Gerald's face is not an attack welling out of mutual irritation and lack of understanding. And the final fight in which Gerald almost chokes Gudrun to death is not occasioned—although it is easy to misunderstand it—by Gerald's jealousy of Loerke. How then are we to grasp the essentially negative nature of their relationship? As we turn the matter in our minds we become convinced to our dismay that discursive language can do no justice to it. Whatever there is between the man and the woman wells up from the depths of their souls; nor is it something to be *understood*, if the term is used to stand for the exhibition of motivations that can be more or less accurately designated in psychological language. But when we turn to the episode of the rabbit and consider the experience between Gerald and Gudrun in the light this episode throws upon it, the whole relationship becomes an object of dramatic aesthesis. What precedes the rabbit episode is crystalized and can now be grasped fully as an object of immediate apprehension, and what follows it takes its significance from it. The rabbit scene is a constitutive symbol. The critic, in the last analysis, is impotent before such a symbol; all he can do is suggest some of the obvious discursive meanings that the scene evokes.

Gudrun and Winifred, Gerald's little sister, want to catch Bismarck in order to draw him, because he looks splendid and fierce. As they are on their way to the hutch Gerald appears, and in the middle of the conversation between him and Gudrun we are told that their eyes meet in knowledge and Gerald finds himself desiring Gudrun. Gerald goes away and Gudrun tries to catch the rabbit, although Winifred warns her that he is a fearful kicker. Gudrun seizes the rabbit by the ears, but he is very strong and in an instant he is lunging wildly and kicking in mid-air. Gudrun is having a hard time holding him when Gerald returns and takes the rabbit from her. The beast lashes out at him also and Gerald, swift as lightning, brings his hand down on his neck. The rabbit emits an unearthly, abhorrent scream and is finally subdued. But nothing but the actual passage will do, although in order for it to have its full effect it must be read in context:

"You wouldn't think there was all that force in a rabbit," he [Gerald] said, looking at Gudrun. And he saw her eyes black as night in her pallid face, she looked almost unearthly. The scream of the rabbit, after the violent tussle, seemed to have torn the veil of her consciousness. He looked at her, and the whitish, electric gleam in his face intensified.

"I don't really like him," Winifred was crooning. "I don't care for him as I do for Loozie. He's hateful really."

A smile twisted Gudrun's face, as she recovered. She knew she was revealed.

"Don't they make the most fearful noise when they scream"? she cried, the high note in her voice, like a seagull's cry.

"Abominable," he said.

"He shouldn't be so silly when he has to be taken out," Winifred was saying, putting out her hand and touching the rabbit tentatively, as it skulked under his arm, motionless as if it were dead.

"He's not dead, is he, Gerald?" she asked.

"No, he ought to be," he said.

"Yes, he ought!" cried the child, with a sudden flush of amusement. And she touched the rabbit with more confidence. "His heart is beating *so* fast. Isn't he funny? He really is."

"Where do you want him?" asked Gerald.

"In the little green court," she said.

Gudrun looked at Gerald with strange, darkened eyes, strained with underworld knowledge, almost supplicating, like those of a creature which is at his mercy, yet which is his ultimate victor. He did not know what to say to her. He felt the mutual hellish recognition. And he felt he ought to say something, to cover it. He had the power of lightning in his nerves, she seemed like a soft recipient of his magical, hideous white fire. He was unconfident, he had qualms of fear.

"Did he hurt you?" he asked.

"No," she said.

"He's an insensible beast," he said, turning his face away.

They came to the little court. . . . Gerald tossed the rabbit down.

It crouched still and would not move. Gudrun watched it with faint horror.

"Why doesn't it move?" she cried.

"It's skulking," he said.

She looked up at him, and a slight sinister smile contracted her white face.

"Isn't it a *fool!*" she cried. "Isn't it a sickening *fool?*" The vindictive mockery in her voice made his brain quiver. Glancing up at him, into his eyes, she revealed again the mocking, white-cruel recognition. There was a league between them, abhorrent to them both. They were implicated with each other in abhorrent mysteries.

"How many scratches have you?" he asked, showing his hard forearm, white and hard and torn in red gashes.

"How really vile!" she cried, flushing with a sinister vision. "Mine is nothing."

She lifted her arm and showed a deep red score down the silken white flesh.

"What a devil!" he exclaimed. But it was as if he had had knowledge of her in the long red rent of her forearm, so silken and soft. He did not want to touch her. He would have to make himself touch her, deliberately. The long, shallow red rip seemed torn across his own brain, tearing the surface of his ultimate consciousness, letting through the forever unconscious, unthinkable red ether of the beyond, the obscene beyond.

"It doesn't hurt you very much, does it?" he asked solicitous.

"Not at all," she cried.

And suddenly the rabbit, which had been crouching as if it were a flower, so still and soft, suddenly burst into life. Round and round the court it went, as if shot from a gun, round and round like a furry meteorite, in a tense hard circle that seemed to bind their brains. They all stood in amazement, smiling uncannily, as if the rabbit were obeying some unknown incantation. Round and round it flew, on the grass under the old red walls like a storm.

And then quite suddenly it settled down, hobbled among the grass, and sat considering, its nose twitching like a bit of fluff in the wind. After having considered for a few minutes, a soft bunch with a black, open eye, which perhaps was looking at them, perhaps was not, it hobbled calmly forward and began to nibble the grass with that mean motion of a rabbit's quick eating.

"It's mad," said Gudrun. "It is most decidedly mad."

He laughed. "The question is," he said, "what is madness? I don't suppose it is rabbit-mad."

"Don't you think it is?" she asked.

"No. That's what it is to be a rabbit."

There was a queer, faint, obscene smile over his face. She looked at him and saw him, and knew that he was initiate as she was initiate. This thwarted her, and contravened her, for the moment.

"God be praised we aren't rabbits," she said, in a high, shrill voice.

The smile intensified a little, on his face.

"Not rabbits?" he said, looking at her fixedly.

Slowly her face relaxed into a smile of obscene recognition.

"Ah, Gerald," she said, in a strong, slow, almost man-like way.

"—All that, and more." Her eyes looked up at him with shocking nonchalance.

He felt again as if she had hit him across the face—or rather, as if she had torn him across the breast, dully, finally. . . . —CHAPTER XVIII

There is a suggestion that the marriage ritual performed by the officiating rabbit is consummated by the blood drawn by the animal's clawing. But if this seems too ingenious, certainly the gash will be recognized by the reader as a variant of the face-slapping episode and an anticipatory summation of their subsequent relationship. One of the themes that the rabbit episode illumines is expressed several times through the novel and comes to indirect and periphrastic expression in Chapter XXI, entitled "Threshold." In the midst of a conversation between Gerald and Gudrun on Birkin's ideal of marriage, we read:

And they both [Gerald and Gudrun] felt the subterranean desire to let go, to fling away everything, and lapse into a sheer unrestraint, brutal and licentious. A strange black passion surged up pure in Gudrun. She felt strong. She felt her hands so strong, as if she could tear the world asunder with them. She remembered the abandonments of Roman licence, and her heart grew hot. She knew she wanted this herself also—or something, something equivalent. Ah, if that which was unknown and suppressed in her were once let loose, what an orgiastic and satisfying event it would be. And she wanted it, she trembled slightly from the proximity of the man, who stood just behind her, suggestive of the same black licentiousness that rose in herself. She wanted it with him, this unacknowledged frenzy. For a moment the clear perception of this preoccupied her, distinct and perfect in its final reality. . . .—CHAPTER XXI

From *Women in Love* it is not possible to discover exactly what their subterranean desire consisted of. But we have already seen what is intended in *Lady Chatterley's Lover*—practices encountered in Krafft-Ebing. Another suggestion of this sort is to be found in *The Rainbow*, in which, describing the love life of Will and Anna, Lawrence tells us that it had become

a sensuality violent and extreme as death. They had no conscious intimacy, no tenderness of love. It was all the lust and the infinite, maddening intoxication of the senses, a passion of death.

And Lawrence continues:

. . . Awful and threatening it was, dangerous to a degree, even whilst he gave himself to it. It was pure darkness, also. All the shameful things of the body revealed themselves to him now with a sort of sinister, tropical beauty. All the shameful, natural and unnatural acts of sensual voluptuousness which he and the woman partook of together, created together, they had their heavy beauty and their delight. Shame, what was it? It was part of extreme delight. It was that part of delight of which man is usually afraid. Why afraid? The secret, shameful things are most terribly beautiful.

They accepted shame, and were one with it in their most unlicensed pleasures. It was incorporated. It was a bud that blossomed into beauty and heavy, fundamental gratification.—CHAPTER VIII

It is not possible to be dogmatic on this question, but I suggest that these passages throw light on a recurrent preoccupation of Lawrence's fictional characters which we have already encoun-

tered in *The Plumed Serpent*. We find the same preoccupation in
the short story, "The Fox." This story is, almost to the end, a
perfectly worked out dramatic situation containing, in the figure
of the fox, a powerfully suggestive constitutive symbol. But all of
a sudden, after the marriage of Henry and Nellie, the story takes
a wholly unexpected and incongruous turn, because Nellie ex-
erted herself in her love towards Henry and he would not have it:

> If she was in love, she ought to *exert* herself, in some way, loving. She
> felt the weary need of our day to *exert* herself in love. . . . No, he
> would not let her exert her love towards him. No, she had to be pas-
> sive, to acquiesce, and to be submerged under the surface of love.[2]

This passage comes all of a sudden, without any relation to
what preceded it, without preparation, and the reader is aware that
the story has taken, for a reason he does not know, a new turn.

These quotations—and many more could be given—enable us to
grasp the fact that the love relationship of some of Lawrence's fictional characters involves, besides their Krafft-Ebing aspect, or
perhaps, because of it, an animal quality of hardness and cruelty.
Their mating, we come to realize, is like the mating of those
insects in which the female kills the male after or even during the
act. This reinforces, in turn, our sense that, in *Women in Love*, the
apparently strong industrial magnate turns out to be the weaker of
the two and the woman knows it from the beginning. She finally
sends Gerald to his death when she is done with him and finds her
true mate in the German sculptor, Loerke. Gudrun murders Gerald without premeditation, guile, or plan, in a more or less unconscious manner, by forcing him to face the frozen emptiness of his
soul. This is not at all clear during the black rite at which the
rabbit officiates. Nor are the premonitions that have preceded the
black rite of their marriage fully clear at this point. They become
clear—in the sense in which an ordered presentation can be grasped
as aesthetically clear—when we manage to comprehend synoptically the whole poem.

It seems desirable to expatiate upon a point already touched on in another connection but not fully elucidated. We have abundant evidence that Lawrence took the account of Gerald as a general law, which may be formulated as follows: industrial magnates are weak and therefore incapable of adequate fulfillment as human beings. But his acceptance of this law does not constitute a fault in *Women in Love*, and the question whether the law is true or false is not relevant, for *Women in Love* has been conceived initially in dramatic terms. What is relevant is that in the novel the way in which Gerald's life is held together externally by the ethics of productivity, the inward emptiness of his life, its tropism towards self-destruction, the eventual failure of his affair with Gudrun and his disastrous fate—all are accepted by the reader as making a harmonious whole. This was the way Gerald was and this was his fate, and there is nothing in his actions or words, nothing in the whole account of him that forces us to recognize the picture as factitious. But a fact and an explanation of a fact are two different things, and if one asks why the combination of traits and inclinations constituting Gerald lead him to his disastrous end, the answer that in fact they do is not an answer to the question. However, it is advisable to reiterate with emphasis that the only admissible question is whether or not dramatically there is a clash or confusion, a disharmony or incongruity, that prevents us from accepting the drama as presented. If there is none, the question, whatever its historical validity or importance, does not point to a flaw because in the novel we find no answer to it. The observation is important not merely because it points to the high achievement that *Women in Love* is generally conceded to represent, but because it calls attention by contrast to the relative failure of those of Lawrence's works in which the component parts are held together mechanically, are tied together by dramatized conceptual means, are, in short, factitious. The contrast marks the difference between the high point of his creative power and lesser expressions of it. It is important to bear in mind that the lesser expressions are by no means negligible, if we are to appreciate the full miracle of his achievement.

That the question of adequate causation does not arise, however, deserves further attention, at least to this extent: Gerald is a successful creation. But when we take it all in and try to see what Lawrence has done and how he has done it, we are forced to reconsider our judgment. Highly as we may have thought of the novel before the critical exploration had done its job, we are now forced to go further and to admit that it is the product of an artistic talent that is quite rare. For it is not in the cattle and the rabbit scenes alone that we find constitutive symbols by means of which Lawrence accomplishes the feat of concentrating meanings and associations he wishes to reveal. The novel presents Gerald by means of a cluster of component constitutive symbols, although, if I am right, all the other symbols occupy a place subordinate to that of the rabbit. Indeed, if the word were not so misleading, because of its polysemic richness, I would say that *Women in Love* is a triumph of *symbolic* art: of art that works, in Mr. Leavis' phrase, from profounder levels and in more complex ways in order to convey more and deeper significance than naturalistic or realistic art is able to.

[3]

Just as the relationship between Gerald and Gudrun is exhibited dramatically, at its full depth, by the powerful symbol of the rabbit scene, so the relationship between Birkin and Ursula is revealed through the symbol of the shattering of the moon, presented in Chapter XIX, entitled "Moony." There is even an interesting parallelism in the two relationships in that corresponding to the quasi-symbol of the mare we find the quasi-symbol of the Mino, in Chapter XIII, by means of which Birkin seeks to convey to Ursula, and Lawrence to us, something of what Birkin has in mind when he says he wants a special kind of love beyond love.

We know a good deal about Birkin before the Mino episode takes place. He first broaches the subject of love in his conversation with Gerald on his way to London. And in the early stages of his relationship with Ursula, after Birkin has finally broken with Hermione, he tries to explain to her, early in Chapter XIII, what he is looking for. He speaks to her about a love beyond love and insists that the ordinary kind of love gives out in the last issues because, at the very last, one is alone, one is a real, impersonal self that is beyond any emotional relationship. For this reason, he tells Ursula, he is not even interested in her good looks. And laying himself open to the obvious retort, he tells her he wants a woman he does not see.

"There is," he [Birkin] said, in a voice of pure abstraction, "a final me which is stark and impersonal and beyond responsibility. So there is a final you. And it is there I would want to meet you—not in the emotional, loving plane—but there beyond, where there is no speech and no terms of agreement. . . ."—CHAPTER XIII.

But Birkin fails in his attempt to make Ursula understand, and the reader is no better off than she is. Her failure stems partly from the fact that Ursula thinks of love in the conventional sense and partly from the fact that she suspects that Birkin has in mind a relationship in which the female is subject to the will of the male. "It is purely selfish," she tells him, and further explanation on his part does not make it clearer to her than it does to us. But while descriptive discourse is of no help, and while it is in any case too early in the relationship for either Ursula or the reader to be able to understand, Lawrence does manage to achieve early in their relationship a dramatic definition of their conflict and their inability to resolve it by the use of the quasi-image of the cat, Mino. In the midst of the discussion:

A young grey cat that had been sleeping on the sofa jumped down and stretched, rising on its long legs, and arching its slim back. Then it sat considering for a moment, erect and kingly. And then, like a dart, it had shot out of the room, through the open window-doors, and into the garden.
"What's he after?" said Birkin, rising.

The young cat trotted lordly down the path, waving his tail. He was an ordinary tabby with white paws, a slender young gentleman. A crouching, fluffy, brownish-grey cat was stealing up the side of the fence. The Mino walked statelily [*sic*] up to her, with manly nonchalance. She crouched before him and pressed herself on the ground in humility, a fluffy soft outcast, looking up at him with wild eyes that were green and lovely as great jewels. He looked casually down on her. So she crept a few inches further, proceeding on her way to the back door, crouching in a wonderful, soft self-obliterating manner, and moving like a shadow.

He, going statelily on his slim legs, walked after her, then suddenly, for pure excess, he gave her a light cuff with his paw on the side of her face. She ran off a few steps, like a blown leaf along the ground, then crouched unobtrusively, in submissive, wild patience. The Mino pretended to take no notice of her. . . .

There is more of this play and finally Ursula breaks out,

"Now, why does he do that?" cried Ursula in indignation.
"They are on intimate terms," said Birkin.

But Ursula thinks Mino is a bully:

"Are you a bully, Mino?" Birkin asked.
The young slim cat looked at him, and slowly narrowed its eyes. Then it glanced away at the landscape, looking into the distance, as if completely oblivious of the two human beings.
"Mino," said Ursula, "I don't like you. You are a bully like all males."
—CHAPTER XIII

The passage is only a small part of a scene too long to quote in full. In the subsequent discussion between the couple the cat is forgotten and Birkin tries to make headway against Ursula's decided and clever resistance to his explanation, but his asseverations and analogies fail. I hope the quotation will help make clear the notion of quasi-symbol. While the Mino scene helps define and serves to sharpen in dramatic terms and, of course, in context, the failure of the couple to come to an understanding, that failure can be and is also conveyed independently. Yet the Mino incident is not a merely external adornment. It is consubstantial with the developing affair. Delete it and important aspects of the drama are lost to our grasp. But what the Mino episode tells us about Birkin's initial failure to convey to Ursula what he means by his love beyond love, it does not tell us *in* as well as *through*, but only *through* itself. What it tells us can be apprehended independently of the Mino scene and is indeed so apprehended later when we grasp the dramatic account of their relationship as it develops.

This reservation does not apply to the moon-shattering scene. Commentary can elucidate the upper layers, so to speak, of its significance; but the reader who has pondered it, knows that what he apprehends dramatically and immediately cannot be successfully translated into discursive terms.

Lawrence begins the moon-shattering scene in a deceptively facile manner. But as he finishes the chapter, the reader is aware that revelations have been made of vast importance; and among these is the central predicament in which Birkin is involved and the crisis to which it leads. There are statements that, made discursively, would have led the police to treat *Women in Love* in the very same manner in which *The Rainbow* and *Lady Chatterley* were treated. The constitutive symbol which is the scene of the shattering of the moon enables Lawrence to make his presentation fully and completely, as I hope to suggest. Ursula set off to Willey Green, towards the mill. And as she walked

She started, noticing something on her right hand, between the tree trunks. It was like a great presence, watching her, dodging her. She started violently. It was only the moon, risen through the thin trees. But it seemed so mysterious, with its white and deathly smile. And there was no avoiding it. Night or day, one could not escape the sinister face, triumphant and radiant like this moon, with a high smile. She hurried on, cowering from the white planet. . . .

The moon was transcendent over the bare, open space, she suffered from being exposed to it. There was a glimmer of nightly rabbits across the ground. . . .—CHAPTER XIX

Walking in a landscape full of night sounds and flooded with moon-brilliant hardness, which makes her soul cry out in her, Ursula finally gets away from the moonlight into the shade, reaches the pond, and notices the water, "perfect in its stillness, floating the moon upon it." Soon she sees Birkin wandering by the edge of the pond, throwing flowers into it, and talking disconnectedly to himself.

"You can't go away," he was saying. "There *is* no away. You only withdraw upon yourself."

He threw a dead flower-husk on to the water.

"An antiphony—they lie, and you sing back to them. There wouldn't have to be any truth, if there weren't any lies. Then one needn't assert anything—"

He stood still, looking at the water, and throwing upon it the husks of the flowers.

"Cybele—curse her! The accursed Syria Dea! Does one begrudge it her? What else is there—?"

Ursula wanted to laugh loudly and hysterically, hearing his isolated voice speaking out. It was so ridiculous.

Then she saw Birkin pick up a stone and throw it in the water. Ursula saw the image of the moon "leaping and swaying, all distorted, in her eyes. It seemed to shoot out arms of fire like a cuttle-fish, like a luminous polyp, palpitating strongly before her." Birkin throws more stones.

Then again there was a burst of sound, and a burst of brilliant light, the moon had exploded on the water, and was flying asunder in flakes of white and dangerous fire. Rapidly, like white birds, the fires all broken rose across the pond, fleeing in clamourous confusion, battling with the flock of dark waves that were forcing their way in. The furthest waves of light, fleeing out, seemed to be clamouring against the shore for escape, the waves of darkness came in heavily, running under towards the centre. But at the centre, the heart of all, was still a vivid incandescent quivering of a white moon not quite destroyed, a white body of fire writhing and striving and not even now broken open, not yet violated. It seemed to be drawing itself together with strange, violent pangs, in blind effort. It was getting stronger, it was re-asserting itself, the inviolable moon. And the rays were hastening in in thin lines of light, to return to the strengthened moon, that shook upon the water in triumphant reassumption.

Birkin tries again and again, throwing more stones, looking for larger stones and throwing them, until Ursula cannot bear it any longer and comes out from where she was sitting and speaks to him.

"You won't throw stones at it any more, will you?"

"I wanted to see if I could make it be quite gone off the pond," he said.
"Yes, it was horrible, really. Why should you hate the moon? It hasn't done you any harm, has it?"
"Was it hate?" he said.—CHAPTER XIX

This scene, it should be remembered, takes place before the relationship between Birkin and Ursula becomes intimate. Birkin has broken with Hermione and has offered Ursula a love beyond love that she cannot bring herself to accept in spite of her feeling towards him. He has spent some time in France, and this is the first time any of his friends or we have seen him since his return. Above all the scene conveys the depth of frustration and the ambivalent and still formless nature of his feelings towards Ursula. But it conveys much more. In the ghastly drama, particularly in the cursing of Cybele, Lawrence gives us the full depth of hopelessness and incoherent disruption from which Birkin is suffering, the threat and the frustration that are tearing him. Mr. Hough observes that Lawrence's mythology is a little rusty. Perhaps. So was his knowledge of the Aztec religion: that was worse than rusty, it was incomplete and superficial. And so, too, I would imagine, was his knowledge of Etruscan archaeology. Whatever Lawrence knew or did not know about classical mythology may be relevant to his biographer who is intent on measuring the extent of his learning;

but it is not relevant to the interpreter of his poetry. Birkin's ravings are fully and adequately expressive. He curses Cybele, the Syria Dea, identified—or was it, confused?—in Greece with Aphrodite. She was a terrible goddess, for she destroyed the sacred king who mated with her on a mountain top by tearing out his sexual organs. She was served by sodomitic priests who dressed as women, castrated themselves, and sought ecstasy in union with her. I take it therefore that Birkin is expressing the ancient and deep-rooted fear some men have felt towards women.

Whether that fear is or is not universal, and what its relation is to the male's vaunted superiority over the female, are interesting questions; but this is not the proper place to ask them. In respect to Birkin, however, it is entirely proper to ask whether the kind of primacy over the female that he claimed and yet the "polarity" he also wanted did not conceal something else: did it conceal a fear, perhaps as deep as, or deeper than, his longing for Ursula? This, I take it, is what, in part, the shattering of the image of the moon tells us. The interpretation is strengthened if we recall what was said in the last section regarding the manner in which Lawrence turns a symbol of generation and fecundity into an object of contempt: specifically, the way in which for the bull he substitutes a bullock. Wanting Ursula, Birkin is also afraid that she will accept him, on any terms whatever. But it is not Ursula alone whom he has feared. He has feared Hermione and has broken with her for what he made to appear to be genuinely good reasons. Are we to gather that Birkin fears women and that at the root of his fear there is a component that he faces in the moon scene but does not dare face in its own literal terms, a component that taken together with his fear of woman leads us to the deep and sickly roots of the conflict between his need for love and his inability to accept or to give love? Critics have generally accepted at face value Lawrence's intention and have failed to notice that it does not coincide exactly with the intention of the novel.

But is this all there is to Birkin's predicament? Cybele's priests are holy eunuchs and are sodomitic. And this is one key to the specific and complex nature of Birkin's predicament. Unless we read the pages following the moon-shattering scene in this context their turgid periphrases will succeed in camouflaging their full import. Let us review Birkin's cogitations the day following his effort to shatter the image of the moon. I shall follow them *au pied de la lettre*. He feels wistful and yearning. But he thinks that perhaps he has been wrong to go to Ursula with the idea of what he wanted. He wonders whether it was really an idea or an interpretation of a profound yearning. If the latter, why was he always talking of sensual fulfillment? The two, he admits, did not agree very well. And facing the contradiction, "suddenly," we are told, he "found himself face to face with a situation." It was, he assures himself, as simple as this—fatally simple. But simple as it may have been for Birkin, for the reader the situation is anything but simple, since the alternatives that Birkin reviews elude his grasp to some extent, and what he succeeds in grasping is a condition that goes beyond a mere division of the soul; it is a distinctly unhealthy condition.

The first alternative that Birkin considers is one that he rejects: "a further sensual experience—something deeper, darker, than ordinary life could give." This experience is defined for Birkin (but not for the reader, or at least not with equal lucidity) by the elegant figure from West Africa that had been the subject of a conversation between him and Gerald the night they spent at Halliday's flat. In that conversation at Halliday's Birkin had told Gerald that the figure was *high* art (he emphasized the adjective), because it embodied hundreds of centuries of pure culture in sensation, culture in the physical consciousness, really ultimate *physical* consciousness (and again the emphasis on the *physical* is Birkin's), mindless, utterly sensual. With the African process Birkin contrasts the process of the white races, having the arctic behind them, the ice-destructive knowledge, the snow-abstract annihilation, which he connects at this time with Gerald. Birkin broods on the African process which, he thinks, involves great mysteries, sensual, mindless, dreadful, far beyond the phallic cult. And he asks himself, "How far in their inverted culture, had these West Africans gone beyond phallic knowledge?" He realizes that they had gone very, very far. He thinks: "Thousands of years ago, that which was imminent in himself must have taken place in these Africans: the goodness, the holiness, the desire for creation . . . must have lapsed." As he broods he realizes that Gerald was fated to "pass away" through the perfect cold that was the way of the white races, with the vast abstraction of ice and snow of the arctic north that lies behind them. Birkin becomes frightened and tired and decides that "he could not attend to these mysteries any more."

Instantly he recollects that there is another way, the way of freedom, the union that he had offered Ursula and that she had rejected because she interpreted it as bullying. Inspired by his recollection he decides that he must go immediately to propose marriage to Ursula. In the Brangwens' living room there is a quarrel between Ursula and her father in Birkin's presence and she then turns down the offer of marriage. But later, recoiling from her impulsive attitude, she turns again in spirit to Birkin and prepares "to fight him" for her belief that love was everything. The chapters that follow in which the couple has the leading role are an account of that fight, with its moments of perfect union and mutual acceptance and its high peaks of erotic ecstasy. In these scenes Lawrence tries to do indirectly what later he attempted to do in *Lady Chatterley* directly—to render in language the felt inwardness of the erotic experience as felt. We have already seen the reason why he often failed.

This is a very inadequate account of the cogitations that occupied Birkin the day after the shattering of the image of the moon. Birkin's thought is presented by Lawrence in three pages whose meaning the reader knows he must grasp, for it is obviously of pivotal importance if one is to grasp clearly what ails Birkin and why he cannot be satisfied with the love Ursula offers him. From these three pages the reader gathers clearly enough that Birkin rejects the African way and decides to seek in his union with Ursula the solution for his desperate problem. But what exactly is the African way that he rejects? And exactly what was *imminent in himself*, that he now emphatically rejects? [3] What kind of goodness and holiness have lapsed in these people, what kind of desire for creation? It cannot be artistic creation, for the West African carving, Birkin had emphatically told Gerald, was a triumph of artistic creation, pure, high art. And what did those who carved it know that he himself did not? And how could he not know it, when he was aware that it was imminent in himself? Exactly what does Birkin mean by "further sensual experience—something deeper, darker, than ordinary life"? What does he mean by the mindless, progressive knowledge through the senses, the principle of knowledge in dissolution needed to produce the long, elegant body of the West African figure? Didn't Birkin, didn't Lawrence know what these phrases intended? A close reading of these three pages, so obviously freighted with meaning, discloses that they suggest vaguely, they intimate, they tease, and in the end they deny the reader the clear understanding he craves. Did Lawrence know the answers to these questions but chose not to tell us in so many words? I think he knew and did not dare tell.

Do the sensual, mindless, dreadful mysteries of an inverted culture coincide with the love play of *Lady Chatterley?* If this is the answer it throws light on an episode presented early in Chapter XXIII, entitled "Excurse," in which, after giving Ursula some rings, Birkin and she quarrel bitterly. After the quarrel Birkin acknowledges to himself that Ursula's accusations were in the main right. "He knew he was perverse, so spiritual on the one hand, and in some strange way, degraded, on the other" (Chapter XXIII). This suggests that he might not have really rejected the African way. For whatever the allusion involves, it is something that, when in a quarrel Ursula throws it in his face, Birkin admits makes him degraded and perverse.

But we are not yet through with the symbol of the shattering of the image of the moon. Another one of the frustrations it expresses is related to two chapters in the book: Chapter XVI, entitled "Man to Man," in which Birkin proposes to Gerald that they swear *Blutbruderschaft;* and Chapter XX, entitled "Gladiatorial," in which Gerald and Birkin wrestle naked in Gerald's living room. The importance of these two chapters must be great because their substance is summed up in the conversation between Birkin and Ursula at the close of the book. Birkin says to Ursula:

> "Having you I can live all my life without anybody else, any other sheer intimacy. But to make it complete, really happy, I wanted eternal union with a man too: another kind of love. . . ."
> "I don't believe it," she said. "It's an obstinacy, a theory, a perversity."
> "Well—" he said.
> "You can't have two kinds of love. Why should you!"
> "It seems as if I can't," he said. "Yet I wanted it."
> "You can't have it, because it's false, impossible," she said.
> "I don't believe that," he answered.

The next line contains only two words: "The End."

It would be delightfully simple if on the basis of this conversation and of Chapters XVI and XX, of which the conversation is the summing up, we could conclude *tout court* that Birkin is frustrated because Ursula's will and Gerald's death defeat his desire for homosexual experience. But in *Women in Love*—as in other major novels of Lawrence's—the treatment of the theme of homosexuality does not lend itself to unambiguous interpretation. Neither the offer of *Blutbruderschaft* nor the wrestling episode nor the closing conversation constitutes positive evidence; with the evidence on hand, an interpretation depends on the meanings we wish to assign to our terms. The term "homosexual" can be used to characterize these passages if we are explicitly clear as to what we are doing: we are using the term in the broad sense we have learned from psychoanalysts. But the passages give us no basis for determining how Birkin's yearning for a friendship with a man would find expression. Did he hope for more than a sublimated relationship?

The problem of homosexuality in Lawrence and in his work is not a simple one, and it is one that many of his critics have treated with less than candor. Some writers have tried to clear Lawrence from the charge. But I am not here interested in Lawrence's biography.

When we interpret Birkin's cravings for friendship with Gerald, we see that the objective intention of *Women in Love* is to represent the incompleteness of Birkin's relationship with Ursula, although that relationship is presented during its rare best moments as giving Ursula complete fulfillment. But only rarely does it give Birkin the fulfillment that it gives Ursula. In Chapters XXIII and XXVII, entitled "Excurse" and "Flitting" respectively, there are passages, it is true, that may be taken as evidence of the complete satisfactoriness of the relationship for Birkin. At the end of Chapter XXIII we read: "She had her desire fulfilled. He had his desire fulfilled. For she was to him what he was to her, the immemorial magnificence of mystic, palpable, real otherness." And later, in Chapter XXVII, there is a passage too long to quote in full from which I pluck the following statements:

She could not know how much it meant to him, how much he meant by the few words. . . . This marriage with her was his resurrection and his life. . . . It was something beyond love, such a gladness of having surpassed oneself, of having transcended the old existence. How could he say "I" when he was something new and unknown, not himself at all?

But in order to assay the novel's meaning properly, such passages must be contrasted with statements such as those found in Chapter XXIII, in which we are told that Birkin found Ursula beautiful, beyond womanhood, but in which we read: "Yet something was tight and unfree in him." With our knowledge of the psychopathology of everyday language, it is pertinent to ask what exactly does it mean when a lover finds a woman *beyond* womanhood. The statement is ambiguous and if the critical detective does not find evidence here, he does find a clue. For if Birkin loved Ursula as a woman, and there were no ambivalence in his love, and she represented for him in the best moments of fulfillment the farthest limit of which Birkin was capable of joy and completion in love, he would find her the essence of womanhood, the crystallization of woman, the embodiment of the Platonic idea of the female; he would find her *beyond* woman in the sense that he found her a woman but unlike the women men mate with, a goddess. On the other hand it may be that the relationship left him tight and unfree, because he found her beautiful beyond *womanhood*, because he was projecting into her, or trying to find in her, what she was not and could not be.

The resolution of this puzzle can at best be merely speculative, in the worst sense of this word, since the ambiguity is inherent in the text and the clues we might find with which to resolve it would call for uncontrolled interpretation. But this much I think we can assert: the relationship between Birkin and Ursula, often contrasted with that between Gerald and Gudrun, and undoubtedly intended by Lawrence to be so contrasted, does not appear on critical examination to be an ideal one. There is no question that Lawrence's intention coincides with that of the novel as regards Gerald and Gudrun; their relationship is destructive, catastrophic. But the relationship between Birkin and Ursula can hardly be said to be an exemplar, to be a "norm" by which to interpret the full disastrous meaning of the other, as Mr. Leavis, among others, takes it to be. Mr. Leavis writes: "In Birkin's married relations with Ursula the book invites us to localize the positive, the conceivable and due—if only with difficulty attainable—solution of the problem; the norm, in relation to which Gerald's disaster gets its full meaning." [4]

The preceding analysis has shown the contrast to be considerably more complex than Mr. Leavis takes it to be. For if the love between Birkin and Ursula illumines the nature of the love between the other couple—and this cannot be denied—it still cannot be taken without extensive qualifications to be a normal marriage or to constitute a norm, even in those high erotic moments

reached occasionally by Birkin and Ursula. To call their relationship a norm by means of which to appreciate the disastrous ending of the affair between Gerald and Gudrun is to fail to perceive
in it that which denies it its character of norm—in either of the
two usual senses of this term. It cannot be a *norm* in the sense
that it is a mark toward which the affair between Gerald and Gudrun *ought* to aspire. There are two reasons for this: the first is that
even when we reckon the rare moments, we cannot separate them
from Birkin's radical dissatisfaction with Ursula and his incompleteness with her; the second is that in spite of his resolution to
abandon "the African way," Birkin does not seem to have abandoned it. Nor can we call the relationship between Birkin and
Ursula a *norm* in the sense that it is the expression of the average
—unless Mr. Leavis is in possession of statistics to which he does
not refer, such as those provided by the late Doctor Kinsey, showing that a significant percentage of the male population of the society constituted by the world of *Women in Love* suffers from
the same frustrations and indulges in the same erotic practices
(the African way?) that Birkin indulges in. But how could Mr.
Leavis or his sociologist have obtained such statistics? The only
way would be that of critics who inquire how many children
Lady Macbeth had.

[4]

These considerations entitle us to arrive at an important conclusion. Put bluntly they show that, contrary to Lawrence's intentions, Birkin's religion of love beyond love, the sort of ultimate
marriage he sought, could not perform for Birkin, when he found
such a marriage, the function that he had hoped it would. Birkin
had hoped that love would give his life center—"seeing there is
no God." But it did not. One could argue that Birkin was incapable of the perfect love for which he yearned or that the love for
which he yearned was not a perfect love—or both, of course. The
religious believer will argue that Birkin failed because there is no

substitute for God. But the observation is here irrelevant. In any case, love did not do for Birkin what he, and apparently Lawrence, had hoped it would do. His craving for the African way and his need for a friendship with Gerald, made impossible by the latter's death, give the lie to Birkin's religion of love and Lawrence's intention. Because I am discussing a novel, I do not mean to say that the religion of love could not have satisfied another man, imaginary or real, under different circumstances. Such a statement, anyway, would be a law of human nature, and I, at least, lack the data to formulate it. All I know of men and their societies would seem to indicate that they find apparently acceptable destinies of the most diverse and conflicting natures. To what extent these diverse ways are, by objective standards, an adequate or a satisfactory realization of the powers of man and hence an expression of the good life, is not a question to be raised here. In any case, to draw a sociological law from the imaginings of a poet—even one greater, more universal, and more healthy than Lawrence—is a foolishness that I am not inclined to commit. All we can assert is that the novel shows that the religion of love failed to satisfy Birkin. Any attempt to go beyond this statement turns a novel into sociology. And the best of novelists can be but very poor sociologists.

What, it will be asked, is the significance of these considerations for our appreciation of Lawrence the poet? We cannot adequately answer the question unless we adopt what may be taken to be an invidious procedure; we must remember the claims that have been made for Lawrence. Let me begin with the claims made by a young critic who recently found a "love ethic" in Lawrence, of which he approves without scruple.[5] We are told that this ethic entails a radical commitment to spontaneous life and to "phallic marriage." Our critic does not explain to us what other kind of marriage there can be between a normal man and a normal woman. Nor why, if it be phallic, it should not also be vaginal.[6]

In a more subtle and in a more plausible manner—for we are now dealing with a more experienced critic—Mr. Leavis makes a somewhat similar assertion. He writes: "My aim, I repeat, is to win clear recognition for the nature of Lawrence's greatness. Any great creative writer who has not had his due is a power for life wasted. But the insight, the wisdom, the revived and re-educated feeling for health that Lawrence brings are what, as our civilization goes, we desperately need." [7]

For the most part, Mr. Leavis writes about Lawrence as Stalinists used to write about the Monstrous Butcher before his death. Only if we digest his study as a whole can we gather the large and complex claims that Mr. Leavis makes for Lawrence. Here and there a very tentative minor criticism is introduced. But on the whole it appears that Lawrence can write nothing less than masterpieces. A close, critical scrutiny of Lawrence's novels reveals, as we have seen, that the matter is not quite as simple as that. What Mr. Leavis' statement means is illuminated by what he says about the difference between *Sons and Lovers* and Lawrence's next two great novels. With *Sons and Lovers*, he tell us, Lawrence

put something behind him. . . . The acute emotional problem or disorder which queered his personal relations and the play of his intelligence has been placed—has been conquered by intelligence, manifesting and vindicating itself in creative art. He is now freed for the work of the greatest kind of artist.

It is *The Rainbow* and *Women in Love*, written during the next few years—the years of the war—that proved him to be that.[8]

That Lawrence was a great artist I do not question. Nor do I question that *The Rainbow* and *Women in Love* are great achievements. But the reader of Mr. Leavis' book can have no doubt that Mr. Leavis assigns, among other values, a high therapeutic value to Lawrence's work. That Lawrence's own life through its whole span was the expression of profound emotional disorder, of obdurate major disharmony, his biography, I believe, amply establishes. But might not Mr. Leavis' high praise apply not to Lawrence the man but to Lawrence the poet, the maker of two great novels and a number of fine short stories? I believe I have shown that if we read *The Rainbow*, *Women in Love*, and *Lady Chatterley* with care we find in them, too, a profound emotional disorder, an obdurate major disharmony, informed with genius as the substance of their drama. To go to these books for the wisdom that our civilization needs, without rigorous discrimination, is folly.

Aside from the moral problem that is posed by the erotic practices of Will Brangwen, Rupert Birkin, and the gamekeeper, Mellors, another observation must be made if we take the novel as anything but a dramatic presentation—if we take it as the source of wisdom or take it as a criticism of contemporary society. Confronted by the values espoused by the two couples in *Women in Love*, we are forced to conclude that Birkin and Ursula stand out in positive contrast to Gerald and Gudrun in their catastrophic relationship. This is clear and unambiguous enough. We must prefer one couple to the other in spite of Birkin's incomplete fulfillment. But Birkin's values involve a repudiation of his world, for in choosing to wander a bit he chooses to escape. Dismissing the ethics of productivity as evil is well enough for himself and his wife. But if it is put forth as a pattern for living, we are forced to ask how we are going to keep body and soul together after quitting our jobs. Who is going to man the boats and railroads that are going to take us on our wandering? Who is going to sow and harvest the wheat and bake the bread? What are we going to buy bread with, assuming that it can be found? Birkin and Ursula had no stated means of livelihood. This is not a fault in the novel. The novel hangs together although Lawrence did not take up that question. But to take the relationship between Birkin and Ursula seriously as a practical solution of our problems is simply silly.

But why do we have to take this novel (or any other novel for that matter) as anything else than what it is, a dramatic presentation? Whatever he may have thought he was doing, what Lawence the artist produced was a creative organization of experience in dramatic and narrative terms which, within its own frame,

is wholly valid, and valid in the only manner in which a novel can and has to be valid—valid aesthetically. If Birkin is not at the end satisfied with his wife but still longs for an "eternal union with a man too: another kind of love," it is Birkin and not mankind who is dissatisfied and still longs; and if Gerald is destroyed, it is Gerald and not all industrial magnates who suffer destruction. And if Hermione feels uplifted when she understands something about the stars, it is Hermione who feels as she does, not all women and all men. And if Sir Joshua the sociologist—I almost wrote the logician and philosopher—is a man "whose mental fibre is so tough as to be insentient," it is Sir Joshua and not all sociologists who are tough and insentient.

We ought to remember also that the values revealed by Lawrence in his novel are not all negative values. The role given carnal love in the novel is, let me repeat, a positive value as Father Tiverton pointed out, when we discriminate between it and those aspects that fall within the province of Krafft-Ebing; the essentially religious reverence for nature we found in Lawrence's response to the Indian dances is also a positive value; the persistent quest for an adequate conception of human destiny is also a positive value of Lawrence's poetry. Nor are these all. But they hardly need be called to the attention of the reader at this late date. What is needed at the moment, if I may be allowed to reiterate, is a study that corrects the exaggerations of such critics as Mr. Eliot or the unintelligent dismissals of Lawrence by such writers as Bertrand Russell, on the one hand, and the abandoned panegyrics of Mr. Leavis on the other. This is the reason I have insisted in this book on pointing out Lawrence's failures and his triumphs, and in pointing out the exact nature of the substance of his triumphs. The required discrimination of the unacceptable values to be found in his work does not mean that his work has no value. It has great value, it has the value of genuine poetry. Lawrence has made it possible for those who read him critically to understand aesthetically, to grasp in the mode of immediate apprehension as-

pects of our contemporary world that, had he left them unin-
formed, would have remained for us mere threatening, oppressive
chaos. He charts our world. Without him and the other poets who
also chart it, we would be likely to be blind to the specific process
of disintegration of which we are the victims.

The Constitutive Symbol

THE TERM "constitutive symbol" has three distinguishable meanings: It may refer to the elementary means we use to grasp the world perceptually, the means which Kantian philosophers call categories, and which give the world the basic order it has for us. Or it may refer to the more or less sophisticated works of art we find in all cultures, however primitive these cultures may be. Or it may refer to components of works of art. It is this third sense of the term that centrally concerned me in the chapters on *The Rainbow* and *Women in Love*, because one of the reasons these two great novels have their high artistic value is that constitutive symbols are among their components. But we cannot discuss this third meaning of the term "constitutive symbol," without first discussing the other two.

In order to make clear what I mean by the term, I shall begin by quoting a statement made by Lawrence which I found in the useful volume edited by Mr. Beal. In an article entitled, "The Dragon of the Apocalypse," Lawrence says: "And gradually we realize that we are in a world of symbol as well as of allegory." A few lines later he continues:

You can't give a great symbol a "meaning." Symbols are organic units of consciousness with a life of their own, and you can never explain them away, because their value is dynamic, emotional, belonging to the sense-consciousness of the body and the soul, and not simply mental. An allegorical image has *meaning*. Mr. Facing-both-ways has a meaning. But I defy you to lay your finger on the full meaning of Janus, who is a symbol.[1]

The hasty explanation Lawrence gives us of this pregnant distinction I would reject in some important respects. In the absence of a full explanation the distinction remains no more than a passing, although a brilliant, *aperçu*. But it is perhaps just as well, since his theoretical efforts, as I have already indicated and as he himself was aware, were more often than not of little value.

A reference to the constitutive symbol, no less suggestive and just as incomplete, is found in Mr. Leavis' study of Lawrence. He tells us that "significance in Lawrence's art is never a matter of a mere intended 'meaning' symbolized; it works from profounder levels and in more complex ways." A few pages further on, discussing Gudrun's wanton provocation of the highland cattle and the violent encounter between herself and Gerald (in Chapter XIV of *Women in Love*), Mr. Leavis writes:

> To sum up the significance [of this incident] is another matter: the whole remarkable chapter is very complex, closely organized, and highly charged. It will be noticed that I have avoided the terms "symbol" and "symbolism" in this discussion: to suggest that the rabbit and the cattle "stand for" this and that would be to suggest much simpler ways of constructing and conveying significance . . . than we actually have.[2]

I subscribe to these statements with the following qualification: For the "never" in the first quotation I would substitute "not always," making it read: "significance in Lawrence is *not always* a matter of mere intended meaning symbolized." When significance is only a matter of meaning symbolized, I shall refer to the symbolic device as a "pseudo-symbol" or a "quasi-symbol," and I shall contrast it with those devices which I call "constitutive symbols," and which are considerably more than a matter of intended meaning symbolized. Observe, however, that scenes that are more than a matter of intended meaning symbolized, or constitutive symbols, must perforce be very rare, even in writers of the highest genius. To produce in a long book a number of "highly charged" constitutive symbols, like those that called forth Mr. Leavis' pregnant statement, is to expect much more of a creative artist, however powerful his genius, than he can give us.

Because the word "symbol" does not have a univocal and recognized acceptation in the English language, there can be no harm in calling the device a "constitutive symbol," although we must recognize that Mr. Leavis' objection to the word is well-founded. Whatever terms we choose, the choice itself is arbitrary and the use of terms a question of stipulation. If what the terms are intended to mean in this essay is defined with a modicum of clarity, they will do as well as any we can invent or find in a dictionary. In order to lighten the presentation, when there is no risk of confusion it is best to speak of the device merely as "symbol." A symbol is to be contrasted with a quasi-symbol or a pseudo-symbol, in which something stands for something else that can be grasped independently of the sign vehicle. Another term for quasi-symbol is "sign" but I prefer the two terms I have adopted in order to distinguish this device from traffic signs, old-fashioned shop signs, and other non-verbal devices of this sort. Our problem, now, is clearly before us. We must try to obtain a working idea of the constitutive symbol in abstract terms and to answer some of the questions the notion raises.

Were a philosopher to ask me what I mean by the term, "constitutive symbol," I would answer that the constitutive symbol is a creative synthesis of empirical matter which manifests itself in dramatic and moral terms and which functions categorially. But I would emphasize the words "creative" and "synthesis." For the constitutive symbol is not arrived at by a mere reshuffling or rearranging of the matter of experience. It is *creative* and it is a *genuine synthesis.*[3]

This is true of the constitutive symbol in any of the three meanings that have been discriminated in the first paragraph of this appendix.

Let us turn to the first of these meanings. A more usual term for it is "category." We have learned from neo-Kantian philosophers, particularly from Cassirer, that the categories with which we grasp the world are not fixed, innate forms, as Kant took them to be, universally valid and susceptible of a neat arrangement in a table of four classes made up of three each. It is best, therefore, to call them "symbolic forms," as Cassirer called them. The world is grasped through, or by means of, symbolic forms. Whether or not there is an a priori element in them, or whether some of them are a priori, is fortunately a question we need not answer. I would suggest that the answer to the question awaits a satisfactory resolution of the mind-body problem. The closer we come to interpreting mind in terms of body, the closer the relationships of perception to apprehension and of experience to somatic grounds are specified by psychology, the more readily must we expect to find in the physical structure shared by the human animal qua animal innate forms that are universal although susceptible of variation through the influence of cultural factors.

A constitutive symbol, in the first meaning, is a symbolic form by means of which the world is apprehended. But in this sense, the symbol is a basic and elementary form. By virtue of its relations to other forms, the world is apprehended as orderly—or, more exactly, as containing such order as the interrelationships among the forms used to apprehend it allow. The apprehension gives the world *meaning*. But the *meaning* that it gives the world is not that which the scientific semiotician is interested in. The semiotician uses the term "meaning" for a relationship in which there are three terms: a sign, a thing that the sign stands for, and the mind, for which the sign functions as sign. But before a mind can make anything stand for something else, both the sign and the thing signified must be grasped by the mind for what they are, each must be given identity, each must be discriminated from other things. I cannot say that a certain kind of pole signifies a barber shop for Americans, unless I recognize the pole and the barber shop as each being what it is in itself and as distinct from one another and from much else. A thing must mean itself before it can mean something else. I have to be able to distinguish it, I have to be familiar with it, before I can use it as sign. And if the scientific semiotician should ask how a thing can mean itself, how meaning can be immanent, can be reflexive and not referential, the answer is that terms like "meaning" and "significance" are legitimately used in two different senses at least, and no one can impose on others his use as the only one that is permissible. One of these senses of "meaning" is that of the scientific semiotician. But his theory assumes that the thing signified by the sign and the sign itself can be grasped directly, independently of any means whatever. And this is indeed the case as regards both sign and thing signified in a realistic epistemology. But the writer holds that both signs and referents must themselves be grasped by means of symbolic forms before anything can be made to stand for anything else. And here the epistemological realist and the neo-Kantian disagree radically. For the latter, the process of perception and apprehension is complex and involves a creative synthesis within a universe of discourse which functions implicitly when that to which the mind turns is grasped as significant or meaningful.

We grasp a thing as significant in a variety of ways: by discriminating it from other things and learning to apprehend it clearly as the thing it is, by learning its use or how it is made, by discerning its position in a chain of familiar events. It may be at bottom a matter of familiarity—but a familiarity acquired through some kind of relation to the thing. However a thing becomes meaningful or significant to us, ordinary things and events attain significance apparently without much effort, and when they attain it we can use them and know their place in our world. This knowledge may be unclear and more a matter of handling the thing or performing the event than the kind of knowledge sought for by the philosopher or the scientist. But for the purposes of ordinary living it is sufficient. When an African native learns to drive an automobile, he has knowledge of the machine without the least knowledge of the physics that makes it possible. He may even acquire an elementary knowledge of the mechanics of internal combustion engines without anything but the most inadequate knowledge of the physical principles that control their operation. Familiarity makes a fork and a chair intelligible under ordinary circumstances. But change the light or setting and they may become puzzling. We refer a familiar object to a context and it is meaningful. For us that thing is a fork and that other is a pencil. The Australian aboriginal who has never seen a fork or used a pencil will be puzzled by them and will initially find them meaningless. An object that enters our purview is instantly categorized, although all too often unsatisfactorily. The Australian aboriginal, I imagine, is not altogether happy calling a fork and a pencil whiteman's thingumajigs, for so long as they remain thingumajigs and nothing else, they remain challenges to his curiosity and sources of irritation to his intelligence. They cease to be challenges and sources of irritation when they become more adequately categorized.

It is at this point that the activity of the poet, the maker of constitutive symbols in the second sense I have referred to, becomes of interest to us. The world in which we live does not consist merely of physical objects that must be discriminated from one another and identified verbally in order that we may live. Ours is a complex world of institutions, values, subtle human relationships, of which we must have knowledge or we run into trouble. To grasp our world in its full axiological density, to acquire a viable sense of our place in it, of the destiny it permits us to achieve, to grasp it as adequately as we grasp a chair or a fork, requires a process of categorization which is both dramatic and moral. We accomplish it, of course, with the same unconscious ease as we acquire the complex forms of our native language. But the actual ease with which we come by the world (and I do not mean, of course, to minimize the difficulties of growing up and of learning to adjust to our social environment and to our own inward demands) should not hide from us that before we can have a world out there, for us, we have to reduce it to order: we must learn what are the direction and force of its energies, what are the values and instrumentalities which are at our disposal, how much room we have and how we can move within it. And all this, let me reiterate, not merely at the physical level but at the level of human relations, which is to say at the moral level. These remarks apply to ourselves as much as they do to the external world, indeed even more so, since self-knowledge may be more painful. Should we fail, or rather, to the extent that we fail, to discover what are the energies and what are their direction and force, we are confronted with failure—a failure we may believe we escape, but the consequences of which are inexorable, since it makes itself felt in our lives not necessarily as punishment but as omission, by reducing our opportunities to develop into the fullness of our humanity as provided by our society. Success, or such success as we achieve in living—and I am not thinking of worldly success, of that which is approved by the world, although I do not underrate the value of this kind of success, I hope—depends, fundamentally, on our ability to make experience whole, to make the world and ourselves intelligible to ourselves and to some extent to make the world and ourselves amenable to control.

My claim is that the world in which we live is made whole when the poet, the maker, subjects its matter to a creative process.

The process of apprehension or the aesthetic process is prior to the artistic process and the latter presupposes the former. For that reason the constitutive symbol, in the second meaning of the term, functions categorially: *it is the means by which we grasp our world at the basic level of ordinary practical living.* When the constitutive symbol is achieved, there is an interanimation between it and the thing or process it symbolizes, a kind of permeation so that for us the world is a world grasped not only *through* the symbol but *in* the symbol also. This is the truth which motivates the efforts sometimes made by critics (in my opinion, erroneously) to find a correlation between the sounds of a line of verse and the things said in it. In the sense of creating constitutive symbols, we are all poets—which is to say, *makers*—but those whom we call poets are more conscious and more skillful makers than the rest of us. And this is the poem's basic and indispensable function: it gives us the world. We read into the world the poem's order and intelligible action; and the nature of the actors and their destinies become the means by which we understand ourselves and our fellows. Note that the poem is a dramatic and a moral category or, more precisely, an organized complex of dramatic and moral categories. It is dramatic in the original sense of the term, since it refers to deeds or acts; and it is moral in the sense that the actions and the judgments of the actors are presented as instinct with values which have a bearing on our weal or woe.

A work of literary art taken as a whole, then, is a constitutive symbol. This is the reason I took pains to show that even an autobiographical novel like *Sons and Lovers*, which appears on the surface to be a faithful representation or imitation of actual events, is the product of a creative act in which not only the selection and organization of its component parts are products of creativity but the rendering of the parts themselves is the product of creativity. In the second sense of the term, any work of art as a whole, whether it contains constitutive symbols within itself as components or not, is itself a constitutive symbol, even though it may appear to be an imitation of reality.

This is more easily seen on a small scale, in short stories for instance, than on a large scale, in novels or dramas. "The Rocking Horse Winner" is a story that critics of Lawrence have tried to interpret in discursive terms. But the attempts, ingenious and even speciously convincing as they may be, in the end must fail. Lawrence wrote a number of short stories which, because he could not finish them, were failures. After carrying the story at a high level of creativity he could not keep up the effort and descended to a lower level, adding material that had not been transmuted thoroughly by the creative imagination. I am thinking of stories like "The Captain's Doll," in which, in order to wind up the story, Lawrence falls back on dreary autobiographical material totally unlike the substance of the first part of the story. This is also true of "The Fox." In this story he starts with an authentic and potent constitutive symbol and ends with the old song and dance about the need of the female to submit and be passive in the sexual act. But if we take the earlier part of this story we find that to assign an external meaning to the fox, and the relations of the girls to it, is to be satisfied with an interpretation of the story that is inadequate. The doll, the fox, the rocking horse are, in the last analysis, beyond elucidation by discursive language. They are constitutive symbols.

The nature of the constitutive symbol is easily grasped not only in powerful constructions like "The Rocking Horse Winner" and "The Woman Who Rode Away" (a story that does not suffer from the faults of "The Captain's Doll" or "The Fox," but which I do not admire because its substance, although wholly transmuted matter is, as I have already noted, wholly negative and masochistic), but in works of larger scale like Kafka's novels. A large number of the efforts to "interpret" *The Trial* or *The Castle* are wholly ridiculous. But even those that are not must in the end fail: if the critic is looking for an exact conceptual statement of their meaning, and one fully congruous with the novels themselves, he is bound to be disappointed. And the reason is that in these works Kafka is offering us a presentation. It is through them that we grasp reality and not the other way. We cannot grasp them through reality. I am overstating my case, for after all without some experience of life, art is meaningless. But there should be no serious harm in an exaggeration that brings to light the important function of art.

We next turn to the third meaning which, as I have already indicated, is the one which is of greatest interest to us in this study: This is the symbol that is a component of a work of art. What I have said about the second meaning of the term applies with very little alteration to the third. It is a complex situation or scene, such as those to which I have called attention in the text and on which I have tried to throw some light, which gathers the significance of events preceding it and illumines the scenes or situations that follow. The scene in which Gudrun slaps Gerald and that in which the rabbit officiates at their marriage in an obscene rite are nucleii that exhibit Gudrun's corruption and power as contrasted with Gerald's corruption and specious power. In the novel the corruption of the woman is not rooted in her lust for sexual excesses. Gudrun is corrupt because she sides with the German artist, who accepts industry. She is stronger because Gerald needs her while she can do without him. Gerald is corrupt because he worships the machine and fails to acknowledge the Eros of the sacred mysteries, as the organizing force which would have enabled him to give his life genuine meaning and character. The moon scene plays a similar role in respect to Birkin. As I tried to show, it reveals the radical predicament in which Birkin finds himself. It is true that Birkin's cogitations the day after the moon episode do not clarify a number of questions they suggest. But the constitutive symbol of the moon episode gives us a powerfully vivid image of the difficulties from which Birkin suffers.

But we do not come to a full understanding of the constitutive symbol until we contrast it with the pseudo-symbol or the quasi-symbol. The meaning of the mare episode can be adequately elucidated in discursive terms and it is, indeed, fully elucidated within the novel. The introduction of it gives the reader the full commitment of Gerald to the ethics of productivity and the concommitant need to achieve dominion over men, animals, and things which that ethic demands.

[2]

A large number of important questions of diverse nature arise when we consider the constitutive symbol. Some of these refer to extremely technical epistemological problems—for instance the question as to the ground on which we know there is a reality that exists prior to, and independently of, the symbol. Since reality appears to us only by means of (through and in) symbols, what evidence do we have for the belief that there is something beyond them? I cannot consider this question here, since it has no proper place in an essay on literary criticism. It has been discussed by professional philosophers and those interested in it are referred to the literature on the subject.[4] However, it must be indicated with emphasis that this problem is a legitimate one, and a critic who accepts the concept of the constitutive symbol must either solve it satisfactorily or must know where to go for a solution of it. Otherwise his critical observations and judgments lack the theoretical basis that I would be the first to insist criticism must have. To be responsible, criticism must be based on an aesthetic which in turn must be based on a complete philosophy, including an epistemology. Criticism that cannot claim such a basis or that is grounded on a syncretistic hodgepodge of theories picked up *en passant* without regard to their fundamental coherence is not responsible.

Although I can, with good conscience, dismiss the epistemological problem that the notion of the constitutive symbol gives rise to, there are others that cannot be so dismissed and the elucidation of which will throw light on the nature and function of the symbol. (1) Is the constitutive symbol a formal or a substantive device? (2) Is there a relation between the constitutive symbol and the so-called heresy of paraphrase? (3) Does not the function that has been assigned to the symbol overlook the fact that some non-literates have no poets? (4) What, if any, is the relationship between the constitutive symbol and Jung's archetypes?

1) In the organismic theory of art on which the contextualist bases his practical criticism, the answer to the first of these questions is that the symbol is both a formal and a substantive device and not exclusively either. For the organicist, the distinction between form and substance can be made only in mind—one cannot be actually separated from the other. Form cannot be formulated in the manner in which the rhyming scheme of a sonnet is formulated, by means of letters. We can direct attention now to form, now to substance. But the form we attend to is always substantial or substanced form and the substance is always informed substance. Unsubstanced or pure form is something that only the Platonic mystic, and he but rarely, can *aspire* to apprehend. This

much at any rate I believe we can with confidence assert: common folk do not claim to have had such experiences. And of course matter utterly free from form is chaos and cannot be thought at all. The symbol is a *formal* device in the sense that we can analyze several component symbols making up a poem and discover how they differ from one another in the roles they play and in the substances they inform. It is a *substantial* device in the sense that the poem or the symbols that may be among its components are constitutive, which is to say that they inform substance that, as Mr. Leavis says, is "highly charged"—with significance, as I imagine he means.

One qualification, however, is desirable. Because the constitutive symbol works from profounder levels and in more complex ways than the quasi-symbol, it is not appropriate to say of it that it is a way of "constructing" significance. Working below the level of consciousness, the constitutive symbol comes about, it grows; the verb "to construct" suggests a mechanical operation like bricklaying or carpentry. For a similar reason I have used the word "device," *malgré moi*. It is hardly the word to employ to refer to the product of that essential mystery which is the creative process. For what do we know about it? The observable steps that psychologists have sorted out, what do they tell us about the dark gestation, about the matter that goes into the formation of the organism that is the poem, about the manner in which the creative mind adds and takes away from the experience that it struggles to inform?

2) The relation between the work of art which is a constitutive symbol and the so-called heresy of paraphrase is easiest to elucidate if we recall that some works of literary art, some poems, do not contain as components constitutive symbols in the third sense to which I have referred. Devoid of constitutive symbols as components, they may be, nevertheless, great works of art. I am thinking, for instance, of the novels of Jane Austen. Her novels seem to give us a report of the actual world in which she lived, nothing ever happens in them that could not have happened to her or her

friends. Her readers seem to be at home in the world of her novels. Allowing of course for obvious differences of time and customs, Emma and Mr. Woodhouse could be English relatives of neighbors of ours. This is true of all of her novels. The Bennets of Longbourn are, like the Woodhouses, people we might have met. Jane Austen's novels could be called "naturalistic" or "realistic," and the theory of imitation *seems* to apply to them so obviously that only academic pedantry would challenge its application to them. Stendhal's epigram, "The novel is a mirror carried along the high road," seems to apply to all of them if we are allowed to qualify to the effect that the notion of Jane Austen carrying a mirror along a highroad is incongruous. "Three or four families in a country village" is what she turns her mirror to. But if we remember what I took pains to bring out in connection with *Sons and Lovers*, it will be granted that the notion that Jane Austen's novels are "reflections," or "imitations," of the world in which she lived is false. Her novels have the high quality they have because she was a *creative* artist and in so far as she was one, her work cannot be a copy or an imitation. It is truer to say that the world imitates the novels than to say the novels imitate the world. They are constitutive symbols—the means through which we organize our experience.

We are now ready to come to the point and explore the relation between the constitutive symbol and the "heresy of paraphrase." Since the literary work of art is a presentation and not an imitation, its meaning is immanent and not referential. It can be apprehended but it cannot be subjected to analysis by which we can distinguish tenor from vehicle and exhibit each separately from the other. This is, of course, as already noted, a matter of degree. For indications can be given as to how to grasp the poem, how to distinguish its form and how to apprehend its substance, although the form is substanced form and the substance is informed substance. But just as in the Leibnizian universe the principle of the identity of the indiscernibles holds throughout, so in the organismic theory of art that has controlled the writing of this

essay, the autonomy and contextual self-identity of a literary work
of art must be asserted. For the individual work of art there can be
no substitutes. There are, of course, similarities and classes, so that
the historical taxonomy of art is not an arbitrary affair. But to the
extent that a work of literary art is excellent, to that extent it is
unique and no substitute can be found for it. This holds, of course,
for all works of art in any medium whatever—although how it
holds for music is a problem of such difficulty, that it is fortunate
I do not have to discuss it here. If you take *Emma* to represent or
imitate life, a discursive account of it can exhaust or come close
to exhausting the novel, and a translation into another language is
possible without loss. But according to such theory the creative
element that *Emma* contains is implicitly denied or overlooked
and it is the novel that is tested by the world that it imitates and
not the world that is tested by the novel. Assert, however, in all
seriousness, that the novel is a constitutive symbol, the product of
genuine creativity, and what you say about the novel is in the last
analysis something which is wholly inadequate to the novel. The
novel is beyond satisfactory translation or the possibility of paraphrase. Let me repeat that all sorts of indications can be given the
reader as to what he will find in the novel. But ultimately he has
to go it alone and enter into the kind of transaction with it that is
the aesthetic apprehension of the intransitive and the immanent
grasp of its meanings.

A number of important qualifications, however, are called for.
The first has already been noted: the question as to whether a
poem can be translated or not, which I have treated as if it were a
question of either/or, is always a question of more or less. The
second qualification is that I do not mean that novels we may call
"realistic" give us a world as real as ours or more real than works
like *King Lear* or *The Trial*. While the world of a novel by Jane
Austen is more like our world than the world of a novel by Kafka,
Jane Austen's novels are just as fictional as the novels of Kafka, although they possess a sense of actuality that we cannot attribute

to the two great novels of Kafka. In this respect there is no difference between one work of art and another.

I would like to add a further qualification, namely that while I am using the term "the heresy of paraphrase," and on other occasions I have referred to "the intentional fallacy," I do so because the labels are in wide usage. But it goes against my grain to speak of "heresies" or "fallacies" in the realm of aesthetics and criticism. In such fields, in which there are as many self-appointed, authoritative revelations as there are writers, and in which councils of bishops cannot be called in order to read out of the church these individuals whose theories differ from ours, to claim for a theory the catholicity or orthodoxy that alone could give us the right to hurl our anathemas against those who disagree with us is to give an impression of egregious presumption. On the theory of imitation it is not heretical to paraphrase or translate a poem, and on a simple two-dimensional theory of mind such as pre-Freudians hold, it is not fallacious to consider the intention of the writer as adequately represented or embodied in what he says about his work.

3) The question as to whether there are or are not poets in non-literate societies is one that will interest anthropologists as well as critics and aestheticians. And it is one that I welcome because it will enable me to further clarify the notion of the symbol and what I take to be the function of poetry.

It is of course true that in non-literate societies there are no poets in the sense in which we find them in ours: there are no men or women who employ their full time and talent in the manner in which Shakespeare, Donne, Jane Austen, and D. H. Lawrence employed theirs. If by the term "poet" we mean the specialist or the professional, it is possible that there may be non-literate societies that lack poets and poetry. But there are no societies that lack the artist, and in making this statement I am backed by the authority of Boas and Robert Redfield. It is possible that in some of the societies that lack poetry—in the sense of linguistic objects—other arts take its place: the dance, elaborations of religious ceremonies —although it would be difficult to conceive of the latter activity carried on without the aid of language. Again, it is also possible that in small, non-literate societies that do not have specialists their absence is made up for by the fact that everybody or nearly everybody in the society is a kind of poet, carrying and passing on the myths in which the vision of life of that society is embodied. This is a question of fact and not to be answered a prioristically. But I find it difficult to believe that there are societies that altogether lack some sort of rudimentary vision of life expressed in myth. Boas some time ago pointed out in his book on primitive art that all peoples have artists, no matter how hard a struggle they have to keep alive. Energy they can ill afford is deviated from the job of survival and put into the creation of works of art, which from the standpoint of survival may seem useless. And Redfield shortly before his untimely end wrote the following:

The peoples studied by anthropologists, taken as whole groups acting and thinking over long periods of time, show a creativeness beyond the demands of subsistence and mere survival. In such a group, however meager its resources and however hardpressed it is to survive, we see some production, an accumulation of generations, in which are expressed imagination, a sense of coherence, a progressive building of some "work of the mind." [5]

Since Redfield had stated earlier in the essay from which I have quoted that man individually and as a group grasps the world as intelligible, I can drop the discussion at this point, for what I am concerned to assert is that it is the poet or the proto-poet, or that faculty in men that constitutes their poetic talent, that is essential for the creation of a world view.

I have been speaking, then, of the poet in two senses: the self-conscious writer of novels or verse or plays, on the one hand, and the myth maker on the other. The former is possible only in certain societies. The latter is to be found in all.

4) The question of the relation between the constitutive symbol and Jung's archetype could, if pressed, lead to perplexing problems of an exasperatingly controversial nature. For this reason I would like to make clear that in the present context I am not interested in the question of whether Jung's genetic interpretation of the archetype and of the manner in which it functions in the process of individuation is valid or not. As is known, Jung traces the symbolic archetype to the primordial experience of the human race and further back to undifferentiated cosmic sources of energy, which he boldly claims the archetype expresses. To the majority of our contemporaries, for reasons we need not go into here, these speculations of Jung are disturbing and even repugnant, although there is nothing in the naturalism that is the reigning philosophical temper of our age that renders these speculations inadmissible—except perhaps that they are speculations as to origins. Fortunately we can avoid these controversial issues, and turn to the similarities and differences between the archetype and the constitutive symbol.

For Jung's definition of symbol we must turn to Chapter XI, entitled "Definitions," in *Psychological Types or The Psychology of Individuation*.[6] Here we find a full discussion of the distinction between what Jung calls a "sign" and a "symbol." The discussion shows that Jung's distinction is, in some important respects, very similar if not identical to that which I have tried to make. The object to which the sign refers is independent of the sign and can be presented or exhibited with full adequacy either by another sign or by direct presentation, whereas that which the symbol conveys or expresses cannot be conveyed in any other manner than by the symbol—or, more precisely, *in* the symbol. Jung also holds that that which the symbol conveys cannot be exhausted by explication, because it is relatively unknown. The symbol, so to speak, is bottomless. The word "tree" refers to a certain thing to which I can point with my finger by taking you to the window and saying, "That, there, is a tree." In Spanish a tree is *un arbol*, and in using the Spanish rather than the English nothing is gained or lost in discursive communication about the thing that both words designate.

But while the sign points to the known or the knowable, and is not incarnate with that to which it points, so to speak, this is not the case with the symbol, which according to Jung expresses or embodies something relatively unknown, something the mind does not fully grasp, having depths that no sounding will ascertain satisfactorily. The symbol, for this reason, is pregnant with meaning—but not the meaning of the sign. The word "meaning" has changed its meaning. The meaning of the symbol is for Jung ultimately a pre-individual, collective experience and finally cosmic energy which it channels into expression. Because they express pre-individual, collective experience, the symbols or archetypes are fully "charged"—to fall back again on Mr. Leavis' useful term. But charged with what? With the pristine reactions of early man and his animal forebears which the symbol expresses for them and still expresses for us? To understand the charge of the constitutive symbol we either have to accept Jung's genetic speculations or substitute our own for his, for the charge must be explained, and it would appear that it has something to do with the depths of the personality, those dark bottoms beyond accessible reach by direct conscious inspection. The fact of the charge, however, and its nature, cannot be put in question, even though we may be at a loss for an adequate explanation of the source of the charge. The charge consists in the power to arouse deep, perhaps totally formless emotion, or if the symbol does not arouse it, to express it objectively, so that we cannot mistake it. And the nature of the charge must be defined, in part at least, by the fascination it exercises, both of fear and attraction, by the sense it carries with it, the ambivalence and the confusion it brings to the surface.

There is an important difference, however, between the constitutive symbol and the archetypal symbol, and this difference is so clearly and precisely stated by Ira Progoff that all I need do is quote his words:

Cassirer proceeds with the idea that man is essentially a symbol-making creature. It would be correct to say that Jung holds the same belief. The difference, however, is that Cassirer understands symbols as instruments which arise out of man's experience in his efforts to further his purposes in communicating with other men and in thinking more efficiently. The question of symbols has, essentially, an epistemological meaning to him. Jung, on the other hand, interprets symbols in terms of the inner functioning of the psyche. Symbols do not arise out of experience as a means of communication in society, but symbols arise out of the spontaneous creativity within the psyche. There is thus a basic difference in the conception of the ways in which symbols function. To Cassirer they are effective as means of knowledge in relation to outer experience; to Jung they are effective in the depths of personality as autonomous channelizers of psychic energy. Symbols operate on a more fundamental level for Jung. When they are understood only as means of communication, they are on the level of consciousness, which is the surface of the psyche; but as autonomous and spontaneous creations carrying large sums of energy, they operate in the unconscious and express basic psychic processes. They are thus much more dynamic factors than mere means of knowledge, and this difference has far-reaching consequences in the two approaches to man.[7]

The difference can be put in a single sentence: Jung is a psychologist and Cassirer is a philosopher whose central concern is epistemology. But the two interests, those of the psychologist and those of the epistemologist, are not necessarily incompatible with one another. In fact, the symbolic archetype, whatever its source, functions in literature and in religion as a kind of means of communication, and this is the reason that so many critics have been so powerfully attracted to Jungian psychology and that Miss Bodkin has written a whole book on the subject of archetypal patterns in literature—in which, incidentally she refers to Lawrence and more specifically to the moon-shattering scene to which so much space was given in an earlier chapter.

Notes

The Two Lawrences

1. This chapter, with slight changes, is reprinted from the *Bucknell Review* (VII,3: March, 1958).
2. This essay was already in its second draft when two noteworthy books on Lawrence were published in close succession: F. R. Leavis, *D. H. Lawrence: Novelist* (New York, 1956), and Graham Hough, *The Dark Sun: A Study of D. H. Lawrence* (London, 1956). Mr. Leavis' book, with the contents of which Lawrence students were already acquainted, I reviewed in the January, 1957, number of *The Sewanee Review*. My reaction to Mr. Hough's book is not fully registered by the references that I introduced into this manuscript after reading his discriminating, thorough, and scholarly examination of the whole range of Lawrence's work. I recommend it highly, although if I were to review it I would have to register my disagreement with Mr. Hough on a number of important points. These two books are in the same class with Father Tiverton's *D. H. Lawrence and Human Existence* (London, 1951). They approach Lawrence objectively and as an artist. Mr. Mark Spilka in *The Love Ethic of D. H. Lawrence* (Bloomington, 1955) attempts the same objective approach, but he does not realize that to find an "ethic" in a poet is to turn the poet into a moralist and to deny him his role as poet.
3. The important essay on "The Novel" is to be found in *Reflections on The Death of a Porcupine and Other Essays* (Philadelphia, 1925). Hereafter referred to as *Reflections*.
4. *Ibid.*, p. 105.

I. *Aaron's Rod*

1. John Middleton Murry, *Son of Woman, The Story of D. H. Lawrence* (New York, 1931), p. 123. John Middleton Murry, *Reminiscences of D. H. Lawrence* (London, 1933), p. 103.
2. For the notion of the quasi-symbol, or pseudo-symbol, see Appendix.
3. The terms "matter for" and "substance of" art mark an important distinction without the grasp of which my analysis of Lawrence's work loses its point and becomes unintelligible. The distinction is elucidated in A. C. Bradley's well-known and still indispensable essay, "Poetry for Poetry's Sake" in *Oxford Lectures on Poetry* (London, 1904), pp. 3 ff. John Dewey borrowed the conception in *Art As Experience*, Chapter VI, "Substance and Form" (New York, 1934), pp. 106 ff. Dewey, however, does not give Bradley the credit that is Bradley's due. By whatever terms marked, the distinction is basic to all organismic theories of poetry or of art in general.
4. Following Mr. Hough's intelligent practice, because of the numerous editions of Lawrence's works, I shall cite chapters in which quotations occur, with the exception of *St Mawr*, which is not divided into chapters. For the short stories, I give no reference. These lines, as noted in the text, are to be found in Chapter IX.
5. *Reflections*, p. 114.
6. F. R. Leavis, *D. H. Lawrence: Novelist* (New York, 1956), p. 28.
7. I have discussed this point at greater length in my review of Leavis' book on Lawrence (*The Sewanee Review*, LXV,1: Winter, 1957).

II. *Kangaroo*

1. Richard Aldington, *Portrait of a Genius, But. . .* (London, 1950), p. 256.

2. Graham Hough, *The Dark Sun: A Study of D. H. Lawrence* (London, 1956), pp. 103 and 106, respectively.
3. Aldington, *op. cit.*, p. 256.

III. *The Plumed Serpent*, I

1. *The Letters of D. H. Lawrence*, ed. Aldous Huxley (New York, 1932), p. 645.
2. *Ibid.*, p. 648. (The italics are his.)
3. *Ibid.*, p. 693.
4. *Ibid.*, p. 719.
5. Oliver La Farge, *Santa Eulalia: The Religion of a Cuchumatan Indian Town* (Chicago, 1947).

IV. *The Plumed Serpent*, II

1. D. H. Lawrence, *Mornings in Mexico* (London, 1927), pp. 97–169.
2. D. H. Lawrence, "New Mexico," *Phoenix* (London, 1936), pp. 141–147.
3. *Ibid.*, p. 142.
4. *Ibid.*, p. 143.
5. E. W. Tedlock, Jr., *A Descriptive Bibliography, The Frieda Lawrence Collection of D. H. Lawrence Manuscripts* (Albuquerque, 1948), p. 194. According to Mr. Tedlock, "New Mexico," which was published in 1931, was probably written in 1928.
6. *Letters*, pp. 571 and 613.
7. *Ibid.*, p. 90.
8. Ada Lawrence and Stuart Gelder, *Young Lorenzo, Early Life of D. H. Lawrence* (Florence, 1931), p. 85.
9. *Letters*, pp. 192, 220, 231, 310, 696.
10. *Phoenix*, p. 145.
11. Mircea Eliade, *Patterns in Comparative Religion*, Sheed and Ward, Inc., New York, N. Y. © 1958, Chapter I.

12. *Mornings in Mexico*, pp. 106–107, 127 f.

13. Ruth Benedict, *Patterns of Culture* (Boston, 1934), p. 93.

14. *Mornings in Mexico*, pp. 141–143, 144, 145 f.

15. D. H. Lawrence, *Etruscan Places* (New York, 1933), pp. 89, 117.

16. D. H. Lawrence, *Apocalypse* (Florence, 1931), pp. 67–69.

17. T. S. Eliot, *After Strange Gods* (London, 1934), pp. 58 f.

18. *Letters*, p. 648.

19. *Reflections*, p. 223 ff.

20. *Apocalypse*, p. 36.

21. *Letters*, p. 241.

22. Henry D. Thoreau, *Walden or Life in the Woods*, Chapter II.

23. *Letters*, p. xv.

24. D. H. Lawrence, *Selected Literary Criticism*, ed., Anthony Beal (London, 1955), p. 156.

25. D. H. Lawrence, *Assorted Articles* (London, 1930), p. 151.

26. *Letters*, p. 693.

27. *Assorted Articles*, p. 152.

V. *Lady Chatterley's Lover*

1. *Letters*, p. 719.

2. *D. H. Lawrence: A Composite Biography*, Gathered, arranged, and edited by Edward Nehls (Madison, 1959), Vol. III, p. 660.

3. *Letters*, p. 690.

4. *Ibid.*, p. 207.

5. Graham Hough, *The Dark Sun* . . . , p. 166.

6. *Reflections*, pp. 104 ff.

7. This erotic solipsism has its root deep in Lawrence's own psychology. His wife has written: "In his heart of hearts I think he always dreaded women, felt that they were in the end more powerful than men. Woman is so absolute and undeniable. Man moves, his spirit flies here and there, but you can't go beyond a woman. From her man is born and to her man returns for his ultimate need of body and soul. She is like earth

and death to which all return." Frieda Lawrence, *Not I, But The Wind* (New York, 1934), p. 57.

8. *Letters*, p. 412: "Yesterday I began to type the *Peace* articles —I want another copy—and I was recasting the second one. But suddenly I felt I was going dotty, straight out of my mind, so I left off . . . I wonder if I *am* a bit dotty." His italics.

9. *Ibid.*, p. 122.

10. *Ibid.*, p. 754.

11. Father William Tiverton, *D. H. Lawrence and Human Existence* (London, 1951), Chapter IV, section II.

12. G. Van Der Leeuw, *Religion in Essence and Manifestation*, translated by J. E. Turner (London, 1938), p. 253.

13. Eliade, *op. cit.*, p. 10.

14. *Ibid.*, p. 31.

15. *Letters*, p. 192.

16. *Phoenix, The Posthumous Papers of D. H. Lawrence*, ed. with an introduction by Edward D. McDonald (London, 1936), p. 173.

17. *Ibid.*, p. 170.

18. *Loc. cit.*

19. *Ibid.*, p. 172.

20. D. H. Lawrence, *Sex Literature and Censorship*, ed. Harry T. Moore (New York, 1953), p. 58.

21. *Ibid.*, pp. 59 f.

22. After this book was finished I came across "A Literary Correspondence" between Edward Dahlberg and Sir Herbert Read in *The Sewanee Review* (Spring and Summer, 1959), in which, among others, Lawrence is discussed. Sir Herbert, by referring to Swift's poem, shows that Lawrence probably never read it. He comments: "There is nothing 'insane' about" it, it is rather "a triumph of reason and common sense" (pp. 424 f.).

23. I wrote these lines sometime ago and I have made the same point in my lectures for a number of years. When I was preparing the final typescript to submit to the publishers I came across the identical argument in an essay by Malcom Cowley in *The New York Times Book Review* of 28 June, 1959. Cowley asks not only what an amateur carpenter will exclaim when he hits his thumb, but what can a lumberjack say when

he wants to start a fight, or how can a father curse his erring son, or a husband his unfaithful wife.

VI. Lawrence Imitates Lawrence

1. In *Sex Literature and Censorship*, p. 120.
2. D. H. Lawrence, *St. Mawr* (New York, 1925), p. 12.
3. F. R. Leavis, *D. H. Lawrence . . .* , p. 279.
4. *Ibid.*, p. 281.
5. *St. Mawr*, p. 41.
6. *Letters*, p. 154.
7. *St. Mawr*, pp. 182 f.
8. *The Tales of D. H. Lawrence*, ed. Aldous Huxley (London, 1934), pp. 664 f.
9. *St. Mawr*, p. 90.
10. Leavis, *op. cit.*, p. 283.
11. *St. Mawr*, pp. 194 f.
12. *Ibid.*, p. 101.
13. Leavis, *op. cit.*, p. 93.
14. See Appendix.

VII. *Sons and Lovers*

1. Nehls, *D. H. Lawrence . . .* , Vol. III, p. 213.
2. *Letters*, p. 79.
3. E. T., *D. H. Lawrence, A Personal Record* (New York, 1936), p. 202.
4. *Ibid.*, p. 201.
5. Allen Tate, *On the Limits of Poetry* (New York, 1948), pp. 128–145, particularly 136 ff.
6. Kingsley Widmer, "D. H. Lawrence and the Art of Nihilism," *The Kenyon Review* (XX,4: Autumn, 1958), pp. 604–616.

VIII. *The Rainbow*

1. D. H. Lawrence, *Selected Literary Criticism*, ed. Beal, pp. 86 and 89 respectively.

2. I owe to the editorial reader of this book, the observation that the erotic and the prenatal symbolism correspond to two kinds of darkness, that of the womb and that of death.

IX. The Form of *Women in Love*

NOTE: Chapters IX and X are expanded and revised versions of an essay that appeared in *The Sewanee Review* under the title, "The Substance of *Women in Love*" (LXVI,4: Autumn, 1958).
1. *Letters*, p. 89.

X. The Substance of *Women in Love*

1. *Letters*, p. 192.
2. *The Tales of D. H. Lawrence*, p. 476.
3. The first American edition (of which I have before me the fifth printing) gives "imminent." And so does the Modern Library edition. But should this be a proofreader's error and should the word be "immanent," the same question must still be asked.
4. Leavis, *D. H. Lawrence* . . . , p. 212.
5. Mark Spilka, *The Love Ethic of D. H. Lawrence* (Bloomington, 1955), *passim*.
6. *Ibid.*, Chapter 8, particularly Section III, pp. 190 ff.
7. Leavis, *op. cit.*, p. xiii.
8. *Ibid.*, p. 7.

APPENDIX
The Constitutive Symbol

1. *D. H. Lawrence* . . . *Criticism*, ed., Beal, p. 157.
2. Leavis, *op. cit.*, p. 220 and p. 230.
3. Since I am speaking to a philosopher, the terms must be taken in their technical acceptation.

4. *The Philosophy of Ernst Cassirer*, ed., Paul A. Schilpp (Evanston, 1949).

5. The contemporary, sophisticated, Anglo-American mind is so deeply instinct with the scientistic spirit that it finds repugnant as well as inadmissible the notion of symbol here advanced. But the need for such a notion has long been felt by many students working in many fields. However incomplete or even defective any formulation of the notion may be—and I concede in advance that the one here proposed is likely to have more than its share of error and lack of clarity—the various formulations of the phenomenon which students are trying to elucidate, each from his own standpoint, cannot be a projection of an idiosyncratic, merely obscurantist mind. In his argument against Bultman's effort to demythologize the Christian religion, Jaspers asserts that myth is not a "cloak" or "disguise" that we put on general ideas, "which can be better or more directly grasped intellectually." (I myself would not use the phrase "grasped intellectually," because myth is as much a product of the intellect as theoretical physics or Mozart's music; it is one of the modes in which the intellect functions.) Jaspers goes on to point out that myths are the carriers of meanings that can be expressed only in their language. "Mythical figures are symbols which, by their very nature, are untranslatable into another language." Karl Jaspers and Rudolph Bultman, *Myth and Christianity. An Inquiry Into the Possibility of Religion Without Myth.* (New York, 1958), pp. 15–16.

6. Robert Redfield, "Anthropological Understanding of Man," *Anthropological Quarterly*, Vol. 32, No. 1, January 1959, p. 18.

7. C. G. Jung, *Psychological Types or The Psychology of Individuation* (London, 1923), pp. 600–610.

8. Ira Progoff, *Jung's Psychology and its Social Meaning* (London, 1953), p. 270.

Index